SLAVERY IN THE CITY

SLAVERY IN THE CITY

Architecture and Landscapes
of Urban Slavery in North America

Edited by
CLIFTON ELLIS
and
REBECCA GINSBURG

University of Virginia Press
CHARLOTTESVILLE AND LONDON

University of Virginia Press
© 2017 by the Rector and Visitors of the University of Virginia
Printed in the United States of America on acid-free paper

First published 2017

9 8 7 6 5 4 3 2

Library of Congress Cataloging-in-Publication Data

Names: Ellis, Clifton, 1956– editor. | Ginsburg, Rebecca, 1963– editor.
Title: Slavery in the city : architecture and landscapes of urban slavery in North America / edited by
    Clifton Ellis and Rebecca Ginsburg.
Description: Charlottesville : University of Virginia Press, 2017. | Includes bibliographical references
    and index.
Identifiers: LCCN 2017001842| ISBN 9780813940052 (cloth : alk. paper) | ISBN 9780813940069
    (ebook)
Subjects: LCSH: Architecture and society—United States—History. | Architecture and society—
    Caribbean Area—History. | Slaves—United States—Social conditions. | Slaves—Caribbean Area—
    Social conditions. | Streetscapes (Urban design)—United States—History. | Streetscapes (Urban
    design)—Caribbean Area—History. | Space (Architecture)—Social aspects—United States—
    History. | Space (Architecture)—Social aspects—Caribbean Area—History.
Classification: LCC NA2543.S6 S59 2017 | DDC 720.1/03—dc23
LC record available at https://lccn.loc.gov/2017001842

Cover art: *Charleston, S.C.* (c. 1850) by J. W. Hill, engraving by Wellstood & Peters. (The Miriam
and Ira D. Wallach Division of Art, Prints and Photographs: Print Collection, The New York Public
Library)

To my sister, Cindy—C. E.

To Anna and Bella, with love—R. G.

CONTENTS

ACKNOWLEDGMENTS

The publication of this book was generously supported by a grant from the Graham Foundation for Advanced Study in Art and Architecture. We thank our superlative research assistant, John Carlos Castillo Marquez, a Ph.D. candidate in history at the University of Illinois at Urbana-Champaign, whose organizational skills and thoughtful insights helped us to perform our jobs as editors more successfully and made this a better volume than it would have been without him.

SLAVERY IN THE CITY

INTRODUCTION

Studying the Landscapes of North American
Urban Slavery

"There was slavery in cities, too?" is a question both of us hear often. As architectural historians who study the built environment of Atlantic slavery, we are accustomed to students, colleagues, and friends expressing bewilderment at this notion. The image of the southern plantation has taken strong root in American popular culture. It is difficult for many to appreciate that, although the majority of enslaved Africans were indeed held on agricultural properties, plantations were by no means the only sites of enslavement.

Antebellum cities and towns could be cosmopolitan, vibrant, fast-changing places. Urban slavery was always more precarious and fragile an institution than plantation slavery. However, the residences, governments, and businesses of North American cities did rely on bonded labor. Slaves lived and worked within institutions like hospitals and convents in towns. They lived in private homes and informal settlements on the edges of cities. The legacy of their presence and their labors is evident still.

This volume presents a strong and irrefutable picture of North America's antebellum urban centers as racially diverse, as economically reliant on slave labor, and, importantly, as material testaments to the skills and talents of African bondsmen. It argues that the practice and conditions of urban slavery shaped and transformed North American cities and towns, from the northern states to the Caribbean. This volume's contributors also make clear that as spatially complex, layered sites, cities accommodated bondsmen's resistance, individual and collective, to their condition. Cities are material monuments to the tensions, conflicts, and often fluctuating and subtle alliances that constituted the shifting sands on which urban slavery often precariously rested.

The authors of the essays that follow come from diverse disciplines, including architectural history, historical archaeology, geography, American studies, and literature. They analyze sites and landscapes that are equally diverse, from the backlots of nineteenth-century Charleston townhouses to movements of enslaved workers through the streets of a small Tennessee town. All share an understanding of the built environment—by which we mean the totality of our human-made surroundings, which can be studied at micro- and macro-scales, and includes everything from household objects to interventions in the natural landscape to buildings—as expressive and constitutive of social relations and as telling of everyday life experiences. Their essays highlight the diversity of the experiences of enslaved urban residents in antebellum cities and towns, even as the essays also articulate the commonalities. The most important of these speak to the conflict and violence inherent in relationships based on brute power. They also articulate the roles of resilience, resistance, and adaptation among enslaved populations in managing the control that slaveholders, urban authorities, and all whites, even children, held over them.

SLAVERY AND THE BUILT ENVIRONMENT

Contemporaries were well aware of the relationship of the material surroundings that sustained, supported, or undermined slavery. Slaveholders adapted old building types and developed new ones with the purpose of employing architecture to subjugate and control their human chattel. It is possible to follow debates in the popular periodicals and books of the time, as editors and responsive readers deliberated on the strengths and weaknesses of various designs and layouts of housing for enslaved workers. City councils throughout North America argued about the construction of architectural features—for example, walls, gates, and bell towers—meant to control the movement of and instill fear in enslaved peoples who found themselves in public spaces. Yet one of the ways slaves expressed their autonomy, restored their dignity, and even achieved their freedom was through manipulation of the very landscapes designed to restrict them.

We, and the contributors to this volume, find historical significance especially in the often-overlooked structures and settings fashioned by people who were not trained as designers. By studying the everyday we can understand better the machinations of the anonymous system of capitalism—agrarian, mercantile, and industrial—and uncover and study the true effects of the mechanisms of a system such as slavery. For example, one important fact that emerges from examining daily, routine experiences of the built environment is that the institution of slavery shaped the landscape of slaveholders too, and consequently their lives. Masters and mistresses were obliged to navigate through an environment they had created to manage the presence of their slaves, and it was not always a pleasant or assuring experience. An editorialist for the *Charleston Courier* lamented, "How many of us retire on a night under the impression that all of our servants are on the premises, and will continue there until morning. And how often it is quite the reverse, especially with our men servants, who are wandering to and fro all night, or are quietly ensconced in some dark retreat of villainy."[1]

Slaveholders looked with suspicion on the landscape they created. Each day when the sun set, a new landscape emerged in which enslaved Africans moved more freely and not always with benign intent. Urban slaveholders responded to this "new landscape" with draconian measures. Gina Haney describes in her essay about Charleston the nightly ritual of signaling the curfew for bonded workers, when the bells of St. Michael's Church peeled each night at nine o'clock and the Night Watch beat in tandem on brass drums. Frederick Law Olmsted described this phenomenon during his visit to the city in 1853: "The frequent drumming which is heard, the State military school, the cannon in position on the parade-ground, the citadel, the guard-house, with its martial ceremonies, the frequent parades of militia (the ranks mainly filled by foreign-born citizens), and, especially, the numerous armed-police, which is under military discipline, might lead one to imagine that the town was in a state of siege or revolution."[2]

Urban slavery in North America continues to be an understudied topic among historians. There has been only one comprehensive study of urban slavery since Richard Wade's 1964 seminal work, *Slavery in the Cities: The South, 1820–1860*. The next major work on urban slavery was Claudia Dale Goldin's *Urban Slavery in the American South, 1820–1860: A Quantitative History* (1976). Wade addressed the socioeconomic conditions that first strained, then undermined, the regime of bondage in the South's metropolises. By 1860 slavery was disintegrating in southern cities. Forty years earlier, the institution had seemed as stable in town as in country. Enslaved individuals comprised at least 20 percent of the population of the major cities. In most places the proportion was much higher, and in Charleston blacks outnumbered whites. Slaves handled the bulk of domestic drudgery, working in shops and factories; building the streets, bridges, and municipal installations; and even acquiring mechanical skills. Within four decades, however, the picture had changed dramatically. A Louisiana planter who was also a frequent visitor to New Orleans noticed this process: "Slavery is from its very nature eminently patriarchial and altogether agricultural. It does not thrive with master or slave when transplanted to cities."[3] Frederick Douglass stated it simply: "Slavery dislikes a dense population."[4]

Since the publication of Wade's *Slavery in the Cities,* little has been written on urban slavery. Cities are complex organisms, and comparative analyses must take into consideration differing racial densities, ward-based politics, and economic bases. The study of urban slavery can be a daunting task, but a few scholars continue to take up the challenge of the topic. Notably, Barbara Jeanne Fields's *Slavery and Freedom on the Middle Ground: Maryland during the Nineteenth Century* (1984), and Midori Takagi's *Rearing Wolves to Our Own Destruction: Slavery in Richmond, Virginia* (2000) build on the work of Wade and Goldin by looking closely at two cities, Baltimore and Richmond, situating urban slavery in the particulars of locality and region. Wade and Goldin sought, in part, to answer the question of whether urban slavery had been a sustainable economic model, and concluded that urban slavery was in decline before the Civil War. Although historians agree that urban slavery declined steadily after about 1820, there remains some disagreement as to why the practice of "hiring out" became less common toward the end of the antebellum period. Wade was the first to explain the seeming contradiction that slavery could flourish in an urban environment, outside the plantation economy. Wade posited that urban slavery, which by its nature had to allow a slave who was hired out much more freedom of movement, association, and negotiation, occupied a "twilight" area between plantation enslavement and freedom. Goldin concluded that market forces caused the decline of hiring slaves out. Fields found that for Baltimore, hiring out declined because the region had a wheat-based economy and an increasingly large immigrant population, against which hiring out could not compete. Takagi's study of Richmond confirms Fields's approach that studying regional economies and immigration offers the most nuanced explanation of this decline.[5]

Despite the relatively few studies of urban slavery, these books and other scholarly works have given us a richer understanding of the lives of enslaved workers who lived in cities. We have more insight into the ways that urban living gave enslaved individuals the opportunity to achieve more autonomy by such practices as negotiating wages for their own benefit, to form strong community networks by founding and constructing churches, and to build solidarity through the establishment of mutual-aid societies. Living in an urban environment, however, did not always benefit the enslaved. Living conditions were not necessarily better than they were on a plantation, and punishment for breaking curfews or laws was swift and often brutal. Separation from family and friends was, as on the plantation, always a possibility.

Scholars of material culture, especially architectural historians, have also studied urban slavery, and to great effect and insight. Analyzing the built landscape has proved to be one of the most profitable ways to recover the lives of the enslaved and the enslaver.

One of the first scholars to look at the material culture of urban slavery was John Michael Vlach. In his "'Without Recourse to Owners': The Architecture of Urban Slavery in the Antebellum South" (1997), Vlach noted that one third of the people living in the largest southern cities—Richmond, Charleston, and Savannah—were black, and that the tasks they performed as city-dwellers made them so much more visible than whites that visitors took the cities to have a large majority of black slaves. Some visitors thought that enslaved individuals constituted as much as two thirds of the population. Vlach studied these and other southern cities to determine where all enslaved workers lived. He found that the larger cities had two venues in which the enslaved were housed. The first can be called a "plantation compound"—a wing or wings attached to the back of the townhouse of the slaveholder, creating an L- or U-shape to the rear of the house. The individuals who occupied these wings were almost always owned by the proprietor of the house and served the household. This arrangement offered the slaveholder maximum opportunity to survey the comings and goings and the work of his or her slaves, and it was the most restrictive of the venues, embedded into the cityscape, out of sight to observers from the street. The second site of worker domiciles was the marginal sections of the city where most of those slaves who were hired out took up residence. These sections had housing that was substandard, ill-situated, and unhealthful.[6]

City officials were most concerned with the marginalized districts of ramshackle housing that hired-out slaves occupied. These districts struck anxiety into the hearts and minds of white city dwellers because the people who lived there had no supervision by white authorities. Thus, the individuals living in these districts moved about the city "without recourse to owners" and were considered a potential threat to white control of the city.

In 1999, Bernard L. Herman took advantage of the growing wealth of archaeologically recovered African American material culture to explore the variations in urban slave living spaces and their settings in Charleston, South Carolina. In "Slave and Servant Housing in Charleston, 1770–1820," Herman explained that on the urban properties of elite Charlestonians, the main dwelling was only one element among many. There were also service units such as kitchens, carriage houses, and washhouses, all of which could include housing for slaves and servants. Different arrangements of these various elements were common during this period, ranging from L-shapes to freestanding outbuildings. What all shared was the existence of a clear division between the main body of the house and its dependencies and the conceptualization of the total lot as a single unit under the control of the white owner.[7]

Some enslaved workers also slept in a main dwelling house, in doorways, halls, and even on pallets in their masters' rooms. Inventories sometimes suggest the presence of worker sleeping quarters in other spaces as well, especially in garret rooms. The presence of slave spaces throughout the properties of urban Charleston suggests that despite the brutal constrains of slavery, the city's slaves were able to claim some measure of privacy and independence in spots located at the very heart of the "urban plantation." Laid bare in the accounts of white life as gleaned from court documents, letters, and diaries—and most vividly in the detailed plans reproduced here—is the sense of the vulnerability of elite power at its most intimate point, the house.

Barbara Burlison Mooney's "Racial Boundaries in a Frontier Town: St. Louis on the Eve of the American Civil War" (2002) takes a close look at how the privileging of demographic data has facilitated erasure of the memory of St. Louis's slave past. Indeed, compared to cities like Richmond, Virginia, or New Orleans, Louisiana, slavery in St. Louis was on a smaller scale. From an outsider's perspective, obvious physical evidence of slavery in St. Louis could be difficult to discern. Writing in the mid-1850s, the German professor Franz von Löher alluded to the veiled nature of slavery: "Generally it is not readily apparent that St. Louis is the major city of a slave state. Only gradually did it emerge that people here are of a somewhat different sort; life here looks wilder and more strident, as if expended faster." English novelist Anthony Trollope claimed that "St. Louis has none of the aspects of a slave city."[8]

Mooney's article reconfigures the city of St. Louis to grapple with its slave past. Studying the narratives of former slaves and using graphic material such as old maps, nineteenth-century perspective views, and twentieth-century measured drawings of historic buildings can help determine black urban territory by defining zones and establishing spatial relationships, connections that might otherwise elude historians. Remapping the black terrain of antebellum St. Louis also makes more clear that racial territory was considered less in terms of specific neighborhoods and more in terms of a system of functional spaces, zones defining habitation, labor worship, terror, and resistance. Replotting the city by race reveals that St. Louis was not characterized by boundless physical and social opportunity, nor by strict separation by race, but by intricately defined, interpenetrating, and often violent white and black territories.

Historian and novelist Lois Leveen used a method of close reading to analyze the spatial aspects of enslavement in her article "Dwelling in the House of Oppression: The Spatial, Racial, and Textual Dynamics of Harriet Wilson's *Our Nig*" (2001). Leveen considers the effects of living in a house that was marked with divisions of race and class through examination of both Frado, a child of an African American father and a white mother, and the white Bellmont family. For Leveen, the act of "dwelling" has the anthropomorphic quality of a narrator or protagonist in the construction of the Bellmont house. Leveen argues that the Wilson's narrative describes hierarchies of power within the private home, and that by doing so, the reader can discern how the private, domestic spaces are the locus in which the dynamics of interracial encounters outside of slavery and the social constructions of race are born.[9]

Leveen describes Frado's literal and metaphorical place of being a "black" body in a "white" house. Such observation ultimately shows the nineteenth-century mindset where "blackness serves whiteness." Leveen also describes the way in which these multiple spaces in the home produce various narratives about Frado and the Bellmonts. Whereas some, such as the Bellmont daughter Mary, would claim to never want a black person inside their home, it was not uncommon among white Americans to feel that blackness or having a "nig" would benefit the white household. Finally, Leveen considers Wilson's "authorial strategy," where she dwells on the home of oppression in order to liberate her own self from the domination of whites and thereby exposes the cruelty and callousness that essentially operates behind the facade of the "happy home."

In her 2010 article "Urban Slavery at Work: The Bellamy Mansion Compound, Wilmington, North Carolina," Catherine W. Bishir studies the Bellamy Mansion compound, completed in 1860 in Wilmington, North Carolina. Bishir shows in unusually concrete and vivid terms how urban slavery shaped domestic architecture in a southern port city. As an urban ensemble that included slave quarters and a carriage house, garden and work yard, cistern and coal cellar, walls and fences, the Bellamy Mansion reveals connections to the institution of slavery in every aspect of the house, from its construction to its design and function.[10]

Drawing on extensive documentation including personal memoirs and slave narratives, this article identifies enslaved artisans and the domestics who cooked, laundered, nursed children, drove the coach, and operated the running water system. From the complex itself we can understand the design of the big house, the work yard, the slave quarters, and the coach house as a working complex posited on slavery. Paths and walls defined and separated black and white activities, shielding kitchen and cooks from dining room and diners. Nearly hidden outdoor staircases allowed slaves to carry baskets of laundry and buck-ets of coal from the ground level to the "parlor" and "bedroom floors" above, and illusionistic facades presented one face to the public street, another to the working domain of slavery in the partially walled rear yard.

The Bellamy family and their slaves occupied the compound for only a few months before the Civil War began. Today the main house is open to the public as a museum of history and decorative arts. The current project is to repair and restore the largely intact slave quarters. The issue of interpreting the slave expe-rience as part of a balanced story of life at the Bellamy complex is an ongoing and consciously addressed challenge.

In her book *Slaves Waiting for Sale: Abolitionist Art and the American Slave Trade* (2013), Maurie McInnis's chapter "Mapping Richmond's Slave Trade in 1853" describes another urban environment, possibly built by slaves and most definitely built for slaves. McInnis reveals the urban landscape of Richmond's infamous domestic slave trade—almost two dozen sites used as "pens" or "jails" to hold slaves awaiting sale. Located among the cooperages and wagon repair shops, slave jails were a prominent feature in the dense bustling business district of antebellum Richmond. From these jails more than a quarter million enslaved men, women, and children were "sold south" to work the cotton plantations of Alabama, Mississippi, Louisiana, and Texas. This complex landscape of com-mon commercial buildings and slave jails now lies beneath interstate exchanges and access roads but has been reconstructed from various maps and records of the period. The reconstruction is instructive as an example of the common practice in the urban South and its resulting landscape of slave trafficking.[11]

This volume, the first compilation of essays that deals directly and exclusively with the role of North American slavery on urban landscapes, material culture, and city life during the antebellum period, contributes to the work of the above scholars, and others, by offering further evidence that we can understand the built environment of North America today only if we take into account the role of slavery in its making.[12] Indeed, it could be argued that slaves were responsible for the built environment of several continents. As Walter Johnson demon-strates in his *River of Dark Dreams: Slavery and Empire in the Cotton Kingdom*, slavery was essential to the development of capitalism during the eighteenth and nineteenth centuries. In 1860, the 4 million enslaved workers in the United

States had an estimated value of $3 billion—more than the combined capital invested in railroads and factories. In 1833, when Britain outlawed slavery in the empire and consequently paid compensation to three thousand Caribbean slaveholders, the cost was 40 percent of the total government budget for that year.[13] Slavery built the landscapes of the Atlantic world. The essays that follow speak to the role of the institution of slavery in the transformation of antebellum cities and towns. They also elucidate the ways that enslaved workers, as inhabitants of these sites, contributed to the formation of their material and social landscapes, past and present. All of this is discernable in the world around us, though sometimes only through close analysis of ruined sites, dusty records, and other data.

Fortunately, historians, architectural historians, archaeologists, and others have taken it upon themselves to study such clues. Their research makes clear that the shaping of the North American landscape has been to a great extent the result of the interplay of forces that variously sustained and challenged slavery. Many of the urban environments that are familiar to us today are the legacy of such violence, as well as of ingenuity, courage, and perseverance.

URBAN SLAVERY INVESTIGATED IN THIS VOLUME

The housing of enslaved workers changed considerably between the late eighteenth and early nineteenth centuries. In his essay, Edward A. Chappell examines the factors that contributed to the changes and what they meant for bonded and free blacks, in the context of prerevolutionary Williamsburg, Virginia, and nineteenth-century Falmouth, Jamaica, a port- and market town of comparable size on the north coast of Jamaica. He also considers the significance of being able to trace the developments across such vast distances. International sentiments about matters such as the growing abolitionist movement may have played as large a role in evolving housing forms as did regional differences.

Virginia's eighteenth-century capital and the associated port at Yorktown illustrate a pattern of relatively unspecialized and inexpensive housing for workers. Jamaica, by contrast, was the principal British colonial exporter in the eighteenth century. Sugar and rum fueled a more expansive economy than that of the rural Chesapeake. There too, however, durable and specialized worker housing was the exception rather than the rule. It was only after the American Revolution that one sees a clear division developing in Jamaica between housing for agricultural laborers and enslaved domestic workers. Indeed, some of the accommodation for domestic workers and free people of color more closely resembled the housing of property-holding whites than it did that for their bound sugar- and cattle-raising counterparts, in quality of finish if not scale and arrangement. The spectrum of housing was far more varied in Jamaica than that in the Chesapeake and Carolinas. This reflected both the amount of wealth and the more diverse West Indian population, economically and racially.

"Appropriated to the Use of the Colored People" takes a critical look at a neglected topic, slavery in the northern states. In it, John Michael Vlach considers the ideological function of the built environment, arguing that the practice of housing enslaved northern workers in marginal spaces served to naturalize their inferior status. In this, northern slaveholders were not unlike their southern counterparts, and Vlach holds that arguments that northern slavery was milder cannot be supported. In this, there are echoes of Chappell's response to the claim that Bermudan slavery was less severe. Vlach has occasionally encountered incredulity and resistance when he tells people he studies slavery in the North. He reports that this essay has been twenty years in the making.

Although historians have documented and interpreted the daily routines and living conditions of enslaved African Americans on plantations for the colonial and antebellum periods, there is less evidence and less analysis of slave life in the households of lesser slaveholders, those who held five to ten slaves. Clifton Ellis's essay uses evidence from the 1798 Federal Direct Tax to reconstruct the city of Annapolis at the end of the eighteenth century in order to investigate the material life and daily routines of slaveholding households. This tax is one of the most revealing and significant sources for historians of material life in the early republic. The tax was remarkably detailed and listed the dimensions of the building, the construction materials, and the number of windowpanes, among other elements. Thus, at the turn of the eighteenth century, the United States had a remarkable record of its built environment. Unfortunately, the 1798 tax lists were lost to fire when the British burned Washington during the War of 1812, and only a few tax lists survived in other locales, such as Annapolis, where officials retained copies of the official roles they had sent to Washington.

By cross-comparing the 1798 tax of Annapolis with property deeds of the period and with the 1800 federal census, it is possible to reconstruct each household in Annapolis, locate that household on a city map, determine the size and construction materials of the house, and populate that house with the free and enslaved members of the household. With this quantitative material at hand, it is possible to then analyze the qualitative environment of a southern urban landscape at the turn of the eighteenth century.

Like most interpretations of urban conditions in the antebellum period, the analysis of late eighteenth-century Annapolis shows a more fluid and freer interaction of enslaved, free blacks, and whites in the city streets. As expected, elite slaveholders had space enough to relegate daily slave movement to spaces that were well defined from those of the white household. But Annapolis had a remarkable percentage of small slaveholding households that had little or no surplus space for slaves to occupy. Thus, the white household and its enslaved servants led a daily life that constantly intersected and overlapped in its routines of work and leisure. Since most slaveholding Annapolis households were small, we must ask ourselves how this spatial proximity affected master-slave relations and at what point the masters of small slaveholding households began to seek more separate spatial spheres for themselves and their slaves. The larger question to be explored is the effect that spatial proximity had on the development of identity that evolved from distinctly different cultures and attitudes toward race.

Gina Haney forces the reader to examine subtle, yet powerful, ways in which race played out on the micro and macro scales of antebellum Charleston, South Carolina. While many scholars have grappled with such issues in urban settings, few have moved beyond examination of architectural evidence to analyze the accompanying sensorial landscapes. The whites who built and regulated Charleston's dense urban fabric, and their slaves who manipulated that urban environment, had to consider many factors including race, gender, architectural settings and spaces, and, as Haney points out, intangible and unpredictable movements, sights, and sounds. Landscapes that white Charlestonians planned and built to define the enslaved status of the city's black residents were used by slaves to their own advantage during specific times of the day and night.

Haney utilizes extant physical evidence as well as primary and secondary sources to develop her point that consideration of the human sensory experience is essential to understanding the life of both the enslaved and the enslaver in antebellum Charleston. Haney's analysis of the sensorial landscape is deepened and made even more convincing by her use of Standpoint Theory as developed by Sandra Harding, Julia Wood, and Patricia Hill Collins, who maintain that an oppressed class of people have a special knowledge of the world from their own perspective that cannot be perceived by their oppressors.[14] Haney's essay is speculative, perhaps, but it is nevertheless extremely valuable for its bold assertion that space does not necessarily have physical or temporal boundaries.

Some historians have suggested that slavery in the city was less harsh than it was on the plantation. Presumably, slaves had more autonomy in the city and moved through the urban landscape with fewer challenges from white authority. The essay by Gina Haney, which deals with urban slavery in Charleston, South Carolina, challenges this view, as does Kenneth Hafertepe in his study of Texas towns. While Haney analyzes the ways in which slaves responded to Charleston's environment, Hafertepe considers the ways in which urban forms were transferred and transformed as slavery moved westward and how this migration affected the apparent autonomy of slaves.

The slave economy of the South dictated that it was cheaper to establish plantation enterprises in virgin soil than it was to renew and tend old tobacco and cotton fields. Thus planters continually pushed westward. The Missouri Compromise and the Compromise of 1850 were the result of southern insistence that slavery must follow an inexorable course westward. Although tobacco, rice, and cotton required different organizational systems, the face of slavery did not change according to the crop. Hafertepe finds the same was true for urban slavery.

As Charles H. Faulkner shows, nineteenth-century Knoxville, Tennessee, was unique among neighboring southern cities in its politics, economy, and racial demography. On the eve of the Civil War, the absence of large plantations in Knoxville's countryside and the small-scale craft and trade composition of its economy distinguished it from many other area towns. More importantly, it was the urban center for the mountainous region of western North Carolina, East Tennessee, and northern Georgia, which favored the Union in the face of national division. The black population of Knoxville from 1820 to 1870 was almost always smaller than that in her sister cities of Nashville and Memphis, remained relatively constant throughout this period, and did not show a significant increase from fleeing refugees and rural migrants in 1870. Another distinction is that in the decade before the Civil War, the free black population increased in Knoxville whereas it stayed the same in Memphis and actually decreased in Nashville. Through a study of documents and historical archaeology, this essay looks at how Knoxville's distinct character influenced the patterns of slavery and its aftermath within its boundaries.

Archaeological excavation of two nineteenth-century slave quarters reveals the construction and size of these buildings and their relationship to the master's residence. White slaveholders were widely distributed throughout the central part of town, resulting in scattered black slave families and neighborhoods prior to emancipation. The city's racial geography—including the close association of enslaved and free blacks and mixed neighborhoods of master and the enslaved—had a strong effect on the postbellum lifeways of Knoxville blacks and the emergence of modem African American culture in this city in the late nineteenth and the early twentieth centuries. Associations of free and enslaved black families and their strong nuclear family orientation appear to have maintained the strength of ethnic bonds in Knoxville's later African American community. However, it has also been suggested that the personalized and paternalistic attitudes of dominant whites among the scattered black families in mixed neighborhoods resulted in a smaller and less assertive African American middle class in this city.

Ever since Richard Wade's groundbreaking work *Slavery in the Cities* was published in 1964, most studies of urban slavery have focused on large southern cities, such as Richmond, Charleston, and New Orleans, which had populations in 1860 of 38,000, 40,000, and 169,000, respectively. There was during the antebellum period a steady decline in the slave population of southern cities, and although scholars still debate the cause for this decline, the essays in this volume are more concerned with the nature and conditions of slave life in the city. The topic of urban slavery continues to provide fresh insights into the lives of slaves in the city.

Yet the term "urban slavery," as we understand it from the study of large cities, cannot be applied effectively to a study of slavery in the smaller towns and hamlets that dominated community life in the South. To be sure, Kenneth Hafertepe contends in this volume that conditions of surveillance that masters created and subversion tactics that slaves responded with find similar architectural expressions in the small frontier towns of Texas. In her essay, *"Henry, A Slave, v. State of Tennessee,"* however, Lisa Tolbert argues that slavery in a small southern town was qualitatively different from slavery in large cities or on plantations.

Tolbert's focus is the small town of Franklin, Tennessee, where a murder trial, faithfully recorded in court records, provides evidence for her thesis. Combined with the recollections of Harriet Jacobs, a slave who lived in a small North Carolina town, Tolbert finds that although small-town slaves, like their counterparts in large cities, also lived out, hired out, and used public spaces, their experience was measurably different. Small-town slaves lacked the anonymity that large urban settings afforded. In the case of Henry, this lack of anonymity had fatal consequences when combined with circumstantial evidence. Yet in the case of Harriet Jacobs, the more intimate environment of a small town protected her from a potentially abusive master. Equally as free in their movements through the townscape as were slaves in large cities, the small-town slave negotiated a landscape that was much more complex in its intimacy among master, slave, and free black.

The experience of small-town slavery was by far the more common experience of what has become known as "urban slavery." Small towns were the focus of community life, and they were the center of slaveholders' social, political, and religious realms. And the landscape that Tolbert explores in Franklin, where slaves made up 42 percent of the population in 1850, was representative of small towns throughout middle Tennessee, all of which had similar demographics. Tolbert's analysis of the slave landscape of a small southern town makes for insightful comparisons with the other studies of the city/town slave experience in this volume.

The misconception that slavery was exclusively a rural phenomenon and the associated implication that urban populations were untouched by the institution is widespread—and pernicious. We are grateful to the authors of the essays in this volume for contributing to a more accurate understanding of slavery's extent and impact throughout the continent, including its cities. They confront directly the significant misapprehension that slavery was a rich man's game, practiced only on the largest, wealthiest agricultural estates in the South. Acknowledging that slavery existed throughout the nation, and was integrated into North America's economy and social structure in multiple ways, calls for reappraisals across many dimensions. Better understanding of the extent of slavery allows us, as a people, to grapple with greater clarity over matters like the contributions of bondsmen to American history and culture and of the long-term consequences of practicing slavery on our shores. These are important questions that Americans continue to face.

NOTES

1. *Charleston Courier,* September 23, 1845, quoted in Maury McInnis, *The Politics of Taste in Antebellum Charleston* (Chapel Hill: University of North Carolina Press, 2005), 181.

2. Frederick Law Olmsted, *A Journey in the Seaboard Slave States: With Remarks on Their Economy* (New York: Dix and Edwards, 1856), 1:404.

3. Quoted in Richard Wade, *Slavery in the Cities: The South, 1820–1860* (New York: Oxford University Press, 1964), 3–4.

4. Quoted in Wade, *Slavery in the Cities,* 4.

5. Barbara Jeanne Fields, *Slavery and Freedom on the Middle Ground: Maryland during the Nineteenth Century* (New Haven, Conn.: Yale University Press, 1984); Midori Takagi, *Rearing Wolves to Our Own Destruction: Slavery in Richmond, Virginia, 1782–1865* (Charlottesville: University Press of Virginia, 2000). See also Ira Berlin and Leslie M. Harris, eds., *Slavery in New York* (New York: New Press, 2005). These essays were published to accompany a major exhibit at the New-York Historical Society. Although none of the essays deals directly with the spatial environment of urban slavery, they demonstrate how slavery shaped the daily experiences of antebellum New Yorkers, and how slavery helped the city to become a world center of commerce and finance.

6. John Michael Vlach, "'Without Recourse to Owners': The Architecture of Urban Slavery in the Antebellum South," in *Perspectives in Vernacular Architecture,* vol. 6, *Shaping Communities,* ed. Carter L. Hudgins and Elizabeth Collins Cromley (Knoxville: University of Tennessee Press, 1997), 150–60.

7. Bernard L. Herman, "Slave and Servant Housing in Charleston, 1770–1820," *Historical Archaeology* 33, no. 3 (1999): 88–101.

8. Barbara Burlison Mooney, "Racial Boundaries in a Frontier Town: St. Louis on the Eve of the American Civil War," in *Identities in Space: Contested Terrains in the Western City since 1850,* ed. Simon Gunn and Robert J. Morris (London: Ashgate, 2002), 10.

9. Lois Leveen, "Dwelling in the House of Oppression: The Spatial, Racial, and Textual Dynamics of Harriet Wilson's *Our Nig,*" *African American Review* 35, no. 4 (Winter 2001): 561–80.

10. Catherine W. Bishir, "Urban Slavery at Work: The Bellamy Mansion Compound, Wilmington, North Carolina," *Buildings and Landscapes: Journal of the Vernacular Architecture Forum* 17, no. 2 (Fall 2010): 13–32.

11. Maurie D. McInnis, "Representing the Slave Trade," in *Waiting for Sale: Abolitionist Art and the American Slave Trade* (Chicago: University of Chicago Press, 2013), 55–84.

12. We are surprised by architectural histories that attempt to do so. For instance, Steven Conn and Max Page, eds., *Building the Nation: Americans Write about Their Architecture, Their Cities, and Their Landscape* (Philadelphia: University of Pennsylvania Press, 2003), runs to more than four hundred pages, less than one of which speaks to the role of slavery in building the American landscape (pp. 157–58).

13. Walter Johnson, *River of Dark Dreams: Slavery and Empire in the Cotton Kingdom* (Cambridge, Mass.: Harvard University Press, 2013); Johnson, "King Cotton's Long Shadow" *New York Times*, March 30, 2013, SR12.

14. See, for instance, Sandra Harding, *Whose Science? Whose Knowledge? Thinking from Women's Lives* (Ithaca, N.Y.: Cornell University Press, 1991); Julia Wood, *Gendered Lives: Communication, Gender, and Culture,* 12th ed. (Belmont, Calif.: Wadsworth, 2016); and Patricia Hill Collins, *Black Feminist Thought: Knowledge, Consciousness, and the Politics of Empowerment* (Boston: Unwin Hyman, 1991).

ARCHITECTURE OF URBAN DOMESTIC SLAVERY IN THE CHESAPEAKE AND JAMAICA

Comparative Evidence

EDWARD A. CHAPPELL

Multiple factors drove change in the housing of enslaved workers and their owners during the late eighteenth and early nineteenth centuries, including development of regional economies within an international mercantile network, Britain's closing of the slave trade, and political reaction to the growing antislavery movement. The change is graphically illustrated by comparison of housing and work buildings from prerevolutionary Williamsburg and Annapolis with Falmouth between 1800 and 1838, a port- and market town of comparable size on the north coast of Jamaica. More broadly, comparison between the practice in the Chesapeake region and Jamaica allows us to recognize temporal change as well as regional variation.

Growing specialization in housing and work spaces reflected varied concerns about the visibility, control, and—selectively—condition of enslaved people, as well as those people's ability to affect their own living arrangements. A careful look at surviving fragments of this material world reveal striking parallels and contrasts over great distances, tangible reminders of the connections wrought by the Atlantic trade and developing international sentiments on the value of humanity. Comparisons are useful at this early stage of studying slavery and housing because it helps us weigh arguments over the influence of regional circumstances.

Virginia's eighteenth-century capital and the associated port at Yorktown illustrate a pattern of relatively unspecialized and inexpensive housing for workers, corresponding to conditions in the rural Chesapeake. Sugar and rum fueled a more expansive economy in Jamaica, the principal British colonial exporter in the eighteenth and early nineteenth centuries. There too, however, durable and specialized worker housing was the exception rather than the rule before the end of the eighteenth century, making it hard to see now above the archaeological record. The sample improves significantly if we look at what can be learned from the houses of owners in addition to front-stage buildings primarily intended for the workers and their work.

It was after the American Revolution that most surviving preindustrial Jamaican houses were built, especially on the wealthy north coast, for owners, their white staffs, and certain enslaved workers. It was then, particularly after Parliament banned the Atlantic slave trade in 1807, that we see a clear division developing between housing for agricultural laborers and enslaved domestic and other high-status workers. In methods of construction, not size and arrangement, some accommodations for domestic servants and especially free people of color came to resemble the housing of property-holding whites as much as it did that for bound sugar- and cattle-raising workers. The spectrum of housing was far more varied in Jamaica than that in the Chesapeake and Carolinas. This reflected both the relative amount of wealth and the more diverse West Indian population, economically and racially. Nevertheless, certain models for housing transcended regions. Close study of urban quarters and service buildings is beginning to reveal similarities as well as variations in buildings among the regions reflecting broadly shared slave owners' perspectives, from the Chesapeake to the Caribbean.

Intending Williamsburg and Annapolis as urban centers for the important tobacco-selling colonies of Virginia and Maryland, Lieutenant Governor Francis Nicholson led design of broad streets grandly arranged in baroque patterns, looking to princely European models for urban space. Both communities flourished, particularly in the third quarter of the eighteenth century, but the two capitals always resembled English country towns, not cities. Houses for white property owners and tenants were nearly all freestanding, often of wood, with few brick rows of the variety built in cities like Philadelphia, Bristol, and

Limerick—or those in more intensely urban communities of the region after the Revolution, including Alexandria, Richmond, Petersburg, and especially Baltimore. Few eighteenth-century houses in either town varied much in form from their rural counterparts.

This was equally true of housing and work spaces for the enslaved half of the population, when their accommodations now remain visible at all. Unfree blacks lived and worked throughout the buildings and yards occupied by residents who owned or rented their time. Personal domestic service, food serving, and house cleaning kept blacks and whites close together. When sleeping, many domestic workers remained nearby, while others removed to attics or cellars. Certain central modes of work, notably cooking and laundering, were emphatically separated from white residents' living space.

Domestic servants who occupied the bedchambers, passages, nurseries, and closets of whites left few records beyond the occasional reference in whites' letters and diaries and physical clues.[1] As late as 1823, a correspondent complained that Williamsburg houses lacked separate quarters, so slaves "have to stay in the basement or garret rooms," an arrangement "you know can not be very agreeable to [white] Virginians."[2] What represents change in this comment is the white residents' increased discomfort with the arrangement.

Two examples of personal or domestic workers occupying attic spaces illustrate modest and exceptional degrees of adaptation. The fine double-pile house the richest Virginian, Robert "King" Carter, built in 1727 beside the governor's residence on Palace Street in Williamsburg includes unspecialized attic space, arguably divided for two individuals or related groups of workers in or soon after 1759. Inside the otherwise open and unfinished attic, a carpenter built a plastered stud partition to separate two habitable rooms. Residents climbed the only stairs in the house, occupying a two-story passage, and they entered the attic, ducking repeatedly under the lowest-set roof timbers. Residents of the inner, south room walked through the outer, north room into their space, which they could lock. Some years thereafter another carpenter applied riven clapboards unevenly above the old plastered partition, indicating that the residents sought full separation between the two rooms.[3] Acting as the sole route of entry, the outer room never offered privacy to its residents. Like attic rooms occupied by many black and white Chesapeake residents throughout the eighteenth century, both rooms were very hot in summer and drafty in winter, without fireplaces or additional finish.

If access to and the character of Carter's attic quarters were characteristically unspecialized, the attributes in the attic of the large Georgian house John Ridout, secretary to Governor Horatio Sharpe, built in Annapolis in 1764–65 were unusually high for a pair of plastered rooms, both with a window, simple trim, and a fireplace. Indeed, the quality of the two rooms could indicate intended use by low-status white members of the Ridout household such as a white housekeeper. The larger of the two rooms, 19 feet 3 inches by 12 feet 9 inches controlled access to two storerooms, while the 9-foot-9-inch by 9-foot other stood alone. While the quality of both rooms offered a modest level of respectability by late colonial white standards, their residents' access was through rustic space. Each resident climbed a stair from an upper passage and walked through the unfinished attic to unlock a door into her or his room. But once past the doorway, they were in their own private space.

Both awake and asleep, domestic workers in the eighteenth-century Chesapeake also commonly occupied spaces or buildings where they and others cooked and washed for their owners or renters. From Maryland south to the Caribbean, before the Revolution, slaveholders employed two principal strategies for separating this messy work from their own more refined rooms, placing it in cellars and separate buildings, both in contrast to the relatively integrated position of cooking and laundry in substantial houses from the mid-Atlantic colonies north to the Maritimes.

Eighteenth-century Williamsburg kitchens were overwhelmingly detached from the main house, either as the sole main-floor space or the largest space in a multi-room structure (fig. 1a–u, w–z). Commonly, too, their design was based on the Anglo-Chesapeake small-house model.[4] At its most basic, the unspecialized form was a single room in which black residents cooked, gathered, ate, and slept (fig. 1a–e). Nearly always it was entered directly from outside, seldom with a porch or other covering.

Certain kitchen residents acquired adjoining space to separate themselves from work and people occupying the core room, by climbing a steep stair to the attic; entering a rear, shed-roofed room (fig. 1f–j); or occasionally stepping into a lateral extension of the cookroom (fig. 1q–s). What marked all these as

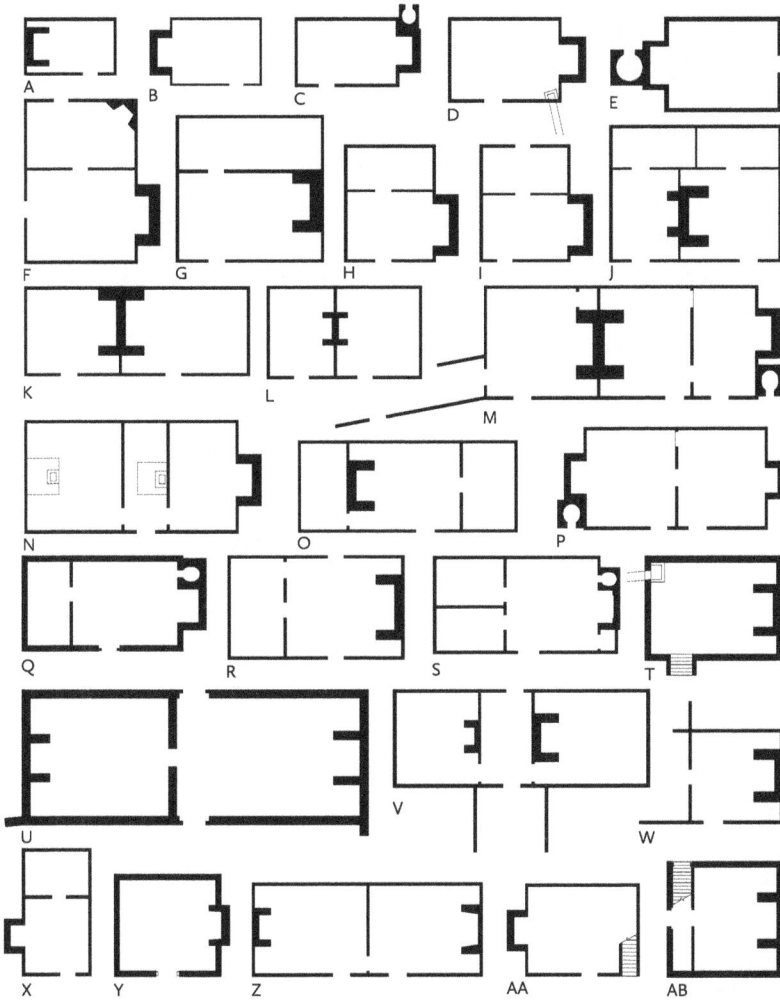

Figure 1. Plans of kitchens and quarters in Williamsburg, Virginia, surviving and based on archaeological excavation: (*a*) tailor Richard Morton; (*b*) Elizabeth Carlos; (*c*) James Moir; (*d*) James Anderson tavern kitchen; (*e*) Robert Carter; (*f*) John Tayloe; (*g*) William Waters; (*h*) James Geddy, Sr.; (*i*) Alexander Craig; (*j*) James Geddy, Jr.; (*k*) Henry Wetherburn's Tavern; (*l*) Anne and Christopher Ayscough; (*m*) Peyton Randolph; (*n*) Philip Barraud; (*o*) George Reid; (*p*) John Greenhow; (*q*) Thomas Everard; (*r*) Nelson and Galt families; (*s*) Market Square Tavern; (*t*) John Palmer's kitchen in the cellar of an outbuilding; (*u*) Governor's Palace; (*v*) John Randolph; (*w*) Lady Susannah Randolph; (*x*) Sarah Byrd; (*y*) Custis; (*z*) Robert Page Waller; (*aa*) Burwell Bassett; (*ab*) Walter W. Webb. (Courtesy of the author)

results of relatively unspecialized planning was that the cookroom remained the core in which people gathered and through which all residents passed to reach ancillary accommodations.

Much is known about the plans of eighteenth-century kitchen-quarters from excavation and a bit of documentation, but only one survives in Williamsburg. What this scant standing evidence suggests is that, with a few high-gentry exceptions, most of the buildings were relatively cheaply built and roughly finished. On balance, the most solidly built buildings had the best chance of surviving.[5]

The one detached kitchen-quarter remaining to the present stands behind the Thomas Everard House, offering a glimpse of how such buildings could evolve and function. It began as a single cookroom, about 18 feet 8 inches by 14 feet 7 inches, rather cheaply framed and enclosed with riven clapboards. The well-heeled Elizabeth Russell probably built it as early as around 1730. Residents of the attic climbed an open ladder to reach their sleeping space, of similar size but limited by the roof slopes. A later owner removed three of the wooden walls and rebuilt them in brick but left the floor as dirt or clay. Finally, in 1773, attorney and sometime-mayor Thomas Everard extended the building with more brickwork, creating a 7-foot-8-inch by 14-foot-8-inch second ground-floor room and a small one above it. By then, all four rooms were plastered and lighted by windows. All the residents gathered in the cookroom, moving from it to the tighter spaces they could call their own.

That Virginia and Maryland owners assumed most of their domestic workers would occupy the room in which the owners' food was cooked is indicated by the regularity with which the cookroom was largest and closest to the main house. George Washington created a complex group of outbuildings at Mount Vernon between 1774 and 1787, some with his purposes so esoteric as "hall for visiting servants," but he mounted his servant bells outside the south end of the house, where workers in the adjoining cookroom would hear them ring. Even at the Virginia Governor's Palace by the 1710s, the cookroom occupied the nearest space in a substantial, brick-walled flanker (fig. 1u).

By around 1750, slaveholders developed a model for quarters, kitchens, and laundries that doubled the Anglo-Chesapeake single-room house, most economically doubling fireplaces in a central chimney (fig. 1j–l). The two rooms

EDWARD A. CHAPPELL

functioned variously for cooking, laundering, and living space in both town and country, and plantation fieldworkers could occupy them removed from domestic labor near owners' houses. Henry Wetherburn built a two-unit work building-quarter with oversized cookroom behind his successful Williamsburg tavern apparently before midcentury, providing space for enslaved servants traveling with their owners as well as those working for the tavern keeper. Such two-room buildings doubled the potential living space for residents, and a pair of front exterior doors allowed independent use, but residents of the attic still spent time in the lower rooms and moved through them to reach their limited private space. Lobbies, passages, and porches were nearly nonexistent. They were then relatively unspecialized in terms of workers' accommodations and owners' control of cooking and laundry work.

More than forty freestanding kitchens are known from eighteenth-century Williamsburg. By contrast, less than a dozen householders followed the alternate strategy of placing a cookroom in the cellar of the main block. There is a single unclear example of a cookroom housed in a rear wing, at the residence of builder Benjamin Powell. Patterns of work were not that altered by Williamsburg cellar cookrooms because cooks still labored on open hearths in poorly lighted rooms, and they or other servants carried the food outside to daylight and into dining spaces on main floors. Delivery of food and retrieval of waste remained outwardly visible, as workers walked outside and into a rear or side door.

Food delivery was equally visible inside, generally through a public stair passage and occasionally through a first-floor bedchamber. At the two-room-plan houses of apothecary and sometime mayor George Gilmer (later Tucker House) and attorney John Palmer, food was carried through the passage and into the eating space. Both before and after alterations in 1752–54 and 1768–72 at the Virginia Governor's Palace, food was similarly carried from outside through a side lobby and backstage room to the main stair hall and dining room. Even at the large midcentury Georgian houses of George Wythe and Peyton Randolph, enslaved staff carried food to the front of the main passage and into the grand dining room, through the same space traversed by the diners, although Randolph's servants reached the passage via a covered way and chamber. Little had changed since merchant Thomas Nelson built his comparably grand Yorktown house with a single passage to the dining room in 1729–30. The articulate British architect Benjamin Henry Latrobe despised such passages in the United States for the very reason that they offered no discrete, independent routes for cleaning and food delivery, likening them to sewers combined with genteel promenades.[6]

Annapolis resembled Williamsburg as a small colonial capital with freestanding houses fleshing out a showy, baroque town plan. Unlike Williamsburg, Annapolis was also a port with wealthy merchant-planters resident rather than arriving seasonally at public times. The richest elites built houses that while not urban in the sense of rowhouses, grew to be more urban in their shielding of service from the public view. They did this by drawing the kitchen into the main block or placing it and domestic workers in an attached flanker. Both differed from the predominant Williamsburg pattern of delivery through fresh air.

Annapolis cellar kitchens more closely resembled English urban practice in providing internal communication. In 1739, Judge John Brice built the first and smallest of what came to be recognized as a distinctively Annapolitan gentry house, with an offset front stair hall giving access to a pair of reception rooms occupying the rear half of the main floor. The pairs of reception rooms and ornamented rear landscapes made such houses double-fronted, more than seen in Williamsburg, and they gave impetus for removing service from the rear view.[7] Brice placed the cookroom in a dark cellar space incorporating an enclosed stair. His enslaved servants carried food up these stairs or a second set to his dining room. Beginning his far grander house in 1764, John Ridout again placed his better-appointed kitchen in the cellar. There, workers brought food up under the main stair and carried it through the hall into the oversized dining room, entering through the same doorway used by the Ridout family and guests. Ridout followed the same model when building his three speculative rowhouses nearby in 1773–74, among the first in the region, by placing cookrooms at the rear of the cellars and connecting them via interior stairs and a passage to a dining room at the back.

An expansive alternative used in late-colonial Annapolis and only once in Williamsburg as well as more often at high-gentry plantation seats was to place cooking and laundering in one of two flankers connected by enclosed hyphens. This resembled the arrangement of earlier Georgian plantation houses like

EDWARD A. CHAPPELL

Carter's Grove (1751–55) and Westover (1750–51, reusing older flankers). But it, as well as later Virginia plantation ensembles at Mount Airy and Blandfield, enclosed the links with walled hyphens, connected the kitchen hyphen with principal circulation space in the main house, and generally enlarged the flankers to provide more rooms. James Brice hugely expanded on his father's house form and connected a cookroom in a dependency by a hyphen to a grand stair hall, and through it to the oversized dining room, in an assertive Annapolis House that rose over six years after 1767. Designer-joiner William Buckland crafted a more stylish version for Matthias Hammond on a nearby street in 1774. There, workers carried meals from the front of a flanker through a brick-walled hyphen to diners in a room overlooking the garden. The route was far from a straight shot: from the cookroom, down hyphen steps and up another short flight into a side stair passage, and from there either through the front passage or a small side room to the dining space.

From the workers' perspective, delivering food had become no easier, with the exception of avoiding the worst weather, because the hyphens offered waiting space closer to the owner without the potential freedom and congeniality of the cookroom or yard. Hyphens were nearly always unheated, but that from the kitchen at the James Brice house included a heated space in which servants could wait adjoining the stair hall, with confined living space above the hyphen as well as upstairs in the kitchen wing. What the multipart houses offered to selected workers was the highly limited possibility of residence in a well-built flanker, sometimes with independent access to one's room through a stair passage, as at John Randolph's seven-part Tazewell Hall in Williamsburg (fig. iv) and Robert Beverley's five-part Blandfield (1769–72) in Essex County.[8] It is worth recognizing, however, that plastered, heated, and relatively well-lighted rooms in large kitchen flankers could house white staff as well as bondspeople, providing more intrusive oversight of the workers.

The hyphens sheltered and hid food delivery from outside and strictly controlled working people's movement, but the people still paraded through elite circulation spaces inside, so old patterns were fit to newly elaborate architecture, and multipart houses represented a mechanism for control more than complete hiding of service. Delivery of food, especially by liveried slaves, remained acceptable and expected. Livery provided a means of theatrically ornamenting scenes of hospitality, costuming workers in fine textiles and fittings that, as matched sets, contrasted with the individualized dress of slave owners' families and guests.[9] Well-dressed black servants cast in supporting roles within eighteenth-century portraits of whites shown in more assertive poses were a parallel portraying orchestrated and controlled relationships between servants and masters.[10] Human objectification aside, livery was a bit like wallpaper in the prerevolutionary colonies, expressing wealth and refinement of the house and the slave owner's ability to drape his property in striking colors and textures. Both represented costly show, a degree of consumption strongly contrasting with the norm of plain walls and barely dressed servers in the houses of earlier and less rich Chesapeake slaveholders. More than one visitor to eighteenth-century Virginia observed that whites visibly ignored the presence of naked or semi-naked youths on the streets and in white houses. Colorful livery and decorative arts sharply focused attention on gentry dining rooms and parlors, settings for the highest-value enactments of Chesapeake hospitality in the last quarter-century of their colonial rule.[11]

By the 1770s, however, the largest house builders sought more subtle arrangements for delivering food and service, buffering servants' movements once they reached inside. Patterns transcended urban-rural distinctions. When enlarging Mount Vernon in 1774–76, Washington built an arcaded, open walk connecting the kitchen in a flanker to an exposed platform giving access to his dining room through a lobby shared by Washington and his butler, William "Billy" Lee, who lived in a room below. Lee managed the family's extensive sets of china and oversaw the transfer of food from the kitchen into serving dishes in a closet off the lobby before it was conveyed to the diners. The covered way partially sheltered and circumscribed servants' movements but left them visible on the side of the house to which most guests approached. Washington's brother-in-law Fielding Lewis built a Georgian house at the edge of the town of Fredericksburg in the same era, with a service route already in mind. Outwardly comparable to Wythe's house, Lewis's Kenmore has a more specialized plan, with a side lobby giving independent service access to a lavish dining room — the largest room in the house — and to the best bedchamber. The cook and other enslaved members of the household lived in a detached, two-room-plan kitchen-quarter from which they carried food across a side yard and up steps to

EDWARD A. CHAPPELL

the small service entry. Lewis had the lobby finished with bright yellow wall-paper to create a striking visual impression when liveried workers stepped into the blue-papered dining room.

The celebration of servitude and such extreme class definition expressed in livery turned cold with the American Revolution.[12] The Revolution and its rhetoric of freedom from slavery and escape from domination cut away at complacency over slavery in the Chesapeake, particularly in the decades imme-diately after the war, before unwavering proslavery doctrine took hold of white southerners. To a new degree, the appearance of slavery discomfited owners and guests in the elite settings of hospitality, where refinement and republi-can virtue were enacted. Enslaved people remained present throughout gentry houses, when cleaning, tending fires, and providing personal service. But own-ers increasingly sought to control that presence at certain times and locations in the house.

In Williamsburg, the Bermudian and young Revolutionary War veteran St. George Tucker moved George Gilmer's old center-passage house from war-battered Palace Street to Market Square. He more than doubled the amount of space between 1788 and 1792, including an expanded dining room in a new lateral wing, above a cellar cookroom and near a detached kitchen connected by an open covered way. Tucker had his builder create an open-ended narrow passage behind the dining room, giving both diners and enslaved servants the same buffered access to the eating space.

The thinkers and penmen of the Revolution and new nation who followed John Adams into the presidency worried about remaking their houses in ways that controlled service access as well as reflected their advancing status, created richer settings for hospitality, and afforded privacy from visitors. Controlled service access, particularly delivery of food, was a chief concern.

Thomas Jefferson executed the most spatially extended and eccentric solu-tion as he recast Monticello between 1796 and 1809, years during which he led a primarily metropolitan life. His cooks Edith Hern Fossett, Fanny Hern, and their helpers prepared meals in a semi-subterranean kitchen at the east (front left) corner of the southeast, L-shaped range, whose productive functions and workers were hidden from the house and lawn. Other enslaved servants carried the food along an embedded masonry-walled and paved path that extended past butler Burwell Colbert's cellar living space, under the entrance hall, and further along the lateral axis to a heated cellar room where servants waited and food could be dressed and staged. Within this room, they mounted a narrow, winding stair to the northwest passage. Walking to the end of the passage, they stepped into a closet-sized space and placed the food on a revolving dumbwaiter. Colbert or a Jefferson family member could then step through a doorway in a sideboard niche off the dining room, spin the half disk around, and move the prepared food to the sideboard or table. Dirty serving pieces and dishes could also be set on the wheel and spun around for the hidden servants to carry back along the circuitous route. Guests and Jefferson's family moved by a different route, primarily entering the dining room from the parlor beyond the entrance hall except when they occupied bedrooms off the passage. Wine too could be exchanged for empty vessels by an unseen worker in the wine cellar, placing full bottles in carefully sized cradles counterweighted to rise into small spaces flanking the dining room fireplace. One cannot help but wonder how Sally Hemings made her way from her single-room log house of around 1793 on Mulberry Row and along a truncated section of the same route, through a cellar room, and up the nearer stair, through the southeast passage, into the library annex and study or the entrance hall to Jefferson's bedchamber, or more publicly from the passage through the hall to the doorway he could unlatch remotely.[13]

More practical and less given to gizmos was James Madison who in 1809–11 remade his two-generation house called Montpelier. Madison, too, nevertheless did substantial surgery, carving a grand new drawing room from two of his parents' principal rooms and building two wings, one for Dolley Madison and himself and another for his partially displaced mother. In the cellar of both wings, his builders created sizable cookrooms equipped with fireplaces and ovens; in the same era they constructed new freestanding kitchens. From the cellar cookrooms, enslaved servants carried food up a stair and through a lobby into the respective dining rooms. There is physical evidence that the younger generation used their internal system, while mother Nelly Madison relied primarily on the old system, having her servants carry food across the yard and through a side door and chamber to her dining room. Madison sought to shield the sounds and odors of the internal kitchens from his family's refined rooms by insulating between the floor joists in these two locations.[14] It is an interesting case because such extreme and clear intervention contrasts with cellar evidence in the 1763 core of the house, where a single small fireplace and remains of a little subfloor pit are the sole physical evidence for enslaved domestics occupying unspecialized space below, semi-directly accessible to the elder Madisons' room only through a steep ladder and a trap door in a closet.

Less famous Chesapeake elites also sought ways of shielding slavery, in towns as well as the country. Norfolk merchant Moses Myers built a fine townhouse in 1797, probably with space for cooking in the cellar. By about 1815 he had built a detached kitchen with room for enslaved staff upstairs. About 1815 he added a fine dining room wing with two sideboard niches and private chambers above. He then had his builders construct a short hyphen connecting the kitchen and the dining room, enclosing the link with movable louvers. Thereafter the wing blocked the public view of the service buildings, and slaves both served the wing and waited in the hyphen, unseen in the open air. The shift to anxious shielding of service is striking, but hiding outside delivery of meals and removal of their remnants was not universal among Virginia elites, as illustrated by Boston architect Alexander Parris's design for the 1813 Virginia Executive Mansion constructed beside Jefferson's capitol in Richmond. The plan of the governors' house functioned much like Fielding Lewis's Kenmore, with dining room and parlor placed at the back and the oversized dining space reached by a discreetly placed service door off the side passage. Just as at Kenmore, in the executive mansion servers carried food and waste outside between the side door and a detached kitchen-laundry, with living space above the workrooms.[15] Likewise, the majority of surviving kitchen-quarters in postrevolutionary Petersburg are freestanding buildings, without covered connections to the houses. A minority are located in Petersburg's cellars and in rear wings.

Service wings offered slaveholders a means of organizing their workers and work while enforcing a degree of segregation as growth of cities accelerated and more rowhouses were built on limited lot frontages after the war. Placing kitchens and workers' quarters in connected or semi-attached rear wings was more common in Philadelphia than in the prerevolutionary Chesapeake, and it became a solution in cities further north as kitchens were moved out of the core of New England houses. Modest Baltimore houses placed cooking in rear wings or cellars even when a single lower room occupied the main block.[16] Southern elites' resistance to direct attachment is most fully expressed in Charleston service wings with exterior circulation to the main house. As early as about 1755, Peyton Randolph built the closest parallel in Williamsburg, a kitchen-laundry-quarter running along the street side of his house lots and connected to a rear chamber by an angled hyphen. Essentially this was an old center-chimney kitchen-laundry, but it appears to have had a third first-floor room and a full second floor of domestic rooms. Perhaps it offered no independent access to the upper rooms, but it was larger and more distinctly urban in its form than other kitchens and quarters in the eighteenth-century town.[17] George Washington built a pair of townhouses for the new capital in 1798 and planned both with a rear kitchen slightly separated from the rear wall rather than attached—close but not quite a wing.[18]

Among the most carefully developed service wings in the Chesapeake was that which Susan Decatur built about 1821 to make the family's grand house on present Lafayette Square rentable a year after the admiral's death. Two floors had single-loaded longitudinal passages reached from a short hyphen. On the lower floor the passage faced the rear yard and opened into four rooms, with at least one residential chamber between the hyphen and cookroom, probably again to house a housekeeper. Upstairs the passage shifted to the outer side, keeping three rooms for enslaved workers away from the street. A large fourth servants' room at the rear spanned the width of the wing and was given windows looking into the street as well as the yard. In short, the eight rooms were effectively bracketed by rooms for superior servants, at front, below, and rear above.

Thinking aesthetically more than socially, Latrobe dismissively referred to attached wings in 1816 as the "frying pan plan" because it gave prominence to the kitchen and, he said, could make it visible from the front entry of the house.[19] But the urban vernacular worked especially well on lots of limited width. Bernard Ghesquirne placed a residential room and small hyphen between his large rowhouse at 202 King Street in Alexandria and its two-story service wing around 1805, using distance and a housekeeper to control access from hearth to table in an elegant dining room. At the Owens-Thomas House in Savannah, another English architect, William Jay, placed cooking in the cellar of the main block and employed a two-story service building with enslaved workers' rooms above a stable set handsomely against the broad rear property line, as far from the owner's house as possible.

Appearances were not the only new concern. As we have seen, the common pattern had been for cookrooms to serve multiple purposes, as a center for gathering, waiting, and sleeping as well as cooking and laundering, and as a common point of circulation to ancillary spaces. Owners' anxiety over the presence and actions of numerous black people in the kitchen grew, particularly in the early decades of the nineteenth century. Virginia owners already worried over unsanctioned access to their houses before the Revolution, and the proliferation of slave insurrections in the southern states and Caribbean after the Revolution put slaveholders on edge about individual acts of retribution as well as coordinated revolt.[20]

Virginia slaveholders concocted peculiar means of continuing use of attic space for housing above a solitary cookroom while avoiding free access to or through the kitchen. At the prerevolutionary Grissell Hay House in Williamsburg between 1815 and 1823, owner Walter Webb replaced the old wooden kitchen with a new brick one offering a separate exterior doorway at the rear giving access to a narrow stair ascending to an attic quarter. On the opposite edge of town, Burwell Bassett built a similar wooden kitchen-quarter, this with one of two front doors opening into a workers' enclosed stair, rising to living space in the garret (fig. 1aa–bb). Soon after finishing a fine Petersburg house in 1839 called Sterling Castle, the owner built a freestanding kitchen-laundry with a third exterior doorway opening into a stairway rising to attic quarters. The above-but-not-in-my-kitchen models were employed in the Virginia countryside as well.[21] Parallels in Charleston included new service buildings and alterations to old ones. The large eighteenth-century cookroom housed a stair to second-floor quarters in Miles Brewton's substantial service building in Charleston, causing a later owner to partition off the steps to separate people's movement through the room where the owner's food was prepared. A simpler alternative used by the Pruden family in an Isle of Wight, Virginia, kitchen simply placed the stair outside, as did Richmond builders at two-story brick kitchen-quarters in the new state capital.

A number of factors led to the development of more complicated work and quartering buildings internationally. As we have seen, one was whites' desire to control activities where their food was prepared. Separating workers into multiple spaces offered owners some hope for greater control: knowing who was where, or at least thinking so. Bernard L. Herman has evocatively observed that urban Charleston slave owners arranged their houses and yards in ways they *believed* would give them more control than they in reality had. But enslaved people also asserted their own desire for separate space and a degree of privacy.[22] They and abolitionists caused owners and apologists for slavery to respond with strategies for what the latter presented as amelioration. Particularly in light of a broad European and American shift toward concern for minimum housing standards, secure and relatively private housing for certain enslaved people found traction. In the Chesapeake, certain planters selectively built model quarters in the second quarter of the nineteenth century, and two-story kitchen-quarters with separate access became an urban parallel.

As I have earlier observed, slave owners also saw variable treatment as a powerful means of control. Tutor Phillip Fithian quoted a Virginia plantation clerk as saying in 1773 that Robert Carter issued a peck of corn and pound of meat to most of his workers and more to his "favorites about the table."[23] Close portraits of Virginia and Jamaica, as elsewhere, reveal owners rewarding and punishing people they owned in a continuous effort to extract the labor and behavior they sought, particularly moving people from domestic service to fieldwork and back to the main house or sugar mill depending on how they and their counterparts behaved.[24] Forced labor relied on incentives as well as physical brutality. Location and quality of housing could be a significant element in this universally harsh negotiation. Domestic work was especially sensitive to interpersonal relations between the owned and owners.

In slaveholding towns and cities from Washington, D.C., and Maryland to Jamaica by the end of the eighteenth century, substantial property owners increasingly addressed concerns for segregation of blacks and whites, separation of cooking and living space, and more private access to living spaces by building more substantial service buildings and quarters, often along one side of their properties and usually behind the main house, in contrast to the rarer and more outwardly formal flankers of big Georgian ensembles like those of prewar Annapolis. Freestanding kitchen-quarters set against a side or rear property line fulfilled white slave-owning desire for more substantial separation from the site of domestic labor and black life, and the scale of two-story varieties provided means of independent access to assigned rooms, more like freestanding houses and duplexes than Robert Carter's attic.

Jamaican buildings for domestic work, quarters, and slaveholders' houses offer a useful comparison because they reflect the different circumstances on Britain's most profitable island colony, where enslaved Africans and African Jamaicans hugely outnumbered white residents, particularly white women; where British abolitionists sought to be more effective in delivering emancipation in the decades after 1790; and where the likelihood of revolt was more tangible. Looking primarily at urban properties, some aspects appear very familiar, representing owners' attitudes toward drudgery that transcend regional circumstances. There, too, broad variation in both urban and rural housing reflected differences in the makeup of West Indian society and economy. The differences are particularly striking in Jamaica.

Most of the enslaved population of eighteenth- and early nineteenth-century Jamaica was rural, predominately sugarcane workers, the majority of the fieldworkers being females. Agricultural labor and sugar processing was brutal work, and most laborers were expected to raise both food and housing for themselves, contributing to a regime that kept natural population growth extremely low. This remained the case even after ending the slave trade in 1807 increased owners' incentive to encourage reproduction.[25]

Production of sugar and rum was highly lucrative for plantation oligarchs, especially on the north coast from the late eighteenth century until the end of slavery in 1834 and full emancipation in 1838. Rich planters made large investments in selected varieties of buildings, increasingly after around 1790. Most dramatically, those investments were directed toward sugar works or factories, storehouses, planter "great houses," and support buildings such as counting houses and hospitals for unwell slaves. Sugar works were the most celebrated architecturally. In the expansive building era after 1790, investment extended to housing for a very small minority of workers—both white managerial staff and certain enslaved domestics—in buildings called "offices" in newspaper advertisements for townhouses and rural properties. It decisively did not extend to the economically most productive people, the sugar workers. Contemporary observers most commonly refer to the fieldworker houses as "huts," though the term appears to reflect their insubstantial nature more than their size. There is little apparent parallel in Jamaica to what southern planters in the United States viewed as model fieldworkers' housing.[26]

Even more than in the Chesapeake, enslaved domestic workers and their children occupied owners' houses, often leaving few physical traces. Maria Nugent, wife of George Nugent, who was Jamaica's resident governor from 1801 to 1805, evocatively chronicled her experiences in Spanish Town and traveling the island. After a ball in St. Ann Parish, she returned to the substantial Seville plantation, laughing as she entered the hall "to see a dozen black heads popped up, for the negroes in the Creole houses sleep always on the floors, in the passages, galleries, & c." A month later, she recounted a story indicating the order of servant precedence reflected in her white personal maid Johnson occupying a bed hung with mosquito netting in her own bedroom and Johnson's *femme de chambre* sleeping on a pallet, apparently outside the door.[27] Half a century earlier and at the other end of the white social scale overseer Thomas Thistlewood noted that over a month in 1755 his cook and principal sexual partner Phibbah slept variously in the cookroom, her separate house, his bedchamber, and "in the hammock in the hall," his largest room.[28]

Jamaica's two urban centers—Kingston, the mercantile port, and Spanish Town, the eighteenth-century capital—are located on or near the south coast. North coast towns grew rapidly after around 1790 as the smaller ports from which sugar, rum, and lesser plantation products like coffee were shipped and where merchants developed supply centers for the plantations and animal-raising "pens." These towns' early evolution coincided with dramatic growth in durable house construction reflecting maturation of creole society there and a broader pattern of rising standards for housing quality in the English-speaking West.[29] The largest of the towns and now the most intact is Falmouth in once sugar-rich Trelawny Parish. Developed after 1770, Falmouth and the nearby countryside offer a spectrum of buildings worth consulting about the material lives of Jamaicans at the height of the island's trade and self-indulgence.[30]

Most emphatically, cooking was removed from principal houses, large and small. There is very little architectural evidence for work fires in the houses of Jamaican property owners or renters. Exceptions are special cases: small fireplaces inside eighteenth-century fortified houses such as Stewart Castle and

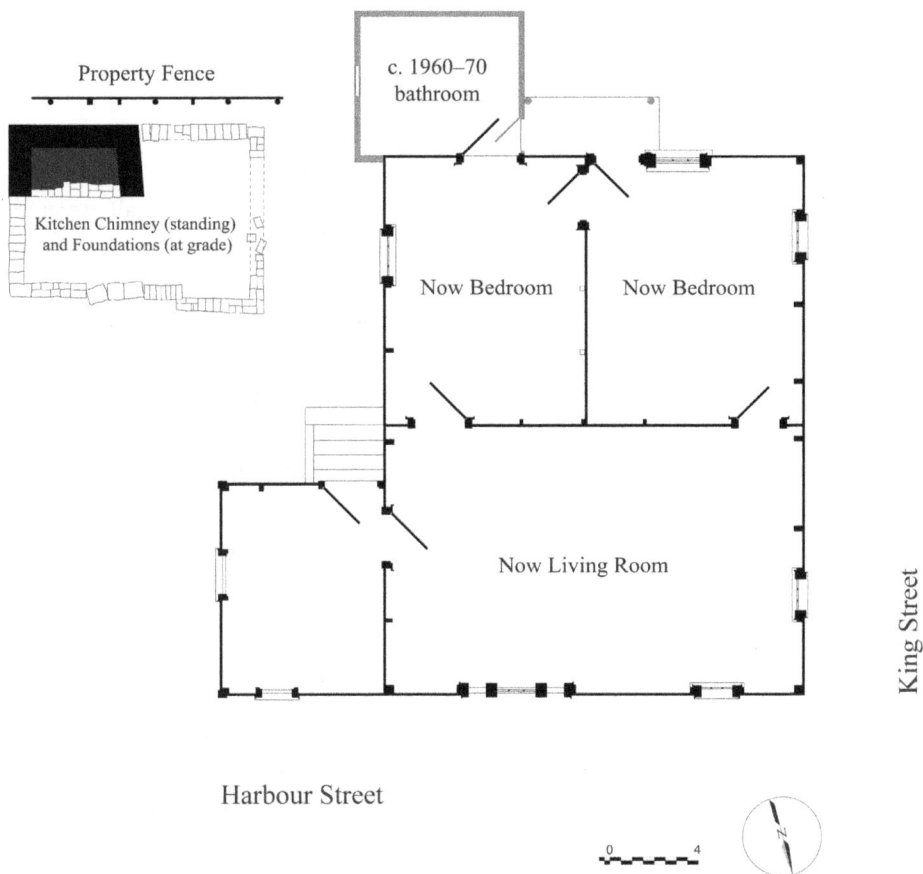

Figure 2. Plan of house and kitchen, 3 Lower Harbour Street, Falmouth, Jamaica. (Courtesy of the author)

Edinburgh Castle, and stew stoves under the piazza at the 1750s Hibbert House in Kingston, the largest surviving urban Georgian house on the island. Chimneys are absent from nearly all early views of urban houses other than workers' quarters combined with cookrooms.

At their most basic, surviving kitchen-quarters are a single small room with a work fireplace and often an oven, freestanding behind or beside the owners' or renters' dwelling house, and open to the roof. They could be close-set if the lot had been subdivided, so a 12-by-9-foot wooden kitchen at 3 Lower

Harbour Street in Falmouth stood only 3 feet 6 inches from the three-room house it served (fig. 2). A more substantial timber building with a 15-foot-by-11-foot-8-inch cookroom and an 8-foot-3-inch-by-11-foot-8-inch quartering space stood only 4 feet behind the 1798 Athol Union Masonic Hall, converted to a Baptist manse in 1832. But another of comparable scale was located 35 feet behind a smaller, two-room house on a deeper lot at 36A Cornwall Street. A small kitchen stands 31 feet behind a substantial Georgian house nearby at 43 Cornwall Street.

All of Falmouth's early houses for free residents are freestanding. The town is without a single row, but the arrangement of the kitchens and quarters conforms to a far more urban pattern than the scattered service buildings and quarters of eighteenth-century Williamsburg, reflecting their later era as well as different place. In nearly every Falmouth case, reflecting a broader Jamaican pattern, service buildings and quarters are set against a lot line, primarily facing the rear yard from one or two sides. Owners preferred using a side rather than rear if there was a single row of rooms but often employed an L-shaped arrangement including the rear property line.

Urban builders favored setting kitchens and laundries against a shared property line rather than a street, often combining the service building's back wall with a property wall or fence, strengthening the barriers between properties. They most often built work fireplaces into this longitudinal rear wall rather than centering chimneys on the transverse partitions, although planters frequently made the latter choice in the countryside, like the Virginians and Marylanders. Living spaces in the best-built Falmouth quarters are generally 9- to 12-feet square, though clearly other enslaved workers occupied smaller spaces, and cookrooms were usually wider.

Work rooms and living spaces could be joined in a single structure or collected into two or more ranges. Behind a moderately large 1805–25 Georgian house at 21 Duke Street, a laundry and kitchen occupied the two largest rooms in an inner range facing residential rooms and a stable backing on the side street (fig. 3). A more unified brick service building grouped four residential rooms with a cookroom running most of the length of a long property line behind a grandly scaled house at 1 Charlotte Street, built or expanded in 1838, at the functional end of Jamaican slavery. A large Regency-style house along

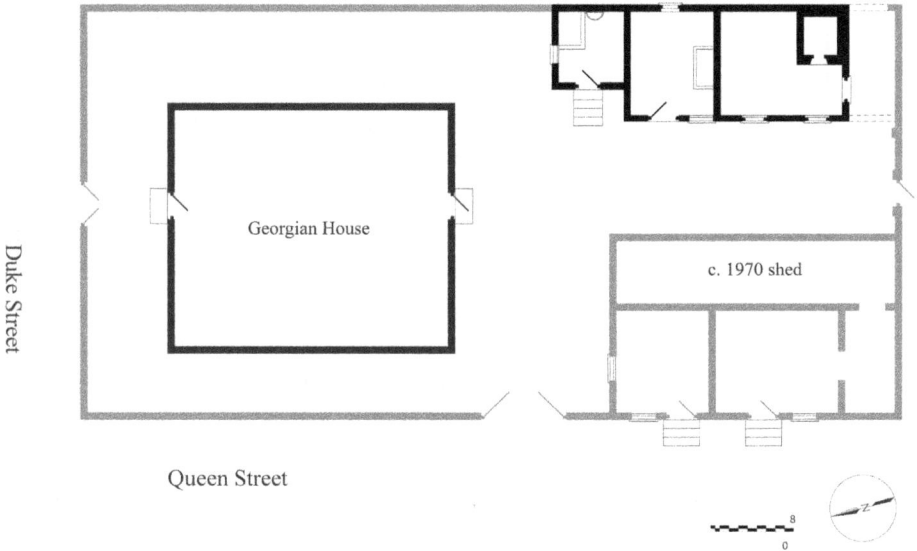

Figure 3. Plan of house and service buildings, 21 Duke Street, Falmouth, Jamaica. (Courtesy of the author)

the western entrance to Falmouth had as many as a dozen 10- to 13-by-14-foot rooms built into side and rear property walls at 20 Duke Street. There is now limited evidence for urban servant halls or larger rooms housing many unrelated people, although enslaved domestics may have waited in a central-rear space in the cellar at the Hibbert House. Alone in Falmouth, a range behind planter John Tharp's 1790–1806 house turned its back on the side street and housed two long rooms, 12 feet 5 inches by 23 to 24 feet, arguably for a servants' hall and office space, with a kitchen and quarters elsewhere on the harbor-facing lot.

Owners increasingly housed individuals, families, or other groups in smaller single rooms, each with an exterior entrance into the yard and no internal communication. An L-shaped range behind a substantial storehouse and residence at 11 Market Street helps us better comprehend how large numbers of such residential rooms could be combined with work space and accommodations for security (fig. 4). Beginning less than 6 feet from the storehouse, a single-story range along a side property wall contains two small residential rooms followed by a larger kitchen and washroom, each with its own door and one or two windows facing the yard, none with internal communication. Starting 3 feet from the laundry, two full stories of quarters extend across the rear of the lot. Here there are four residential rooms on the ground level and five above, reached by exterior steps and a porch. All nine rooms have a single doorway and window, each pair sharing a wallpost for economy, and none have internal communication. At the center of the lower range is a smaller room, 8 feet by 9 feet 6 inches, its front wall pierced by curved air slots rather than windows. The slots are similar to those added to an exterior stone wall in the large 1798 slave hospital at Great Hope in Trelawny Parish, where they clearly were intended to provide modest ventilation while denying communication with people locked inside. An observer can argue over whether the Market Street room too is a lockup or a more mundane storeroom, but owners confining and punishing workers was a central element of Jamaican slavery, and a secure storeroom was likely to be pressed into service in the absence of a specialized lockup.[31] Falmouth and other towns offered public provisions for incarceration and punishment of enslaved people and "apprentices."

In short, the Market Street wings accommodated domestic work, separate quarters for about eleven solitary individuals, or upwards of thirty people if living in groups, and a space arranged for security. At the earlier and far grander Hibbert House, there appear to be three floors of quarters on all three outer sides of the merchant's rear yard. Such large numbers of residential rooms as seen off Market and Duke Streets suggest substantial populations of workers in town, people owned or rented by the white resident, or spaces rented by nonassociated slaves or their owners. Enslaved workers commonly found their own urban lodging in Jamaica when distant from their masters, and white or mixed-race tradesmen could rent housing for teams assembled from various slave owners for project work in town. The process continued into the "apprenticeship" era before full emancipation in 1838.

Newspaper ads for urban houses after 1790 listed "Negro rooms" as part of their value. Robert Ewart offered to sell or rent his house in Church Street, specifying that it included " very good negro rooms, a wash-house and storehouse . . . all new and built of brick." Joseph F. Lions advertised Falmouth accommodations in 1836: "To be leased or rented, a Range of Negro Rooms in Duke-Street, suitable either for a Mason's or Carpenter's gang."[32] The ads

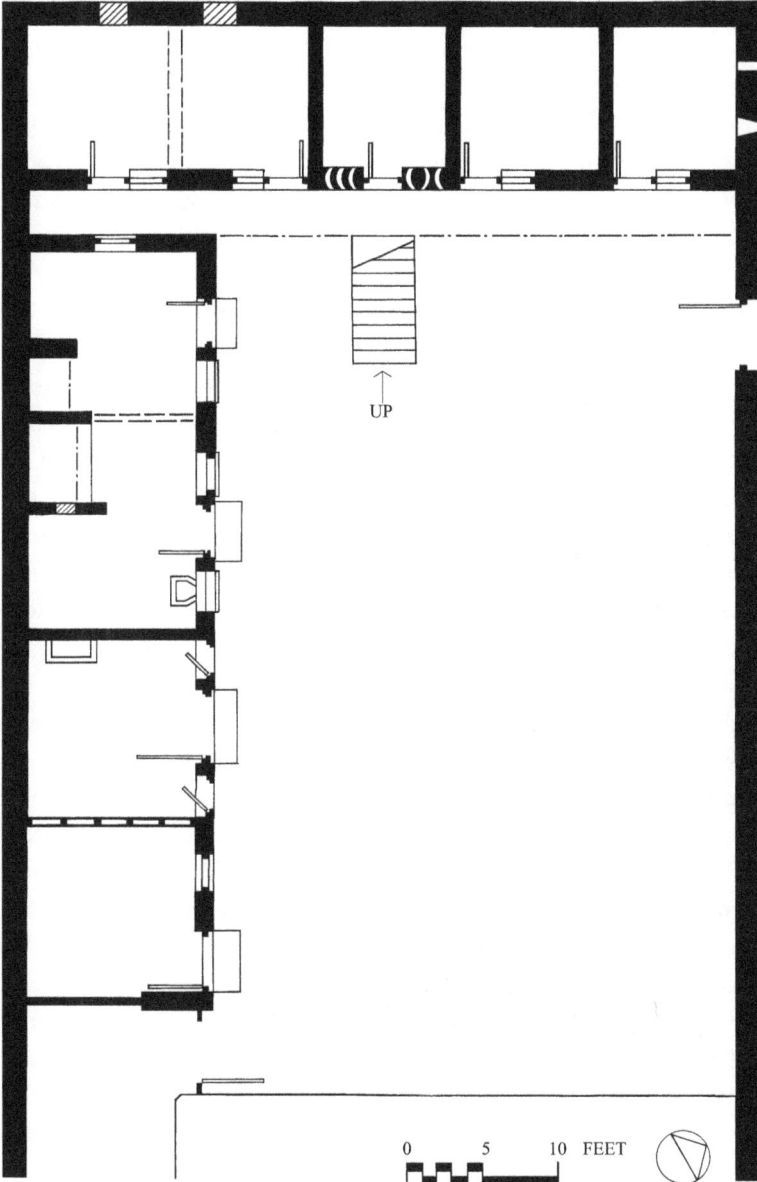

Figure 4. Plan of work yard, kitchen, laundry, "Negro rooms," and secure room, 11 Market Street, Falmouth, Jamaica. (Courtesy of the author)

indicate that certain groups of Negro rooms, houses, and yards were developed independent of owners' houses for income production, especially in Kingston. Edward George Matthew offered in Hannah's Town "six good Negro Rooms &c. well adapted for a Negro Yard." An advertiser in 1825 offered to exchange "a small upstairs dwelling" for four hundred pounds or "a Piece of land with Negro Rooms of equal value."[33] A small house in Kingston was offered in 1831 with "a negro yard . . . with twelve negro rooms, kitchen &c., &c." on another street, presumably intended for renting.[34]

On properties occupied by whites as well as enslaved people, surveillance was paramount, or its intent. Small or large, most Falmouth houses were entered from a side or rear yard, and virtually all the residences located above storehouses were so reached, within view of the workhouses and quarters. Especially for elite householders living over storehouses, reception rooms usually faced the street, as in Charleston rather than Annapolis, and private rooms overlooked the yards, their buildings, and their residents. In some cases, as in a refined apartment at the Moulton Barrett House, 7 Market Street, there was a small, well-ventilated, comfortable space projecting from the rear of the second-floor residence, arranged to have full view of the work-quarter ranges.[35] There was, then, elevated owners' eye contact with every worker's door and window.

Hiding the delivery of service affected Jamaican houses very little. Enslaved servants carried food and removed waste from the same rear and side doors and stairs used by owners and guests, particularly in storehouse-residences where upper exterior doorways were limited and everyone walked down an axial passage. Rear piazzas and rare interior cellar stairs, as at the Hibbert House, generally opened into central circulation space rather than providing direct access to dining rooms. If the caricatures produced by English artists are believed, scantily dressed servants hauled wine and food and stood by as whites "creolized," sprawling informally with their feet on railings or tables, up until the end of slavery. While most rooms were secured with locks on doors, nearly all circulation spaces as well as primary reception rooms were not closed off by doors. Once inside the main exterior doors of an urban house, one could reach the often-distant best room without encountering architectural obstacles.

Plantation service and quartering ranges adjoining great houses were closely related to urban counterparts in scale and arrangement. Such unbalanced

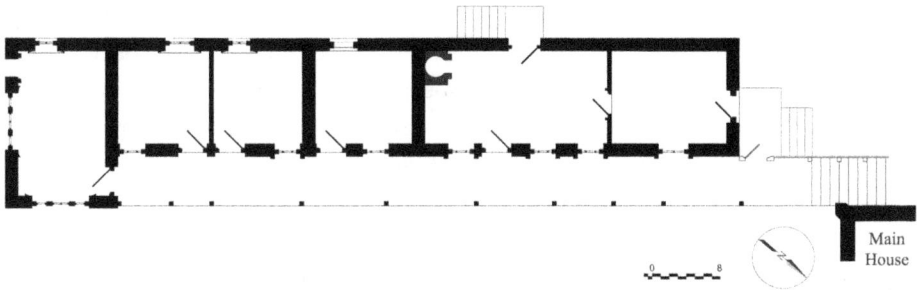

Figure 5. Plan of service and quartering wing, Vale Royal, Trelawny Parish, Jamaica. (Courtesy of the author)

and detached or barely attached plantation wings could be found in the late antebellum Chesapeake, as at the grand temple-form Berry Hill in Halifax County, but they were much more common in Jamaica, making them relevant to the urban story. Two Trelawny Parish examples illustrate the point. A 72-foot-by-18-foot stone-walled kitchen-quarter stands several feet behind John Tharp's house at Good Hope, facing the rear yard. At Vale Royal, a long single brick range contains, starting just next to the great house's rear steps, a housekeeper's front room connecting with a large cookroom, then three smaller and noncommunicating domestic workers' quarters, concluding with a large and well-lighted rear room, probably for a white bookkeeper or attorney (fig. 5). So the cooking and enslaved servants were bracketed by representatives of the owner. All are reached from a porch extending from the steps to the supervisory room and facing the yard.

As in houses in town, work rooms and living spaces could be assigned to separate structures. Certain Montego Bay merchants built fine houses in villa-like locations on hills above the town. Grove Hill now has the most intact 1800–1830 service buildings and rooms intended for enslaved domestic workers. These illustrate a range of accommodations. Attached to a 20-foot-by-12-foot-9-inch cookroom are two such spaces, 10 feet by 12 feet 8 inches and 13 feet 8 inches by 12 feet 9 inches, the latter provided with two windows for favored workers. By contrast, three workers' rooms attached to a vehicle house range from 8 feet by 8 feet 7 inches to 10 feet by 12 feet 6 inches, each with an exterior door and one to two windows. The best spaces open onto a ground-level porch.

At the 1790–1820 Arcadia, also in Trelawny, there is a two-room ground-floor kitchen-laundry with two upper residential rooms behind the little neo-classical owner's house and a more specialized quartering range above storage far to one side of the house. Stone steps rise in a characteristically elaborate Jamaican manner to a lateral passage in the larger building, giving independent access to six rooms. Reminiscent of the spatially efficient Decatur quarters and ranges at a number of other Jamaican plantations, the passage stops short at the ends, so that the outer rooms extend the depth of the building. All six rooms are reached through their own doorways from the passage, but the two large rooms both also communicate with an adjoining room. As a result, the building offered the owner a number of choices, depending on who he favored for better accommodations. He could house six individuals or groups in an equal number of rooms, or he could give to favored staff pairs of connecting rooms. A more compact version of specialized plantation quarters placed three residential rooms behind a long porch facing the rear yard and kitchen block at Itopia in St. Ann Parish. Here smaller end rooms flank the porch. The best of the Arcadia and Itopia accommodations were likely built for the white male workers usually employed on substantial sugar estates, but the surviving plantation quarters as well as those in Falmouth indicate some of the range of enslaved worker accommodations seen in the Caribbean and not in slaveholding states.

Construction methods and finish link the 1790–1838 urban quarters and kitchens to these plantation offices, and the ranges of rooms off Market and Duke Streets suggest that not all the substantial plantation accommodations were intended for whites. At least among surviving elite buildings, the immediate plantation offices can be seen as increasingly built of materials similar to those in the adjoining mansion houses. In 1815, William Robertson offered to sell a well-furnished pen just outside Kingston featuring "a good upstair house with stores below built of the best hard bricks, cook room, wash house and buttery of the same."[36] The best Falmouth ranges too were brick-walled, presented as part of the owner's or renter's substantial ensemble, but commonly they were of somewhat inferior material, such as masonry-filled rough frame or rubble stonework when the main house was brick or ashlar stone. The most elaborate kitchen-quarters like that at Vale Royal had glazed windows, planed overhead framing, and plastered walls. This was the highest end. In the well-built Arcadia

EDWARD A. CHAPPELL

housing, some of the plaster was applied to wattle-like lath with frames left partially exposed, and rough wall rendering was often used inside Falmouth and smaller plantation offices like a kitchen-washroom at Spring Vale in Trelawny. Even superior Jamaican quarters usually had shuttered and unglazed windows.

The surviving Falmouth offices and their plantation counterparts stand in most dramatic contrast with more rudely built "huts" of agricultural and some-times urban workers, built of unworked earth-set poles and wattle or shaped studs with clay filling or board siding above sills and stone foundations, and covered by thatch or shingles. Huts were commonly gathered in what were called "Negro villages" on plantations and, at least in the eighteenth century, on the edges of Spanish Town, Port Royal, and Kingston.[37] Thistlewood recorded one day in April 1752 that he worked with five enslaved people building "a hut so large as may shelter all the Negroes from a shower of rain. Laid it out, and put up the frame myself, about 18' by 10', 6' 6" to 7'-high." Thistlewood distin-guished between huts and more finished building constructed by carpenters.[38] The amelioration-minded owner Matthew Lewis optimistically claimed in 1816 that the sugar workers' houses on his Cornwall estate in Westmoreland Parish "are composed of wattles on the outside, with rafters of sweet-wood, and are well-plastered within and whitewashed; they consist of two chambers, one for cooking and the other for sleeping," but archaeological excavations have found a general pattern of separate cooking and absence of window glass.[39]

Historian B. W. Higman has suggested that many of the "Negro village" houses consisted of tall roofs nearly reaching the ground, somewhat like con-temporary thatched Cuban tobacco houses. St. James planter John Baillie testi-fied to Parliament after the 1832 Jamaican revolt that fieldworkers he owned in-sisted on living in separate houses, resisting his attempts to accommodate them in stone-walled barracks.[40] Archaeologist Douglas V. Armstrong excavating in the slave village at Drax Hall in St. Ann Parish found a late eighteenth-century, three-room house just over 29 by 14 feet and an early nineteenth-century house measuring 11 feet 5 inches by 12 feet 6 inches. More recently, Hayden Bassett estimates that houses he excavated at Tharp's Good Hope village were roughly 21 by 12 feet, although the stone foundations of a superior quarter near the Tharp house were 15 feet 10 inches by 14 feet 6 inches.[41] More slave village exploration is warranted, but at this point it seems that fieldworkers and craftspeople may have chosen to build "huts" somewhat larger if less substantial than the rooms assigned to domestic workers on comparable plantations and in town after the late eighteenth century. This then raises the question of whether the owner-built rooms were for smaller numbers of residents. Skilled tradesmen living in the villages had more opportunity for negotiation with whites as well as more access to materials for houses than did their fieldworking family members and neighbors.[42] Yet it is evident that slaveholders commonly chose to make their "Negro rooms" smaller than huts agricultural workers and plantation tradesmen had agency to build for themselves. In addition, owner-built housing removed residents' ability to make choices for themselves about character and visibility. Professional construction directed by owners often increased their surveillance.

The variety of Caribbean accommodations extends to many small, carpenter-built wooden residences that shared the streets with larger merchant houses and stores after about 1790. In Jamaican towns, many of the houses commonly containing two to three rooms with glazed windows, movable louvers for ventilation, raised floors, exposed and finished joinery, refined trim, and separate cooking structures of some substance were built by free people of color in the decades before and soon after emancipation. In size, number of rooms, free-standing position, quality of finish, and light, the houses of these predominantly free people contrasted with even the best work buildings and quarters occupied by enslaved domestics. While most cane workers built their own small houses with predominantly unfinished material, certain successful mixed-race tradespeople employed professional builders to produce tidy houses that often incorporated finish and controlled access approaching that seen in houses and storehouse-residences of Falmouth merchants (fig. 6). The houses reflected the ability of some to both choose their own accommodations and make them comfortable.

The majority of urban free people of color before 1838 were women who employed education, personal relationships with white men, income, and evangelical religion to establish themselves as free and property owning. Some ran well-regarded taverns and owned slaves. Certain sons from mixed-race unions also made their living in trades centered in towns like Falmouth. In a colony where elite white women were the smallest minority, and rich planters and merchants openly lived with women of color and regularly applied to the governing

Figure 6. Two-room house, 31 Duke Street, Falmouth, Jamaica. (Courtesy of the author)

assembly for the right to free and provide support for their partners and children, economic lines did not follow the absolute racial rules of mainland slave-holding colonies and states. Further, D. A. Dunkley shifts attention away from white interests to that of black Jamaicans buying themselves out of slavery from the 1790s until 1834.[43] Particularly in Kingston and the towns, free people of color played economic roles limited or disallowed from Maryland to Alabama. On the island, the relatively small numbers of whites, outnumbered as much as ten to one, had reason to seek support from free people of mixed race, particularly when concerned about the threat of revolt. Enslaved Jamaicans' active resistance as well as developments in St. Dominque and the Haitian Revolution brought realistic worry to slaveholders, as expressed in guarded steps like their 1797 act supporting Christian conversion through the Anglican Church.[44]

White Jamaicans brutalized the large majority of the population, people who performed forced labor, built their own ephemeral houses, and sought to feed themselves and their children. Little of what antebellum Chesapeake slaveholders thought were model houses were built on the island for sugar workers.

Urban Negro rooms were generally mean, smaller, and without the variety that field laborers could bring to their own construction. Favored African Jamaican domestic workers could, on an ever insecure basis, be housed in quarters with substance and a modicum of comfort, as part of a broader movement toward durable building. Such housing as well as hospitals created some appearance of amelioration, which slaveholders held up as a shield toward abolitionists after the 1780s, as British public opinion turned against them. This and other superficial forms of amelioration swayed neither the residents nor their distant advocates. Within four decades, the revolt of enslaved Jamaicans and the work of those abolitionists would bring the lucrative system to an end.

NOTES

The author acknowledges kind help from Hayden Bassett, Brent Fortenberry, Ke Vaughn Harding, Cathy Hellier, and Jonathan Owen.

1. See, for example, *Journal and Letters of Philip Vickers Fithian,* ed. Hunter Dickinson Farish (Williamsburg, Va.: Colonial Williamsburg, 1943), 242, 246 (1774); *The Journal of John Harrower, an Indentured Servant in the Colony of Virginia, 1773–1776,* ed. Edward Miles Riley (Williamsburg, Va.: Colonial Williamsburg, 1963), 87 (1775).

2. Unknown to Dr. A. D. Galt, 1823, Galt Papers, Special Collections, E. G. Swem Library, College of William and Mary, Williamsburg, Va.

3. This was probably in the decade after 1761 when the house was owned and occupied by the Robert Carter who after the Revolution manumitted the largest number of enslaved people in the Chesapeake before the Civil War. See Andrew Levy, *The First Emancipator* (New York: Random House, 2005).

4. Bernard L. Herman, "Slave Quarters in Virginia: The Persona behind Historic Artifacts," in *The Scope of Historical Archaeology,* ed. David G. Orr and Daniel G. Crozier (Philadelphia: Laboratory of Anthropology, Temple University, 1984), 253–83.

5. For example, archaeology has uncovered evidence for a number of eighteenth-century buildings in Williamsburg constructed with earthbound framing posts, but none appears to have survived far into the following century. Some thirty outbuildings survive postdating the eighteenth century, suggesting later buildings were better built.

6. Benjamin Henry Latrobe to William Waln, March 26, 1805, quoted in Michael W. Fazio and Patrick A. Snadon, *The Domestic Architecture of Benjamin Henry Latrobe* (Baltimore: Johns Hopkins University Press, 2006), 186.

7. The Robert Carter House is the only similar Williamsburg house; it too acquired formal landscaping at the rear but never a cellar cookroom.

EDWARD A. CHAPPELL

8. Singleton P. Moorehead, "Tazewell Hall: A Report on Its Eighteenth-Century Appearance," *Journal of the Society of Architectural Historians* 14, no. 1 (March 1955): 14–17.

9. Linda Baumgarten, "'Clothes for the People': Slave Clothing in Early Virginia," *Journal of Early Southern Decorative Arts* 14, no. 2 (November 1988): 33–37; Linda Baumgarten, *What Clothes Reveal* (Williamsburg, Va.: Colonial Williamsburg Foundation, 2002).

10. Elizabeth L. O'Leary, *At Beck and Call: The Representation of Domestic Servants in Nineteenth-Century American Painting* (Washington, D.C.: Smithsonian Institution Press, 1996).

11. Ebenezer Hazard attributed Williamsburg ladies' sangfroid to familiarity with the practice. Fred Shelley, ed., "The Journal of Ebenezer Hazard in Virginia," *Virginia Magazine of History and Biography* 62, no. 4 (October 1954): 410.

12. Not entirely cold, however. George Washington ordered livery lace in 1784, and President Thomas Jefferson ordered livery for his servants, even as he dressed in relative modesty. Baumgarten, "'Clothes for the People,'" 35–36; Baumgarten, *What Clothes Reveal,* 131.

13. Jefferson installed an esoteric brass night bolt on the hall-bedroom door. These were English mechanisms usually operated from the resident's bed. Edward Chappell, "Thomas Jefferson's Night Bolt" (unpublished report, 2016). Examples survive at Hampton Court Palace and Ball's Park, a country house in Hertfordshire.

14. Similarly, Washington placed a plaster surface on the underside of flooring below his study to shield it from his cellar cookroom, which seems ultimately to have been little used for cooking.

15. William Seale, *Virginia's Executive Mansion: A History of the Governor's House* (Richmond: Virginia State Library and Archives, 1988).

16. Mary Ellen Hayward, *Baltimore's Alley Houses* (Baltimore: Johns Hopkins University Press, 2008).

17. Randolph's service building is known from archaeological remains and its partial appearance in two early photos. The building underwent changes in the mid-nineteenth century, so it is not certain it began with two full stories, but its dearth of wealthy owners after circa 1800 suggests it always had a full upper floor, rather than being subsequently expanded.

18. Joseph Manca, *George Washington's Eye: Landscape, Architecture, and Design at Mount Vernon* (Baltimore: Johns Hopkins University Press, 2012), 34.

19. Benjamin Henry Latrobe to Christopher Hughes, October 4, 1816, quoted in Fazio and Snaden, *Domestic Architecture of Benjamin Henry Latrobe,* 723n13.

20. Farish, ed., *Philip Vickers Fithian,* 242–43, 245 (1774); Alan Taylor, *The Internal Enemy: Slavery and War in Virginia, 1772–1832* (New York: Norton, 2014).

21. An 1840–50 example similar to the two Williamsburg examples survives at Cherry Walk in Essex County.

22. Bernard L. Herman, *Town House: Architecture and Material Life in the Early American City, 1780–1830* (Chapel Hill: University of North Carolina Press, 2005),

119–54; James O. Breeden, ed., *Advice among Masters: The Ideal in Slave Management in the Old South* (Westport, Conn.: Greenwood Press, 1980), 125. Slavery advocate Nathaniel Beverley Tucker is said to have built in the early 1840s the 25-by-15-foot house (probably with a heated main room and unheated inner room) located some 250 feet from his Williamsburg house at the request of family nurse Polly Valentine. Patricia M. Sanford et al., "Archaeological Investigations at the Brush-Everard Site, Williamsburg, Virginia," report, Colonial Williamsburg Foundation, 1999, 90–91; Ywone Edwards-Ingram, "Master-Slave Relations: A Williamsburg Perspective" (M.A. thesis, College of William and Mary, 1990), pt. 2, 111.

23. Farish, ed., *Philip Vickers Fithian*, 50–51 (1773).

24. Rhys Isaac, *Landon Carter's Uneasy Kingdom: Revolution and Rebellion on a Virginia Plantation* (Oxford: Oxford University Press, 2004); Trevor Burnard, *Mastery, Tyranny, and Desire: Thomas Thistlewood and His Slaves in the Anglo-Jamaican World* (Chapel Hill: University of North Carolina Press, 2004).

25. Richard S. Dunn, *A Tale of Two Plantations: Slave Life in Jamaica and Virginia* (Cambridge, Mass.: Harvard University Press, 2014).

26. Edward A. Chappell, "Housing Slavery," in *The Chesapeake House,* ed. Cary Carson and Carl R. Lounsbury (Chapel Hill: University of North Carolina Press, 2013), 173–78.

27. *Lady Nugent's Journal of Her Residence in Jamaica from 1801 to 1805,* ed. Philip Wright (Kingston: Institute of Jamaica, 1966), 81, 84–85 (1802).

28. Douglas Hall, ed., *In Miserable Slavery: Thomas Thistlewood in Jamaica, 1750–86* (Mona, Jamaica: University of West Indies Press, 1999), 67.

29. Edward A. Chappell, "Housing a Nation: The Transformation of Living Standards in Early America," in *Of Consuming Interests: The Style of Life in the Eighteenth Century,* ed. Cary Carson, Ronald Hoffman, and Peter J. Albert (Charlottesville: University Press of Virginia, 1994), 167–232.

30. Ivor C. Connolley and James Parrent, "Land Deeds That Tell the Story of the Birth of Falmouth," *Jamaica Historical Society Bulletin* 11 (2005): 383–409; Louis P. Nelson and Edward A. Chappell, eds., *Falmouth, Jamaica: Architecture as History* (Kingston, Jamaica: University of West Indies Press, 2014).

31. Matthew Lewis, *Journal of a West India Propertier,* ed. Judith Terry (Oxford: Oxford University Press, 1999), 237–38.

32. *Daily Advertiser* (Kingston), February 11, 1791, 3; *Supplement to the Falmouth Post,* October 25, 1836, 1. In 1824, George Kiesselbach offered to sell or rent his Kingston house, which he claimed to have eleven bedrooms as well as "seven Negro Rooms and a large oven and baking house." *Jamaica Journal*, November 20, 1824, 807.

33. *Kingston Chronicle,* April 23, 1822, 3; September 14, 1825, 3.

34. *The Watchman and Jamaica Free Press* (Kingston), May 7, 1831, 8. By contrast, another small Kingston house was offered in 1831 with a shop and "one negro room, kitchen, house

stable, &c." B. W. Higman, *Slave Population and Economy in Jamaica, 1807–1834* (Mona, Jamaica: University of West Indies Press, 1995), 60–61.

35. Edward A. Chappell and Louis P. Nelson, "Falmouth, Jamaica: Early Housing in a Caribbean Town," in Nelson and Chappell, eds., *Falmouth,* 34, 64–67.

36. *Kingston Chronicle,* March 4, 1815, 2.

37. Higman, *Slave Population,* 61.

38. In another diary entry he noted, "Negroes getting thatch and putting up a hut for Peggy." Thistlewood nevertheless also referred to the workers' residences as houses, such as "Negroes putting up Maria's house," in November 1786. Hall, ed., *In Miserable Slavery,* 47, 153, 311.

39. Lewis, *Journal,* 70–71.

40. B. W. Higman, *Jamaica Surveyed* (Kingston: Institute of Jamaica, 1988), 245, 250.

41. Douglas V. Armstrong, *The Old Village and the Great House: An Archaeological and Historical Examination of Drax Hall Plantation, St. Ann's Bay, Jamaica* (Urbana: University of Illinois Press, 1990), 101, 113; Hayden F. Bassett, "The House-Yard Revisited: Domestic Landscapes of Enslaved People in Plantation Jamaica," paper, Annual Conference of Society for Historical Archaeology, Washington, D.C., Jan. 8, 2016; Bassett to author, personal communication, February 4–5, 2016, Digital Archaeological Archive of Comparative Slavery, Monticello, Charlottesville, Va., http://www.daacs.org.

42. Higman, *Slave Population,* 168–69.

43. Lucille Matharin Mair, *A Historical Study of Women in Jamaica, 1655–1844* (Mona, Jamaica: University of West Indies Press, 2006); D. A. Dunkley, *Agency of the Enslaved: Jamaica and the Culture of Freedom in the Atlantic World* (Lanham, Md.: Lexington Books, 2013).

44. Orlando Patterson, *Slavery and Social Death: A Comparative Study* (Cambridge, Mass.: Harvard University Press, 1982), 257–61; Hilary McD. Beckles, "Social and Political Control in the Slave Society," in *General History of the Caribbean,* vol. 3, *The Slave Societies of the Caribbean,* ed. Franklin W. Knight (London: UNESCO, 1997), 213; Dunkley, *Agency of the Enslaved.*

"APPROPRIATED TO THE USE OF THE COLORED PEOPLE"

Urban Slave Housing in the North

JOHN MICHAEL VLACH

Chattel slavery was practiced for more than two centuries north of the Mason-Dixon Line. Assumed for most of the twentieth century to have been a more benign variant of the brutal lifelong servitude established in the South, some writers even remarked that northern slaves could consider themselves fortunate to have ended up in a region where the system was so "mild" and their treatment seemingly so fair.[1] While this assertion has recently been challenged by a wide-ranging set of revisionist studies focused expressly on the impact of African bondsmen and -women in the northern states, no investigator has ever described in any detail how and where slaves were housed. This matter is important because the spaces and places to which northern slaveholders assigned slaves reveal that their housing served as a key element within a punitive system intended to confine and discipline enslaved workers as well as to mark them as property.

Slavery in the North was practiced more selectively than in the southern states and was implemented most often in urban settings. While the practice of bound labor was gradually abolished as various state legislatures judged human bondage to be morally repugnant, in some states slavery persisted well into the nineteenth century. New York did not abolish slavery until 1827. While New Jersey embarked on a program of gradual emancipation in 1804, many captives were not freed until after 1840, and eighteen of them were finally liberated in 1865 by the passage of the Thirteenth Amendment. Even though African American slaves formed only a small percentage of the total northern population, there were nevertheless more than forty thousand of them in 1790 with the greatest number—over thirty thousand—concentrated in New York and New Jersey, mostly in those counties bordering the Hudson River.[2] Given the systematic inequities upon which any practice of slavery was based, it should not be surprising to learn that northern blacks were routinely brutalized. Runaway advertisements appearing in local newspapers provide evidence of vicious beatings; a slave from Morris County, New Jersey, described only as Joe was, for example, identified as having his back "much scarified and in lumps by whipping." Recent excavations of the skeletal remains in the African Burial Ground in lower Manhattan reveal a slave population that was malnourished and literally worked to death.[3] The architecture of slavery in the North, in particular the system of buildings and spaces created to shelter captive African and African American workers, similarly reveals the day-to-day animosity faced by enslaved people. Animosity was expressed in part through white efforts to maintain racial segregation, which, in turn, was enforced through a wide range of building types.

TYPES OF SLAVE QUARTERS

Something like the social separation found on southern plantations was enforced on the larger northern farms that were operated with slave labor. For example, on the western shore of Narragansett Bay in Rhode Island, there were about two dozen sizable estates, each containing thousands of acres. William Robinson, one of the more prominent members among Rhode Island's planters, was reported in 1751 as the owner of seventy slaves.[4] Large-scale plantation slavery was practiced in several other places as well. Samuel Brown of Salem, Connecticut, is alleged to have brought in sixty slaves to clear his lands in 1720, and British traveler William Strickland, while touring the Hudson Valley in 1794, noted, "Many of the old Dutch farmers in this country have 20 or 30 slaves about their house."[5] Since the early settlers of New Jersey were offered a bounty of seventy-five acres for every slave they brought into the colony, there was ample incentive to develop sizable slave-operated estates.[6] Even in Pennsylvania, often noted as a stronghold of Quaker antislavery sentiments, there were noteworthy cases of the use of slave labor and the creation of racially segregated landscapes.[7]

Determining exactly what types of buildings planters built to house slaves at these various estates is difficult since so few of those structures have survived. This is understandable given the fact that the buildings in question were constructed mainly during the colonial period and thus, in most cases, had already disappeared by the first decades of the nineteenth century. Fortunately, something of the nature of northern slave quarters can still be determined by reviewing various documents and testimonies. Wilkins Updike, a direct descendant of Narragansett planter Richard Smith, wrote in 1847 that "some of the large mansion-houses of the slave-holders, with spacious gable roofs, are now standing, the garret-rooms in which, with their out-houses, were the sleeping places for slaves."[8] Indeed, Richard Smith's inventory of 1692 indicates that at least eight slaves were quartered in his own stone house.[9]

Since the planters of the western Narragansett Bay region owned significant numbers of slaves, we can infer from Updike's description that the typical slave workforce was divided into two groups: one that worked as house servants and was provided with shelter in the attic of the slaveholder's house and another, presumably larger, group that was assigned to agricultural tasks. This second group was quartered in cabins or sheds located out in the fields and pastures. Probate inventories compiled in South Kingston, Rhode Island, confirm that Updike's characterization of slave housing holds as well for the farms of Samuel Hazard, George Hazard, and Rowland Robinson.[10] However, given the absence of any known examples of standing slave quarters in Rhode Island today, we are left with crucial questions regarding the design, size, and mode of construction for these buildings. Still we can confidently assume that they were modest structures and, further, that they were not any better built than the houses of the ordinary New England laborer. Sarah Knight visited one of these houses in 1704. She wrote of it: "This little Hut was one of the wretchedest I ever saw [as] a habitation for human creatures. It was supported with shores enclosed with Clapboards laid on lengthways, and so much asunder, that the Light came in throu' everywhere; the door tyed on with cord in place of hinges; the floor

JOHN MICHAEL VLACH

the bare earth."[11] Knight's account also makes it clear why so few eighteenth-century buildings designed expressly for any agricultural laborer, black or white, remain to be found in the northern landscape — they were often so poorly constructed that they were destined to stand for a few decades only.

Some of the wealthiest settlers of New York obtained large land grants called manors that encompassed 100,000 acres or more. These holdings were often worked by considerable numbers of slaves as well as other tenants. In some years there were as many as thirty slaves at Philipsburg Manor in Westchester County, while according to the federal census of 1790, Robert Livingston had that year forty-four slaves at his Rensselaer Manor near Albany. Lewis Morris seems to have been the largest slaveholder in New York; at the time of his death in 1691, there were some sixty slaves at his Morrisania Manor in Westchester County.[12] The slave houses at many of these sites have vanished with time. At Philipsburg, even though the manor house, mill, and other work sites have been either preserved or restored as components of an open-air museum, the former "Negro House," which may have sheltered about twenty people in 1750, remains merely a conjectural site lacking enough structural evidence to establish either its size or appearance.[13] Similarly, little can be said at this time of the former slave quarters at nearby Van Cortlandt Manor located in Croton-on-Hudson. The federal census of 1790 records Pierre Van Cortlandt as the owner of eight slaves, probably his house servants. Since there was no sleeping space for these slaves in the manor house itself (although some of them may have bedded down on the kitchen floor located on the lower level of the house), it is most likely that they were quartered in a small building placed out in the yard behind the house close to the other service buildings. Only a scatter of bricks measuring approximately 15 by 20 feet and some fragments of crockery and pipe stems lying about 150 feet north of the old manor house survive to suggest the former presence of this building.[14]

What some of these vanished New York slave quarters may have looked like can be inferred from several structures that survived into the twentieth century. There is a standing quarter next to the Mabee house (also spelled Mabe, Mebie, and Mabie) outside of Rotterdam Junction in Schenectady County (fig. 1). The details of the building's construction are consistent with Dutch architectural practices of the early eighteenth century; the Mabee slave house is basically a

Figure 1. Jan Mabie House, River Road (State Route 55), Rotterdam Junction, Schenectady County, New York. (Historic American Buildings Survey, Prints and Photographs Division, Library of Congress, Washington, D.C., HABS NY,47-ROTJ,1-1)

framed structure encased with bricks.[15] Planned as a one-room dwelling, the building has as well a reasonably large cellar and a high loft space because of its steeply pitched roof. Arranged with its narrowest dimension at the front, the quarter's facade is pierced only by a single, centrally located door. One senses immediately that this structure, despite its generous proportions and sturdy construction, was intended to be less than a home. The building has the austere, functional look of a box meant to hold property, and a slave quarter was exactly that, a container for human chattels, an outbuilding rather than a house. Placed in front of and slightly to the side of the main house so that the two buildings have an L-shaped arrangement, the slave quarter instantly conveyed to all visitors the authority and social position of Mabee family. It was clear to all that the Mabees were wealthy enough to own slaves that would tend their house and fields.

Another building that can be used to recover some of the history of New York slave quarters previously stood at the "The Flatts," a property situated along the banks of the Hudson River just north of Albany. Purchased by Philip

JOHN MICHAEL VLACH

Pieterse Schuyler in 1672, succeeding generations of the Schuyler family would add many buildings to the estate. A memoir penned by Anne McVickar Grant in 1808 confirms that the Flatts was definitely worked by slaves during the regime of Philip's grandson Colonel Philip Pieterse Schuyler. Recalling the period between 1758 and 1768, she noted that "in summer negroes inhabited slight outer kitchens in which food was dressed for the family."[16] Her passing reference to "slight outer kitchens" may describe a group of slave houses that once stretched across the roughly two-mile expanse of the Schuyler estate. While none of these structures survive, they were likely framed cabins similar in design to a kitchen that once stood just behind the Schuyler residence. This building, staffed by a slave cook and presumably one or two assistants, probably served as a quarter as well, but the cabins for those who "wrought in the fields" were probably smaller and less well constructed than this kitchen.

In the town of Commack, Long Island, a slave house once stood prominently in front of the Caleb Smith house (fig. 2).[17] It was, like many other slave quarters, a rectangular, one-room frame structure with a loft space large enough for sleeping. The four slaves who are listed as belonging to the Smith family in the federal census of 1790 are alleged to have been quartered in this building. Given the proximity of the quarter to the main house and the fact that its rear door opened to a pathway leading directly to the cellar entrance of the Smith residence, it seems likely that some of the former occupants of this cabin were charged with domestic duties. That the front and rear facades of this little house were carefully designed with an evident concern for balance and symmetry stems, most likely, from the fact that the house was so visible from the road and thus would have been seen by passersby. While slave houses were commonly little more than framed boxes covered by a gabled roofs, to have such an expediently built structure standing in plain view would have reflected poorly on the Smith family. Consequently, the Smith house quarter was better built than most.

Hendrick I. Lott inherited a 124-acre farm in Kings County, New York, in 1796 and immediately began to improve the property by more than tripling the size of his residence and adding other barns and sheds. He also had a detached stone kitchen built next to his house.[18] Here he quartered at least a few of his

Figure 2. Caleb Smith slave house, Commack, Suffolk County, New York. (Historic American Buildings Survey, Prints and Photographs Division, Library of Congress, Washington, D.C., HABS NY,52-COM,1A-1)

five slaves. The fact that the new kitchen was constructed in stone masonry can be explained as a reasonable precaution against the danger of fire, but that it was so visible signals that spatial protocols for signaling racial segregation were in force. These were attitudes that Lott no doubt learned from his father, Johannes, who had been among the largest slaveholders in Kings County.[19]

The social separation of slaves from their owners is also encountered in Connecticut. In 1740, Godfrey Malbone, known as one of richest merchants of Newport, Rhode Island, purchased over three thousand acres of farmland in eastern Connecticut near the town of Brooklyn. A 1764 document of transfer indicated the considerable prosperity of this estate for, in addition to a vast herd of cattle, 600 sheep, 180 goats, and 150 hogs, a group of 27 slaves are listed as well; 18 of them are mentioned by name.[20] Godfrey Malbone, Jr., took charge of this large Connecticut plantation in 1768, residing in a building described as a "great rambling plank house built for a tenant." While his plantation house

JOHN MICHAEL VLACH

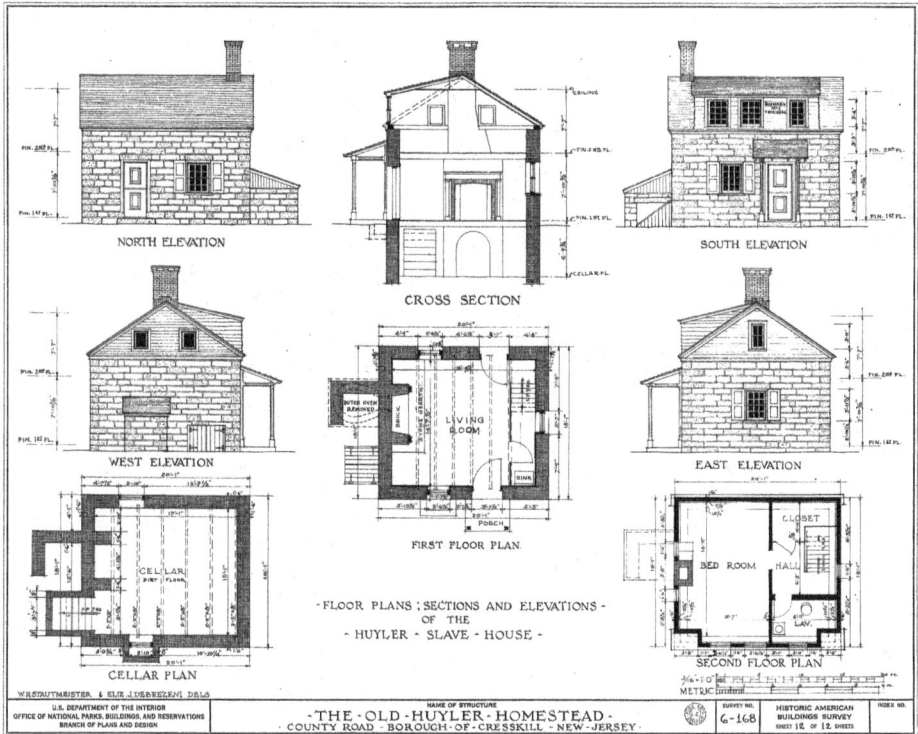

Figure 3. Measured drawings of the slave house at Captain John Huyler Homestead, 500 County Road, Cresskill, Bergen County, New Jersey. (Historic American Buildings Survey, Prints and Photographs Division, Library of Congress, Washington, D.C., HABS NJ,2-CRESK, 113)

was rather plain, Malbone's status as a planter was certainly signaled by the line of slave cabins that stood along the road just south of his residence.[21] These slave quarters were remembered by eyewitnesses interviewed in the 1930s, but none of these buildings remains standing today.

The single-room house was also the main building type used by New Jersey slaveholders as a freestanding quarter. In a reminiscence of northern Bergen County, John J. Haring recalled that "nearly every house had a small, square, stone structure known as an out-kitchen"; he added, "these kitchens were largely appropriated to the use of the colored people."[22] An example of this building type stands today near the Huyler house in Cresskill (fig. 3). Square in plan and roughly 20 feet on a side, the building is a story-and-a-half in height, and, like the Mabee slave house, it contains both a cellar and a sleeping loft. Constructed in 1836 out of the cut blocks of the red sandstone that are so typical of older Bergen County buildings, the house stands in front of and slightly to the side of the Huyler residence.[23]

An earlier Bergen County kitchen-quarter can be found at the site of the John A. Haring house near Rockleigh. This house was built in 1805, and the kitchen, reported as staffed by a slave cook, was added in 1808. Constructed of stone blocks, the kitchen measures roughly 16 by 17 feet and is now flanked by framed additions. The first floor of the kitchen contained a wide, jambless fireplace and was equipped with an impressive domed oven while the loft apparently provided a place to sleep.[24] Located usefully near to the dining room, the kitchen nevertheless stood apart from the main house—although by a distance of less than 3 feet. This outbuilding was marked as a subordinate structure not only by its small size but also by its placement slightly forward of and to the side of the house. The L-shaped layout of the Haring house and kitchen follows the pattern for slave quarter placement found at other Dutch sites as well as some early southern sites.[25] A third surviving out-kitchen, consisting of first-floor cooking space with a loft area above, stands adjacent to the Berrien house in Somerset County, New Jersey. As indicated in Peter Berrien's will, this building also served as a slave quarter as he owned three slaves, two men and a woman, a sufficient number to maintain his house and to prepare and serve meals.[26]

Southern slaveholders also had an impact on the northern states. Joseph Speed moved from Mecklenburg County, Virginia, to Tompkins County, New York, in 1805, where he purchased 964 acres of farmland in order to establish the plantation he called Springfarm. He not only built for himself a southern style I-house, a two-story dwelling that was one-room deep and two-rooms wide with fireplaces at the gable ends, but he also constructed a row of log cabins for his slaves.[27] Of these structures, only the farmhouse still stands. Other southern families made similar treks into the Finger Lakes region of New York. Peregrine Fitzhugh, also a Virginian, brought a gang of forty slaves to clear his lands at Sodus Bay between 1796 and 1800. A little later, in 1803, Robert Rose, originally from Stafford County, Virginia, began to develop an estate that he called Rose Hill on the shore of Seneca Lake. He is alleged to have quartered the majority of his thirty-seven slaves in a string of log cabins set at the edge of the lake well below the bluff where his own eight-room house was located.[28] Since the site was thoroughly rearranged by a new owner after 1835, none of the original character of the first farm remains. A much more imposing Greek Revival mansion was constructed as the prime residence, and Rose's home was turned into the carriage house. With the end of slavery in 1827, all the slave cabins disappeared as well. Of Rose's many outbuildings, only the detached kitchen, which probably doubled as a quarter for the slave cook, still stands at the rear of the newer temple-form house.

Standing just behind Morven, the mansion built in Princeton, New Jersey, for Richard Stockton during the 1750s, is a two-story brick and stone building where he is believed to have kept most of his slaves (fig. 4). Measuring 45 by 17 feet overall, the building was constructed in several stages. First to be built was a stone icehouse containing a deep storage vault for blocks of ice and an upper room that served either as an office or as an additional storage space.[29] The quarters for Stockton's slaves were located in a brick structure that abutted the western edge of the icehouse. Preliminary archaeological probes suggest that this structure was first configured as a row of brick rooms that was longer than the present building.[30] Since the quarters were raised to two stories in 1848 by Robert Field Stockton, Richard Stockton's grandson, it is evident the first slave quarter was only one story in height.[31] Because the building has been reconfigured several times, it is difficult to determine the layout of even the 1848 quarter. It would seem, however, from the pattern of the fenestration and evidence in the building's plan, that during the early decades of the nineteenth century the quarter probably contained several square rooms that measured 15 feet on a side.

A trustworthy total for the size of Stockton's slave workforce also remains elusive, as does a clear plan for their quarters. But given the labor required to run both a three-hundred-acre livestock farm and a large mansion, an estimate of between fifteen and twenty slaves would seem reasonable. In letters written by Richard Stockton, Jr., in 1784 and again in 1790, the enslaved population is described euphemistically as "our outdoor family."[32] We can surmise then that over the last two decades of the eighteenth century, this "family" was large enough to constitute a sizable work gang. While it is unlikely that Robert Field

Figure 4. Measured drawing of icehouse, Morven, 55 Stockton Street (U.S. Highway 206), Princeton, Mercer County, New Jersey. (Historic American Buildings Survey, Prints and Photographs Division, Library of Congress, Washington, D.C., HABS NJ,11-PRINT,7-A- [sheet 2 of 2])

Stockton still owned any slaves at the time of his 1848 renovations, the 1830 federal census does record three slaves in his household along with one "free colored" male.[33]

Among the most elaborately finished of all the surviving northern slave quarters is one of the dependencies at Cliveden, the Georgian manor house built as a summer retreat for Benjamin Chew in Germantown, Pennsylvania, in 1763.[34] The Cliveden slave building and a similar but smaller structure that served as the kitchen were paired behind the main house where together they defined the edges of a rear courtyard (fig. 5). The walls of the quarter were constructed with irregular courses of native stone; all of them were exposed except for the front wall, which was covered with a smooth coat of plaster and incised to simulate the appearance of cut stone blocks. The front facade was outfitted as well with elaborate moldings echoing the decor of the main house. Measuring approxi-

Figure 5. General view of rear elevations of house, addition and wings, from north—Cliveden, 6401 Germantown Avenue, Philadelphia, Philadelphia County, Pennsylvania. (Historic American Buildings Survey, Prints and Photographs Division, Library of Congress, Washington, D.C., HABS PA,51-GERM,64-9)

mately 18 by 36 feet, the building consisted of two rooms of equal size on each of its two floors. The first floor probably functioned as a laundry while the two rooms above were sleeping rooms.

Chew, who served from 1774 to 1784 as chief justice of the Pennsylvania Supreme Court and then as president of the High Court of Errors and Appeals until 1808, was a wealthy man. Owner of a large plantation near Dover, Delaware, he was also a major slaveholder. He constantly shuttled slaves between his plantation and his Germantown residence.[35] Clearly, a large staff of servants was required to run Cliveden and to tend to the needs of his family and of the constant stream of prominent visitors. Documents filed by Chew with the Pennsylvania Assembly in 1780 show that he then owned thirteen slaves in Philadelphia County, seven adults and six children capable of performing rudimentary tasks.[36] These people were the occupants of the Cliveden quarters.

CONCLUSION

The structures and spaces in which northern slaves were housed varied widely across the region. They included multiunit buildings with as many as ten rooms as well as more ubiquitous single-room houses. Even one-room dwellings differed from place to place since they might be built in frame, brick, logs, or stone using Dutch or English techniques, and might be designed with cellars and lofts or confined to merely a single ground-floor space. Slave quarters could be as elegant as the quarters at Benjamin Chew's Cliveden or as plain as the kitchen at the Berrien house. Considering as well all the additional ad-hoc spaces that could be designated for slave use in service wings, sheds, cookhouses, stables, lofts, cellars, garrets, and attics, one might conclude that there was no discernable pattern to the architectural treatment of northern slaves. Yet one theme is clear in all of these quartering spaces: slaves were "exiled" from the heart of the white household. This separation was easy to establish when enslaved blacks were placed away from the house in a different building. However, even when slave space was incorporated into a slaveholder's house, a sense of separation could still be achieved, although to a lesser degree, by the placement of walls, doors, stairways, and corridors. Scale, like placement, was also used consistently to distinguish black space from white; freestanding slave houses were always smaller than their owners' houses, the rooms always more compressed and less accommodating. It is significant that often attics and cellars, spaces that were not even legitimate rooms, were judged appropriate for slave use.

All across the North slaveholders used built form in a consistent manner to mark, underscore, and even enforce social difference in terms of status and race. A slave building or space was, then, more than a shelter; it could also be seen as an instrument, albeit a passive one, of chattel slavery. While not as terrifying as the whips used to administer floggings or as oppressive as the iron collars fashioned with long spikes intended to keep slaves from running away into the woods, the architecture of slavery was crucial for the maintenance of the ideological foundation of slavery. By creating or identifying separate marginal spaces and consistently placing slaves literally out, away, apart, down, at the back, to the side, or confined in storage areas within them, slaveholders not only made slaves' inferior social position visible; they also made their low status seem natural and their harsh treatments seem justly deserved. The various tactics of subterfuge that oppressed peoples like African American slaves might have used to respond to their circumstances constitute what anthropologist James C. Scott has called "the weapons of the weak."[37] The power wielded by northern slaveholders as they positioned black people in the landscape suggests that in slave housing, they had found an ominous "weapon of the strong."

NOTES

1. Among the most significant works in the recent upsurge of interest in northern slavery are William D. Piersen, *Black Yankees: The Development of an Afro-American Subculture in Eighteenth-Century New England* (Amherst: University of Massachusetts Press, 1988); Graham Russell Hodges, *Slavery and Freedom in the Rural North: African Americans in Monmouth County, New Jersey* (Madison, Wis.: Madison House, 1997); Hodges, *Root and Branch: African Americans in New York and East Jersey* (Chapel Hill: University of North Carolina Press, 1999); and Gary B. Nash, *Forging Freedom: The Formation of Philadelphia's Black Community, 1720–1840* (Cambridge, Mass.: Harvard University Press, 1988). The most succinct synthesis of this attention to African Americans in the northern United States is provided by Ira Berlin in *Many Thousands Gone: The First Two Centuries of Slavery in North America* (Cambridge, Mass.: Harvard University Press, 1998), particularly chaps. 2, 7, 9. To bring this surge of academic interest in the history of northern slavery to a wider public, the New-York Historical Society staged a major exhibition in 2005 that was accompanied by a collection of essays by eleven prominent scholars; see Ira Berlin and Leslie M. Harris, eds., *Slavery in New York* (New York: New Press, 2005).

2. Leon F. Litwack, *North of Slavery: The Negro in the Free States, 1790–1860* (Chicago: University of Chicago Press, 1961), 3; Giles R. Wright, *Afro-Americans in New Jersey: A Short History* (Trenton: New Jersey Historical Commission, 1988), 18.

3. Graham Russell Hodges and Alan Edward Brown, eds., *"Pretends to Be Free": Runaway Slave Advertisements from Colonial and Revolutionary New York and New Jersey* (New York: Garland, 1994), 240, 7; Harriet Jackson Scarupa, "Learning from Ancestral Bones: New York's Exhumed African Past," *American Visions* 9, no. 1 (1994): 18–21.

4. William Davis Miller, "The Narragansett Planters," *Proceedings of the American Antiquarian Society* 43 (1933): 71. See also Rhett S. Jones, "Plantation Slavery in the Narragansett Country of Rhodes Island, 1690–1790: A Preliminary Study," *Plantation Society* 2 (1986): 161.

5. Ralph Foster Weld. *Slavery in Connecticut* (New Haven, Conn.: Yale University Press, 1935), 6. Strickland is quoted in A. J. Williams-Meyers, "The Arduous Journey: The African-

American Presence in the Hudson-Mohawk Region," in *The African-American Presence in New York State History: Four Regional History Surveys,* ed. Monroe Fordam (Albany: New York African American Institute, 1989), 22.

6. Rosalie Fellows Bailey, *Pre-Revolutionary Dutch Houses and Families in Northern New Jersey and Southern New York* (New York: William Morrow, 1936), 266.

7. Jacob Painter, *Reminiscence: Gleanings and Thoughts* (N.p.: N.p., 1871), reports that early in the eighteenth century in Delaware County, "part of the slaves lived with their master's family, the others had separate cabins on the farm where they lived separately" (1, no. 1:12). One of these farmers, Jacob Minshall, received slaves from the West Indies including an African man known as Oran Hazzard (1, no. 2:15).

8. Wilkins Updike, *History of the Episcopal Church in Narragansett* (Boston: Merrymount Press, 1907), 208–9.

9. Cited in Robert K. Fitts, "The Landscapes of Northern Bondage," *Historical Archaeology* 30 (1996): 57.

10. Ibid.

11. Sarah Knight, *The Journal of Madam Knight* (1704; rpt., Boston: D. Godine, 1972), 13.

12. Edwin Olson, "Negro Slavery in New York, 1626–1827" (Ph.D. diss., Columbia University, 1938), 40, 42; Frederic Shonnard and W. W. Spooner, *History of Westchester County, New York* (1900; rpt., Harrison, N.Y.: Harbor Hill Books, 1974), 152–53.

13. *Philipsburg Manor: A Guidebook* (Tarrytown, N.Y.: Sleepy Hollow Restorations, 1969), 35; Jacob Judd and Paula Sampson, "Archaeological Study of Philipsburg Upper Mills," n.d., 30, unpublished manuscript, Historic Hudson Valley, Tarrytown, N.Y.

14. Joseph T. Butler, *Van Cortlandt Manor* (Tarrytown, N.Y.: Sleepy Hollow Restorations, 1978), 34; Architects Office of Colonial Williamsburg, "Archaeological Report of the Restoration of Van Cortlandt Manor at Croton-on-Hudson for Mr. John D. Rockefeller," May 1, 1959, xxx–xxxii, unpublished manuscript, Historic Hudson Valley.

15. Helen Wilkinson Reynolds, *Dutch Houses in the Hudson Valley before 1776* (New York: Holland Society, 1929), 105–6; Dell Upton, "Dutch," in *America's Architectural Roots: Ethnic Groups That Built America,* ed. Dell Upton (Washington, D.C.: Preservation Press, 1986), 48–49; Clifford W. Zink, "Dutch Framed Houses in New York and New Jersey," *Winterthur Portfolio* 22 (1987): 278–81.

16. Quoted in Reynolds, *Dutch Houses in the Hudson Valley,* 59, 61.

17. See American Institute of Architects, Long Island Chapter, *AIA Architectural Guide to Nassau and Suffolk Counties, Long Island* (New York: Dover, 1992), 167, which indicates that the Caleb Smith house was moved to a museum park in nearby Smithtown in 1955.

18. Bailey, *Pre-Revolutionary Dutch Houses and Families,* 63–64; Charles Andrew Ditmas, *Historic Homesteads of Kings County* (Brooklyn: C. A. Ditmas, 1909), 37–41.

19. Richard Shannon Moss, *Slavery on Long Island: A Study in Local Institutional and Early African-American Communal Life* (New York: Garland, 1993), 71.

20. Howard W. Preston, "Godfrey Malbone's Connecticut Investment," *Rhode Island History* (October 1923): 2.

21. Susan Jewett Griggs, *Early Homesteads of Pomfret and Hampton* (Abingdon, Conn.: N.p., [1950]), 96. Griggs also provided an interesting anecdote about the Malbone slaves that suggests this group of slaves was sent to Connecticut as a reward for saving one of Malbone's slave ships from being captured by pirates. She also described an annual election ceremony held at the site: "Pero, an intelligent negro, son of an African king, usually held the office" (97).

22. John J. Haring, *Floating Chips: Annals of Old and New Times* (1924), quoted in Firth Haring Fabend, *A Dutch Family in the Middle Colonies, 1600–1800* (New Brunswick, N.J.: Rutgers University Press, 1991), 65. A similar observation was made by Benjamin Meyer Brink about Ulster County, New York, which is located a few miles north of the Bergen County line. He wrote of the typical Dutch farmhouse: "Behind the house was the great kitchen. Here was the domain of the negro women of the household if such there were." Benjamin Meyers Brink, *The Early History of Saugerties, 1660–1825* (Kingston, N.Y.: R. W. Anderson and Son, 1902), 214.

23. Because the Huyler outbuilding was not constructed until 1836, it is possible that this structure, which is identified as a slave house, may never have held any slaves. Gradual emancipation laws for New Jersey were enacted in 1804 so that the local slave population was much reduced by 1836; there were then 2,254 slaves living in New Jersey in 1830 as compared to 12,422 in 1800. However, it should be noted that the Huyler family did have a history of owning slaves. Even as late as 1830—when their household included three free black men and four free black females—the federal census indicates that they still owned one female slave. Some descendants of these African Americans continued to work for the Huylers until 1880. It is likely then that the spatial arrangements initiated during the period of slavery were continued deep into the nineteenth century. Despite the late date of its construction, the Huyler outbuilding can still provide us with insights into earlier Dutch architectural practices; in form, size, construction, placement, and function it differs very little from the slave houses that were built during the previous generation. See Catherine Fogarty, John E. O'Connor, and Charles F. Cummings, *Bergen County: A Pictorial History* (Norfolk, Va.: Donning, 1985), 47; *A Town Called Cresskill* (Cresskill, N.J.: Borough of Cresskill, 1994), 5, 7–8, 11; and Wright, *Afro-Americans in New Jersey*, 80.

24. John T. Boyd, Jr., "Some Early Dutch Houses in New Jersey," pt. 2, *Architectural Record* 36 (1914): 149, 154, 156.

25. The Haring house site plan has the same L-shaped configuration as the Mabee farm and the following southern homesteads: St. John's, St. Mary's City, Maryland (1678); King's Reach, Calvert County, Maryland (1695); and the Clifts Plantation, Westmoreland County, Virginia (1670). Cary Carson, "Doing History with Material Culture," in *Material Culture and the Study of American Life,* ed. Ian M. G. Quimby (New York: Norton, 1978), 53; Den-

nis J. Pogue, *King's Reach and 17th-Century Plantation Life* (Annapolis: Maryland Historical and Cultural Publications, 1990), cover illustration, 11; Frazier D. Neiman, *The "Manner House" before Stratford* (Stratford, Va.: A Stratford Handbook, 1980), 15–16.

26. Bailey, *Pre-Revolutionary Dutch Houses and Families,* 433.

27. Almyra Morgan, *The Catskill Turnpike* (Cayuga, N.Y.: Daughters of the American Revolution, 1929), 146. See also "Hundred Year Farm," *Tompkins County Farm Bureau News* 6 (May 1949): 1. On the southern I-house, see Henry Glassie, *Pattern in the Material Folk Culture of the Eastern United States* (Philadelphia: University of Pennsylvania Press, 1968), 64–69, especially figure 19-B.

28. Kathryn Grover, *Make a Way Somehow: African-American Life in Northern Community, 1790–1965* (Syracuse, N.Y.: Syracuse University Press, 1994), 16–18, 75–76; H. Edmond Wirtz and H. Merrill Roenke, Jr., *Rose Hill: A Greek Revival Mansion—History and Restoration* (Geneva, N.Y.: Geneva Historical Society, 1984), 17–18.

29. Alexander O. Boulton and Judy Ridner, "Morven's Slave Quarter," November 1987, 6, unpublished manuscript, History Department, College of William and Mary, Williamsburg, Va.

30. Dr. Anne Yentsch, History Department, Armstrong State College, Savannah, Georgia, personal communication, June 19, 1995.

31. Alfred Hoyt Bill, *A House Called Morven* (Princeton, N.J.: Princeton University Press, 1954), 98.

32. Ibid., 62, 68.

33. Boulton and Ridner, "Morven's Slave Quarter," 4.

34. Frank Cousins and Phil M. Riley, *The Colonial Architecture of Philadelphia* (Boston: Little, Brown, 1920), 87–91.

35. William H. Williams, *Slavery and Freedom in Delaware, 1639–1865* (Wilmington, Del.: Scholarly Resources, 1996), 230.

36. Nash, *Forging Freedom,* 15; Gary B. Nash and Jean R. Soderlund, *Freedom by Degrees: Emancipation in Pennsylvania and Its Aftermath* (New York: Oxford University Press, 1991), 147.

37. James C. Scott, *Weapons of the Weak: Everyday Forms of Peasant Resistance* (New Haven, Conn.: Yale University Press, 1985).

JOHN MICHAEL VLACH

CLOSE QUARTERS

Master and Slave Space in Eighteenth-Century Annapolis

CLIFTON ELLIS

Until recently, scholars had few opportunities to analyze the architectural expressions of other classes of people who populated the towns and countryside of the eighteenth-century Chesapeake. Most contemporary travelers, for example, record only the material culture of the gentry, and their few references to other classes of people are oblique or must be inferred.

Archaeological evidence, however, combined with documentary sources, such as census, tax, probate, and inventory records, allow scholars to consider a larger, more inclusive landscape. The Federal Direct Tax of 1798 is one such source. A tax on dwellings and other building types, the 1798 direct tax offers an opportunity to examine a cross section of early America's architectural material culture. Unfortunately, only fragments of the 1798 tax list survive, most of the lists having been destroyed when the British burned Washington, D.C., during the War of 1812. Fortunately, a few of the government assessors copied their lists before sending them to the national capital, depositing the copies with state or local officials, and it is these copies that now survive in local, state, and private archives. One of the few lists that survived intact is that for Annapolis, Maryland, and a close reading of this tax list can reveal the attitudes and intentions of Annapolis slaveholders, as well as the regional differences in the ways that slave spaces were arranged in urban environments.[1]

On July 9, 1798, the U.S. Congress passed "An Act to Provide for the Valuation of Lands and Dwelling Houses and the Enumeration of Slaves within the United States." Congress, worried that a war with France was imminent, sought to raise revenue for its underfunded army and navy with this tax, initially intended to be an annual tax. The U.S. Treasury estimated that the country had 570,000 dwellings, a figure it arrived at by dividing the nation's population by seven, the average number of people who occupied a house, according to the treasury's reckoning. In addition, each able-bodied slave was to be taxed. The tax would raise $2 million in its first year.[2]

This was the first federal property tax to be levied on U.S. citizens. The tax was very specific in that it called for detailed descriptions of the building. The assessor was charged with recording the dimensions of each building on a property and the materials from which the buildings were built. Initially, the assessors were charged also with recording the number and dimensions of the windows and the number of glass panes in each window, but that part of the assessors' charge, known as the "window tax," was later dropped after much resistance among property owners. Although this bold move by the federal government to exercise its power to tax was met with varying degrees of resistance, most of the tax was eventually collected.[3]

In order for scholars to analyze the tax list for Annapolis, it first had to be transcribed and entered into a database. Property owners were then located on a map of Annapolis that had been prepared by Edward Papenfuse and Jane McWilliams with funding from the National Endowment for the Humanities. Papenfuse and McWilliams traced the property transactions for each city lot, from the founding of Annapolis in 1718 to 1800, identifying owners and the succession of changes in property boundaries, and thus created a resource known as the Annapolis Lot Histories and Maps. After locating the properties from the 1798 tax on this map, the property owners were cross-referenced with the U.S. Census of 1800, which revealed the numbers of whites, free blacks, and slaves within each Annapolis household. With the full integration of the 1798 tax, the Annapolis Lot Histories and Maps, and the 1800 census, it is possible to place these buildings in a much larger, comparative context and to speculate about the significance of this landscape to its inhabitants.[4]

The 1798 Federal Direct Tax is unusual in that, by law, it was meant to be a detailed description of real property, that is, specific types of buildings such as dwelling houses, commercial buildings, and other building types located on an assessed property. The surviving 1798 tax lists, whether whole or fragmented, are thus tantalizing glimpses of the built landscape of the United States at the very end of the eighteenth century. Reconstructing this landscape, albeit on paper, is important because the reconstruction offers the opportunity to populate that landscape through census records, and once populated, interrogate that landscape in light of the social, political, and economic forces that shaped and built it. Particular to this essay, the question centers on the issue of slavery and their quotidian negotiation of that landscape.

The city of Annapolis enjoys a fair prospect on a peninsula bounded by the Severn and South Rivers, near their confluence with the Chesapeake Bay. The land undulates gently over the peninsula and is cut by creeks within steep ravines and punctuated by knolls that rise prominently within the site. It was one of those knolls that Governor Francis Nicholson made the focal point when he laid out the baroque town plan in 1694, reserving it for the seat of government and calling it Public Circle (fig. 1). To the west, he located Church Circle on another rise of ground, reserving it for the newly established Anglican church that would soon be built. With these two foci of government Nicholson hoped to neutralize the Catholic faction in the colony by emphasizing the Protestant king's new administration of his colony, Maryland. From these circles of power, streets radiated out and down the gentle hill to the waterfront. Duke of Gloucester Street ran along a high ridge from Church Circle until it made a quick descent to the water. By the end of the colonial era, the gentry of Annapolis had claimed the high ground of the city, building impressive townhouses. The houses of Matthias Hammond, William Paca, Samuel Chase, Upton Scott, John Ridout, and Charles Carroll, among others, dominated the city and rivaled the civic and religious centers that the baroque plan were meant to emphasize. By 1800 Annapolis had grown to a city with a population of 2,213, including 646 slaves and 273 free blacks.[5]

The conscientious work of Jonathon Jacobs, the tax assessor for Annapolis, allows us to populate Nicholson's baroque plan of Annapolis with the various buildings that had been constructed by the end of the eighteenth century. Figure 1 shows each property parcel in Annapolis as it existed in 1798, as well as the

■	=	extant
□	=	not standing
◼	=	extant, but not listed
b		bake house
g		granary
k		kitchen
m		milk house
o		outhouse
of		office
sm		smoke house
st		stables
w		wash house
p		poultry
c		carriage

N

Harbor

Harbour Street

King George Street

Market Street

College Avenue

Prince George Street

Raleigh 51

Hulme

Cornhill Street

Church Street

State House Circle

Francis Street

Main Street

Duke of Gloucester Street

Fleet Street

Market Space

Church Circle

Charles Street

School Street

Ridout 112

Charles Carroll House

Southeast Street

Conduit Street

Shipwright Street

Cathedral Street

Figure 2. Ridout Row (1774), Duke of Gloucester Street. (Historic American Buildings Survey, Prints and Photographs Division, Library of Congress, Washington, D.C,, HABS MD,2-ANNA,22-3)

location of each dwelling and outbuilding on the tax list. Extant buildings are marked in black. Remarkably, 30 percent of the buildings assessed in Annapolis for the year 1798 survive to this day.

In keeping with his charge, Jacobs duly noted the materials from which the buildings were made. Forty-one percent of all the assessed dwellings in Annapolis were built of brick. Two dwellings were built of stone, and the rest were frame. The assessor recorded no log dwelling houses. When François de la Rochefoucauld-Liancourt in his travels through the United States described the inhabitants of Annapolis as "in general, families in easy circumstances," he was most likely referring to the unusually substantial brick houses of Annapolis's merchant elite. Brick dwellings were an unusual sight in the eighteenth-century Chesapeake. Twenty percent of these dwellings, however, were listed as being in bad repair. By 1798 Baltimore was eclipsing Annapolis as a center of trade, and the percentage of properties in bad repair may reflect the declining prosperity of Annapolis. Nevertheless, some of the houses still stand in Annap-

(*Opposite*) Figure 1. Map of Annapolis showing property lines and buildings as listed in the 1798 Federal Direct Tax. Extant buildings are shaded gray. (Redrawn by William Pellicani from the author's drawing; reconstruction of this map made possible by a grant from the Maryland Historical Trust)

olis, and they give us a good idea of what the assessor had in mind for each of these categories.[6]

A group of three fine townhouses in Duke of Gloucester Street, known as Ridout Row (fig. 2), exemplifies the type of house that the elite of Annapolis could afford and that the duke admired. Each member of the Ridout family who owned one of these houses was assessed a thousand dollars for a finely finished three-story brick house, over a cellar, that measured 30 by 40 feet. Each property had a frame stable as well that measured 14 by 12 feet. The assessment put the Ridouts in the top 10 percent of property owners in the city.

On the other end of the economic scale was Christopher Hohne's house in Corn Hill Street, which is no longer extant. Hohne owned "one frame dwelling house 18 feet by 16 feet single story." This property was worth $150, which put Hohne in the bottom quarter of owners in Annapolis. Of the middling sort was Absalom Ridgley, who owned a house at 51 Fleet Street. Ridgley was assessed for "one brick dwelling house two story 16 feet by 24 feet. One frame stable 16 feet by 18 feet" (fig. 3). Both of these buildings were in bad repair, but Ridgley's property was worth $350, which put him in the fiftieth percentile of Annapolis property owners.

One characteristic that towns and rural areas shared was the presence in the yard of outbuildings dedicated to such functional tasks as food preparation, processing, and storage, all of which were subject to taxation and thus recorded by the tax assessors. Largely missing from the surviving assessments of Annapolis, however, is the listing of slave dwellings. Jacobs recorded no slave dwellings in the city of Annapolis, but he did record slave dwellings in Anne Arundel County, the county surrounding Annapolis. It is unlikely that the conscientious Jacobs would have purposely or inadvertently omitted a taxable building in Annapolis such as a slave quarter, so we are left with the question of whether slave dwellings were more common in rural areas. Parts of Jacobs's assessment for Anne Arundel County are missing and thus do not offer a good comparison by which to answer the question. However, the 1798 tax list for one rural area, Wye Hundred in Queen Anne's County, still survives. It serves as a comparison with Annapolis (fig. 4).

Wye Hundred had a white population of 1,044 divided among 171 households, averaging 6.1 people per household, close to the 7 people per household

Figure 3. Absalom Ridgley House, 51 Fleet Street, last quarter of the eighteenth century. (Courtesy of the author)

calculated by the federal treasury. Wye Hundred had a free black population of 78 divided among 15 households, just under 6 people per household. The slave population totaled 683, or a little over 37 percent of the total population of Wye Hundred. A vast majority of the 171 households in Wye Hundred held slaves, with 96.9 percent of the property-owning households and 84.8 percent of tenant households being slaveholders. Of these 171 households, only 23 had slave quarters on the property, and of those 23 households, each had only a single slave quarter. Thus, just over 13 percent of the rural households provided separate living quarters for slaves.

In comparison, Annapolis had a white population of 1,294 divided among 246 households, averaging 5.2 people per household, below the 7 people per household calculated by the federal treasury. The free black population num-

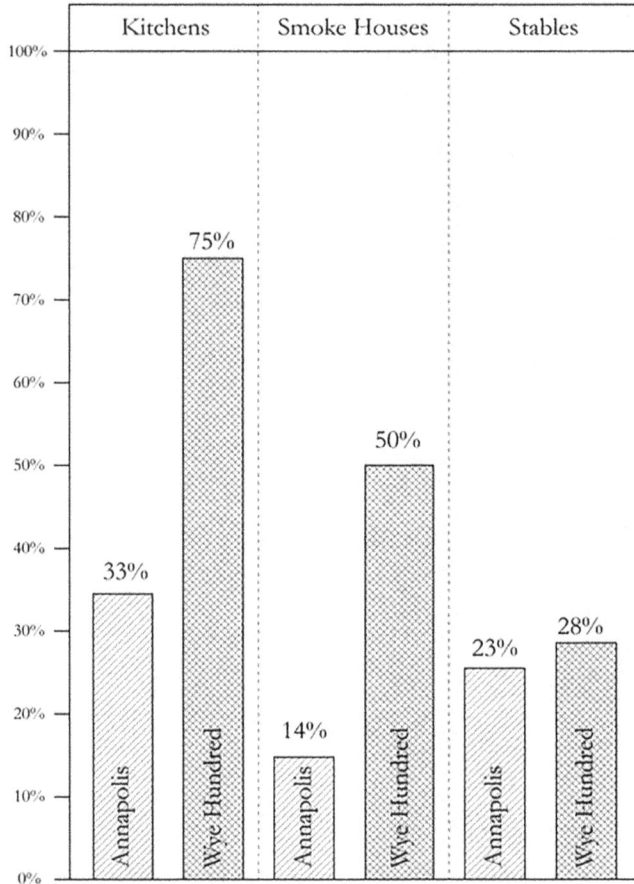

Figure 4. Comparison of outbuildings from the 1798 Federal Direct Tax between Annapolis and Wye Hundred tax districts. (Graphics by William Pellicani)

bered 273 among 40 households in Annapolis, 6.8 people per household. Annapolis had a slave population of 646, meaning that 29 percent of the city's population was enslaved. In total, 41.4 percent of Annapolis households owned slave, with 15 percent of tenants and 26.4 percent of property owners holding slaves. Although a substantial number of households owned slaves, no slave dwellings are recorded.

It has been commonly held that, in the absence of slave quarters, slaves slept in agricultural outbuildings such as barns and tobacco houses, but the field evidence is scant. Documentary sources hint at this practice, but the samples of both extant buildings and documents cannot allow a generalization. More proof has been found for slaves occupying kitchen lofts and secondary spaces, such as cellars, within the dwellings of their masters. Field investigations of Wye Hundred on Maryland's eastern shore by Orlando V. Ridout uncovered numerous examples of slaves occupying secondary domestic spaces, such as kitchen lofts, on both rural and urban sites. In the town of Centreville, Queen Anne County, Maryland, five of the eight houses listed in the 1798 tax list still survive, and they provide evidence that masters housed slaves within the house itself, in cellars and garrets. Joseph H. Nicholson, for example, owned a large, two-story brick house that was home to three whites, one free black, and seven slaves. The cellar had a large cooking fireplace and brick-paved floors, and the garret shows evidence of whitewashing, usually an indication of human occupancy. The evidence indicates that Nicholson assigned these spaces to his slaves as sleeping quarters. Since none of the townhouses had service stairs, slaves moved up and down the main stairs of the house, just as their masters did. In Annapolis, Mary Ridout's four slaves might have slept in the loft of her frame stable, but this space was most probably unheated and not suitable for year-round occupancy. Most likely, Ridout's slaves bedded down in the cellar and garret of her townhouse.[7]

Archaeological excavations in the cellars of gentry properties in Annapolis have uncovered collections of pins, beads, and other objects associated with African American life, which suggest that slaves probably occupied cellar and garret spaces year round. Anne Elizabeth Yentsch, who excavated the site of Governor Charles Calvert's house on State Circle where such pins and beads were discovered, notes that European women did not wear beads until the mid-nineteenth century and concludes that the beads belonged to the enslaved women who served the Calvert household. The beads at the Calvert site, dating to between 1727 and 1734, included jade, coral, turquoise, lapis, and white quartz. Yentsch also found larger glass beads of various colors—red, blue, green, orange, yellow, and white—as well as small bells that female slaves wove into their hair. If slaves were allowed such adornments, showing African customs, they probably were allowed other things like African cloth or hairstyles. Slaves evidently adorned themselves regularly, suggesting that slaveholders considered this personal allowance an insignificant indulgence. It seems that in some gentry households, those large enough to have secondary spaces such as garrets, cellars, or kitchen lofts, slaves had dedicated sleeping spaces. The personal items associated with the slaves spaces further suggest that these spaces might have been inconvenient enough to the surveillance of their masters that slaves were able to establish and sustain a distinct identity.[8]

Compared to the accommodations of Mary Ridout's house, the sleeping arrangement of Richard Owens's five slaves is less certain and more typical of slaves in Annapolis. Owens's house, no longer extant, was a one-and-a-half story frame structure measuring 32 by 20 feet on School Street. The dimensions of the house suggest that it probably had two rooms on the first floor with a loft or garret above the stairs. With no outbuildings on the property, Owens's slaves must have bedded down for the night either in the garret or in a downstairs room. In such a household, the contact between slave and master was intimate indeed, offering little if any time away from the master. Slaves living in such circumstances most likely had to find moments of bonding outside their master's household.

Slaves living in urban conditions performed a wide range of chores. In households with a larger number of slaves, the work might be divided, usually along gender lines, with women working in the house. Women would have swept and scoured floors; washed, dried, and mended clothes; cleaned hearths; and cooked, among other things. Men might have been employed inside the house, but most likely would be assigned to such tasks as tending animals kept on the town property, cleaning out the stables, and tending vegetable or flower gardens. Whatever their duties in the household, slaves would have passed their masters many times a day. How master and slave negotiated these frequent interactions is a matter of speculation—did the master acknowledge the slave or vice-versa with a verbal greeting, a nod, or direct eye contact? Or did they pass each other without acknowledgment?

In general, there is little evidence for daily interactions between slave and master, but the evidence we do have shows that slave owners could be almost oblivious to the presence of their slaves. The daily routines of slaves as they moved about their master's house or through the city created a regular familiarity that could make them almost invisible to their masters and other whites in the city. Bernard L. Herman has noted examples in which slaves depended on this "cloak of familiarity" as a means to achieve their own ends, whether it be theft or insurrection. For example, an enslaved woman of Richmond named Sally stole into the shop of her master, James Boyce, and slipped out again, taking with her items from the shop, including several shawls, cloaks, and bolts of cloth. Sally exited the shop through the family dining room where a Mrs. Boyce was entertaining a guest, unnoticed by either. Sally's usual presence within the house while performing various tasks gave her a cloak of familiarity that made her bold feat possible. In another example, Billy Robinson, a slave whose master had hired him out in Charleston and who was a defendant in the famous Denmark Vesey slave insurrection trials, claimed that his collusion with other conspirators was impossible because his room was so closely surveyed by his white landlord, Andrew Miller. Miller testified that it was impossible for Robinson to have conspired because Robinson's room was always within his vision. But a fellow slave testified, to Miller's disbelief, that he had indeed conspired with Robinson in his own room. Miller's disbelief shows just how invisible an enslaved individual could be in the midst of the daily routines of white life.[9]

The evidence from Richmond and Charleston is found in a close read of the court records of those cities. Other examples exist in county and city court records across the slaveholding South, but no such records have been found for Annapolis. Nevertheless, these examples suggest that slaveholders of Annapolis must have experienced a similar inattentiveness to slaves within their houses, and it helps explain how someone like Richard Owens was able to maintain such a large number of slaves in a small house.

Some slaves living in Annapolis were hired out, living in the city apart from their masters, who remained in the countryside. These slaves worked on the wharves and in the shipyards, as watermen, at various other trades, or as domestic servants. They often were responsible for hiring themselves out, and thus could negotiate their wages above the sum they would owe their masters, thereby earning money of their own. By the late eighteenth century the practice of hiring out slaves to urban centers was growing more common. Tax and census records for Annapolis do not indicate whether a slave was hired out, but those slaves who were working for hire in Annapolis would have rented space from an Annapolis property owner, thus adding to the slave population in the city.[10]

Since there were no quarters for slaves mentioned in the Annapolis tax list, where enslaved people formed friendships, engaged in courtship, and lived their lives is still a subject of speculation. Slaves might have slept in garrets or cellars, but their lives were lived to a large extent in the streets and interstitial spaces of the city itself. Racial boundaries in both the dwelling and the city in late eighteenth-century Annapolis were fluid. Another site in Annapolis, Bloomsbury Square, provides an example of just how ambiguous the racial boundaries were. Governor Francis Nicholson laid out Bloomsbury Square just north of State Circle in 1718 and named it after the fashionable neighborhood in London. He intended the square to be a center of gentry society, but the square never achieved its intended status, and by 1798 only two substantial brick dwelling houses stood on the site.

William Whetcroft owned three properties in Bloomsbury Square that he rented out. Francis DeLaland rented a two-story brick house, with a single-story brick kitchen and an old frame stable in bad repair. DeLaland owned four slaves whose living space is, as usual, a matter of speculation. Whetcroft also owned two frame dwelling houses on Bloomsbury Square known to the assessor as "Red Row." Both of these houses were single story. One measured 56 by 18 feet, while the other measured 44 by 16 feet, and both were in bad repair. The assessor noted that both of these properties were "occupied by free black people, names not known." The 1800 Annapolis poll book, however, identifies three of the occupants of these houses as Africa Green; his wife, Sarah, and her daughter, Kitty.[11]

Thus, one block from the state capitol, there lived two groups of free black people and one household of enslaved blacks in the same square. This juxtaposition of free and enslaved blacks coupled with the lack of an architecturally defined space for slaves on other properties suggests that Annapolitans had little concern for defining racial boundaries in their city. No one objected to free blacks living next door to them, and evidently felt that free blacks offered little threat to the order of their world.

Although slaves in Annapolis had no space that they claimed as their own, they nevertheless laid claim to the city. Slaves gathered when they could, and their culture of gathering was a sharp contrast to that of their white owners. Slaves and probably their free black friends played banjos, fiddles, flutes, horns, and drums as others danced, chanted, and sang. A distinct African American culture was on display. It was called "tumultuous" by their white masters, a word that meant such occasions were marked by disorder, noise, and seeming violence. During the first quarter of the eighteenth century Governor Alexander Spotswood of Virginia sought to outlaw such gatherings, but to no real effect. Governor Charles Calvert of Maryland chose not to outlaw the practice but instead to hold the slave owners responsible for the conduct of their slaves during such gatherings.[12]

These gatherings offered slaves an opportunity to develop and maintain a distinct identity, and in this context, the beads that Yentsch discovered in gentry households take on more significance as a way to maintain African cultural traditions of personal adornment. William Bosman, a Dutch trader who at the end of the seventeenth century spent several years on the Guinea coast of West Africa, noted that West African women dressed finely. Bosman specified their pride in clothing, commenting that "the women's dress is richer than the men's. Ladies plat their hair very artfully, and place their fetishes, coral and ivory, with a judicious air and go much finer than the men." This tradition of personal adornment survived enslavement, and black women continued to dress well whenever they could in the colonial South. In Virginia, John Davis observed in 1803 that "the girls never failed to put on their garments, their bracelets, chains, rings, and ear-rings" before visiting their neighbors on a Sunday. Personal adornments were part of claiming and proclaiming a social and cultural identity distinct from that of their masters.[13]

The free black and enslaved communities of Annapolis offered a place within the larger Chesapeake region that runaway slaves could hope to exploit. In November 9, 1797, the *Maryland Gazette* reported that two "runaway lads" were in the custody of the sheriff, Richard Harwood. One was a twenty-year-old from Worcester County and the other, aged eighteen, was from Baltimore. In April 27 of the same year, three more runaways were reported in the *Gazette,* one from Anne Arundel County; one from Georgetown, outside Washington, D.C.; and a female slave from Louden County, Virginia. All had run away, evidently hoping to blend into the slave and free black community of Annapolis.

Runaway slaves might have been trying to contact slaves in Annapolis who could give them refuge or direct them to places of refuge. An urban setting that was accustomed to seeing blacks on errands by themselves or going to or from work might provide a place for refuge. Slaves in Annapolis were not confined to the town's limits. They had family connections that reached well into the hinterlands as far as Potomac Falls, and they were allowed to venture abroad unsupervised to visit wives and husbands. One Annapolis slaveholder reported a midnight encounter with a group of ebullient slaves returning to Annapolis on a Sunday night after visiting relatives in Georgetown. The white traveler expressed no surprise or disapproval at the encounter, but rather noted only their jolly mood and the fine night air. Both urban and rural slaves maintained a large network among themselves, which provided them with a distinct identity, one not determined by their masters, and a certain amount of autonomy.[14]

Annapolitans saw no need to modify the baroque elements of their city's plan as more slaves and free blacks appeared on their streets and in their yards. Designed to emphasize a new political and social order after the colony passed from proprietary to royal control, the Annapolis plan focused attention on the church and the statehouse, both symbols of royal dominion. The radiating streets precluded the regular and even division of lots, giving rise to a variety of lot forms and development. Again, the gentry were quick to acquire and develop the most desirable lots with an eye to the fashionable expression of their status. They gave little thought to architectural forms that would help regulate the lives of their slaves. The observation that Annapolitans had a more fluid sense of racial boundaries is illuminated more when compared with Charleston, another port city with a slave population.

Charleston's regular grid quickly developed and expanded, and by the mid-eighteenth century, Charlestonians had regularized the expression of their urban form. The Charleston single house is set flush to the street with the principal facade facing a side garden (fig. 5). Behind this lay the other distinctive feature of Charleston's urban form, the backlot. By 1797 Charlestonian's were ordering their urban lots in a way that clearly defined their notions of racial boundaries. Kitchens, stables, carriage houses, and other support buildings clustered toward the rear of the lot while the main house stood at the front. Walls, most often built of brick, defined the boundary lines of the backlot while

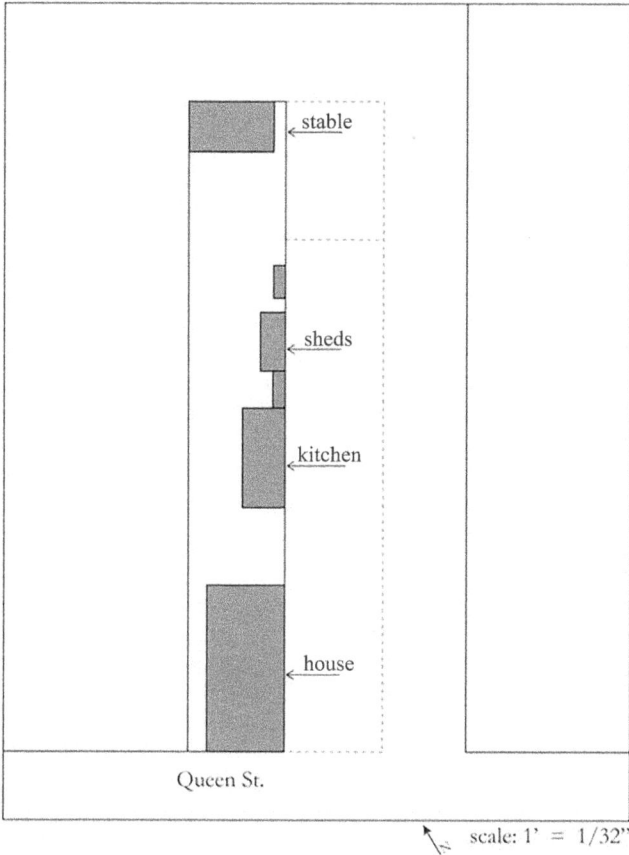

Figure 5. Queen Street house, Charleston, S.C. (Courtesy McCrady Plat Collection, no. 3736, Register of Means and Conveyance for the County of Charleston, January 11, 1797, redrawn by William Pellicani)

gates closed off entrances. Two entrances offered access to this compound. One opened from the street onto the piazza of the main house. The other opened into the side yard and led the way to the backlot.[15]

Charleston was the center of the slave trade on the East Coast and had a much larger slave and free black population than Annapolis. Slave traders brought African and Caribbean slaves to Sullivan's Island near Charleston, where they were kept during a period of "seasoning" as they awaited their fates on the auction blocks in Charleston and elsewhere. Charlestonians had vivid memories of the Stono Rebellion in 1739, and of the slave rebellion in St. Dominque. In 1797, two French slaves were executed for their part in a slave plot to "burn Charleston and act as they formerly had done at St. Dominque."[16]

Slaves and free blacks were also a threat to the economic order. White workingmen vigorously protected their economic interests against encroachment by slaves and free blacks, who competed with them for jobs. In 1793, white coopers formed a union to mitigate the evils of slaves who were "selling their commodities and working at their Trades much lower, and at much cheaper Rates." For wealthy Charlestonians, the presence of slaves was a promise of economic expansion, but for working-class Charlestonians, slaves were a threat to their livelihood. For all Charlestonians, slavery carried with it the potential of social unrest—even violent rebellion.[17]

Thus, Charleston slaves lived in the distinct and architecturally defined backlot. Unlike Annapolitans, Charlestonians were quick to define racial boundaries both in their domestic realms and in the larger civic realm. Charlestonians sought to mitigate their fears by ordering their city in such a way that ensured they could observe and control their slaves and the free black population. Despite a domestic compound designed to survey and control slave movements, and despite city ordinances regulating slave movements within the city, slaves and free blacks moved around largely at will and when they chose. If white Charlestonians were lax at the enforcement of their ordinances, despite the lessons of the Stono Rebellion, perhaps it is because they felt that they had sufficiently ordered their built environment to give them at least a sense of security.

The evidence for Annapolis, however, shows little concern for an architectural expression of slave spaces. Slaves and free blacks of Annapolis lived in and moved through an urban landscape that offered few barriers. Unlike Charleston, however, Annapolis was not a center of slave importation and slave trade, and consequently, the population of Annapolis, white and black, was relatively stable. With the growth of Baltimore, Annapolis declined as an economic center and settled into its role as a political center. There was little competition among slaves, free blacks, and whites for employment, which might have led to attempts to regulate more closely the racial boundaries of the city. Perhaps more importantly, Annapolis never experienced the regular and large influx of slaves directly from Africa and the Caribbean that Charleston did. The slaves and free blacks of Annapolis were a relatively stable population, and in a city of little more than two thousand souls, easily identifiable, recognizable within the community.[18]

This is not to say that slaves and free blacks who lived in Annapolis were not perceived as a potential threat to the social order. In 1723, Governor Calvert signed the death warrant of a female slave convicted of murder. He ordered that her body "be hanged up in Chains on the Gallows there to remain until she be rotten." In the 1930s, former slaves still recounted this brutal act of intimidation in their narratives for the Federal Writers' Project.[19] The black population of Annapolis surely knew its place in the scheme of things. Boundaries did exist—psychological and social boundaries. But these boundaries found little expression in the way Annapolitans ordered either their domestic or their civil landscapes.

NOTES

1. 1798 Federal Direct Tax, microfilm, M3468–M3481, Maryland State Archives, Annapolis.

2. Lee Soltow, "Egalitarian America and Its Inegalitarian Housing in the Federal Period," *Social Science History* 9, no. 2 (Spring 1985): 199–213.

3. Paul Douglas Newman, *Fries's Rebellion: The Enduring Struggle for the American Revolution* (Philadelphia : University of Pennsylvania Press, 2004), 79–112.

4. Edward Papenfuse and Jane McWilliams, Annapolis Lot Histories and Maps, 2 vols., unpublished report, SC 829, Maryland State Archives.

5. Mark P. Leone and Silas D. Hurry, "Seeing: The Power of Town Planning in the Chesapeake," *Historical Archaeology* 32, no. 4 (1998): 34–62.

6. François La Rochefoucauld du Liancourt, *Voyage dans les Etats-Unis d'Amerique, fait en 1795, 1796, et 1797* (Paris: Du Pont, Buisson, Charles Pougens, 1799), 6:93.

7. Orlando V. Ridout, "Reediting the Architectural Past: A Comparison of Surviving Physical and Documentary Evidence on Maryland's Eastern Shore," *Buildings and Landscapes: Journal of the Vernacular Architecture Forum* 21, no. 2 (Fall 2014): 88–112.

8. Anne Elizabeth Yentsch, *A Chesapeake Family and Their Slaves: A Study in Historical Archaeology* (Cambridge: Cambridge University Press, 1994), 193–94. Yentsch applied postprocessual theory in her study of the Calvert site. While some applications of that theory do lack rigor, it revolutionized archaeological interpretation. Reviewers of Yentsch's use of postprocessual theory praised the conclusions she made using this theory. I have

followed Yentsh's use of postprocessual theory, using a standard of reasonable—not simply plausible—deduction, and being cautious not to go beyond Yentsch's lead.

9. Bernard L. Herman, *Town House: Architecture and Material Life in the Early American City, 1780–1830* (Chapel Hill: University of North Carolina Press, 2005), 149; Herman, "Slave and Servant Housing in Charleston, 1770–1820," *Historical Archaeology* 33, no. 3 (1999): 88–101.

10. Ira Berlin, "Time, Space, and the Evolution of Afro-American Society on British Mainland North America," *American Historical Review* 85 (February 1980): 57–59; Ulrich B. Phillips, "The Slave Labor Problem in Charleston District," in *Plantation, Town and Country: Essays on Local History of American Slave Society,* ed. Elinor Miller and Eugene Genovese (Urbana: University of Illinois Press, 1974), 13.

11. David S. Bogen, "The Annapolis Poll Books of 1800 and 1804: African American Voting in the Early Republic," *Maryland Historical Magazine* 86, no. 1 (1991): 57.

12. Yentsch, *A Chesapeake Family and Their Slaves,* 178–79.

13. Ibid., 178–96. Yentsch quotes from John Davis, *Travels of Four Years and a Half in the United States of America: During 1798, 1799, 1800, 1801, and 1802* (London: Edwards, 1803), 372.

14. Yentsch, *A Chesapeake Family and Their Slaves,* 177–78.

15. John Michael Vlach, "'Without Recourse to Owners': The Architecture of Urban Slavery in the Antebellum South," in *Perspectives in Vernacular Architecture,* vol. 6, *Shaping Communities,* ed. Carter L. Hudgins and Elizabeth Collins Cromley (Knoxville: University of Tennessee Press, 1997), 150–60.

16. Peter H. Wood, "Anatomy of a Revolt," in *Stono: Documenting and Interpreting a Southern Slave Revolt,* ed. Mark M. Smith (Columbia: University of South Carolina Press, 2005), 59–73.

17. "To the Honorable David Ramsay President, and the Honorable Members of the Senate of the State of South Carolina," petition, December 11, 1793, microfilm, reel 2, frames 832–34, South Carolina Department of Archives and History, Columbia.

18. Barbara Jeanne Fields, *Slavery and Freedom on the Middle Ground: Maryland during the Nineteenth Century* (New Haven, Conn.: Yale University Press, 1985), 40–62.

19. Yentsch, *A Chesapeake Family and Their Slaves,* 184.

UNDERSTANDING ANTEBELLUM CHARLESTON'S BACKLOTS THROUGH LIGHT, SOUND, AND ACTION

GINA HANEY

The Charleston backlot—or the "yard" as antebellum Charlestonians called that area behind their city houses in which their slaves lived and worked—was a separate and distinct realm within the urban landscape of the antebellum city, and scholars have scrutinized its spatial arrangement as a material manifestation of the contentious relationships between masters and enslaved people. There is no doubt that slaveholders envisioned walls, gates, fences, and the like as elements to control the behavior of slaves, but architecture was only the most visible component of Charleston's deeply textured urban landscape. As the following 1804 advertisement from the *Charleston Courier* suggests, whites employed bells not only to summon but also to establish control and gain a sense of security:

William Hedderly,
    House Bell-Hanger, Bell Founder, & c.
    FROM LONDON
    No. 86, Queen-Street, two doors west of King-Street
    [William Hedderly] begs leave to inform those ladies and gentlemen
who are building new houses, or who may wish to have Bells hung that he
has on hand a great variety of the best materials, both patent and common,

for hanging Bells in the neatest and most modern taste. . . . Alarms Bells fixed at outer doors, so as to prevent any person from entering in the night without alarming the family. . . .

W. H. solicits those ladies or gentlemen who maybe inclined to favour him with their orders, to be particular in directing as above as there has been a number of persons greatly disappointed by the misapplication of their servants.[1]

The advertisement also suggests that white Charlestonians, "the family," were fearful of unregulated movements at night, and that "servants" were often blamed for the "misapplication" of bells. This paper goes beyond investigation of the city's material fabric to explore its meaning as sensorial landscape where movement, bells, drums, voices, and light brought new meanings to architectural settings.[2]

Slaveholders often remarked on the importance of spatial and temporal order as essential to overall societal order.[3] The role of sound and time in the city's landscape is illustrated in the lyrics of a song known to black Charlestonians in the early nineteenth century about an enslaved person who finds herself abroad after curfew (fig. 1):

> Oh! Dear! I can't get out,
> For I'm in dis lady's garden.
> Bell done ring and drum done beat,
> And I'm in dis lady's garden.[4]

This one short stanza is replete with references to the tangible and intangible forces that guided the daily routine of black and white, enslaved and not enslaved, Charlestonians. In quick order we learn of an enslaved black woman's distress and anxiety at being trapped, unable to "get out," presumably out of a specific space: a supposedly typical emotional response to aural and physical phenomena that, from one standpoint, were common to the urban experience. The second line tells us that the space is a garden—a lady's garden, which conjures up images of a carefully tended, genteel botanical enclosure. The third line emphasizes the illicit nature of the visit. The sound of drum and bell signaled

GINA HANEY

Figure 1. *Charlotte Helen Middleton (Mrs. E. P. DeWolf) and Nurse Lydia, 1852,* by George Smith Cook (American, 1819–1902). Ambrotype on glass. (Courtesy Gibbes Museum of Art/Carolina Art Association, 1937.05.10)

the curfew in Charleston and were warnings to blacks that they must leave the streets and return to their houses or their masters. Those slaves caught without a pass in the streets after curfew could face incarceration and whipping. The last line repeats the second line, but now with a new significance to the implications of trespass and its consequences. The garden is transformed from a space of botanical delights to a space of entrapment, for women and by women, in which discovery could lead to an even more permanent state of confinement in the workhouse. The song recalls one of the systematic, aural devices employed by white Charlestonians on a public scale to control the movements of slaves and the success of the city's black population in circumventing such schemes.

Because of their status, disenfranchised peoples often develop multiple perspectives on how to understand their world and their place in it, and thus are motivated to understand the perspectives of elites in order to subvert, where possible, the power of the privileged. This song is attributed to the enslaved woman called Lydia, who is pictured in figure 1. If the song is examined within the tenets of this "standpoint theory," as defined by Patricia Hill Collins, Sandra Harding, and Alison Wylie, Lydia's perspective may provide a more objective and complete insight into the conflicted landscapes of the city. Therefore, Lydia, as a black, enslaved woman, would have a deeper sense of knowing due to her marginalized gender, race, and economic status. She knew intimately the backlots and alleys of Charleston. She was equally observant of the environment of her white masters, and her point of view has a depth and nuance that the slaveholder does not or cannot perceive.[5]

URBAN SPACE

Lydia's song depicts a particular moment in Charleston's history when anxiety over unregulated slave activities had increased dramatically and white Charlestonians were attempting to place black Charlestonians in various states of virtual lockdown. The specter of slave uprising was deeply imbedded in the minds of white Charlestonians. The Stono Rebellion of 1739 and the Haitian Revolution of 1791–1804 were especially violent and created what became a constant dread of the possible gruesome scenarios that might await the white citizens of Charleston. The Haitian Revolution was by far the largest of all slave revolts;

by its conclusion, the most productive colony of the day had been decimated and its ruling class eradicated. However, the 1822 failed plot for a slave rebellion, master minded by Denmark Vesey, himself a former slave living in Charleston, marked the beginning of a new era in the city's attempts to control its black population.[6]

In response to Vesey's plan to murder slaveholders and free slaves, a law was enacted requiring all free black males over the age of fifteen to either be sold into slavery or taken by a white guardian. This law also established the right to enslave any free black who left the state of South Carolina and then returned. In addition, the Negro Seaman's Act required that all black sailors on board vessels entering Charleston harbor be confined by lock and key until the departure of the ship. If the captain of the vessel refused or could not pay the cost of food and lodging incurred by this preventative incarceration, the black sailor—chattel or not—could be sold into slavery. Vesey's plot was all the more threatening considering the demographics of the city. The first federal census in 1790 revealed that Charleston's slaves accounted for slightly over half of the population. This trend continued, and in 1830 more than 57 percent of Charleston's population was enslaved. In addition to their majority, black Charlestonians constituted in the United States the most ethnically diverse community of enslaved persons directly from West Africa.[7]

Period accounts describe in vivid detail the variations in skin color and the striking manners by which these different African ethnic groups distinguished themselves: the scarification of faces, limbs, and torsos, indicating tribal membership; the sharpening of teeth into fangs; and the babel of languages heard in the street. Such exotic physical characteristics were intimidating to those whites who described them, and the fact that scarification and sharp teeth were noted at all is telling of the unease that these visual experiences caused the chroniclers.[8] An editorialist for the *Charleston Courier* lamented: "How many of us retire on a night under the impression that all of our servants are on the premises, and will continue there until morning. And how often it is quite the reverse, especially with our men servants, who are wandering to and fro all night, or are quietly ensconced in some dark retreat of villainy."[9]

In an attempt to prevent the clandestine meetings among slaves and free blacks that had led to Vesey's plot, city officials instituted a night curfew—

nine o'clock during winter and ten o'clock in summer—which forbade slaves and free blacks to be in city streets after dark without a written pass. During the first quarter of the nineteenth century, when the curfew was enacted, Charlestonians, black and white, began to observe a daily ritual revolving around light and sound. With unbroken regularity, after sunlight faded in the city's streets, the sharp, high-pitched peal of the bells of St. Michael's Church sounded over the rooftops and the low, deep boom of bass drums rolled through the streets. Charlestonians came to call the event the "drum beat," and its effect struck fear in the slave population. Slaves ran through the street "to get to their places of abode, many of them in great trepidation, uttering ejaculations of terror as they ran." J. S. Glennie, a Scotsman visiting the United States, witnessed the visual and aural effects that sunset brought to Charleston's urban landscape and noted that "[at] night I was struck by the sudden disappearance of all the Negroes in the streets." Bernard Karl, Duke of Saxe-Weimar Eisenach, visiting Charleston during the winter of 1825, wrote that "Charleston keeps in pay a company of police soldiers [which] owes its support to the fear of the Negroes. At nine o'clock in the evening a bell is sounded; and after this no Negro can venture without a written permission from his master." When Frederick Law Olmsted visited Charleston in 1853, he described the city as it came under curfew with the beginning of the "drumming": "The frequent drumming which is heard, the State military school, the cannon in position on the parade-ground, the citadel, the guard-house, with its martial ceremonies, the frequent parades of militia (the ranks mainly filled by foreign-born citizens), and, especially, the numerous armed-police, which is under military discipline, might lead one to imagine that the town was in a state of siege or revolution."[10]

For more than a half century, white Charlestonians laid siege to their own city on a nightly basis, transforming the meaning and experience of every space they occupied. Englishwoman Fanny Kemble reported that in the evening, there was "a most ominous tolling of bells and beating of drums . . . and the guard was set [out] every night as if an invasion were expected. In Charleston, however, it is not the dread of foreign invasion, but of domestic insurrection that occasions these nightly precautions." Mrs. Kemble opined that "I should prefer going to sleep without the apprehension of my servants' cutting my throat in bed."[11]

GINA HANEY

The sudden disappearance of slaves after dark was all the more extraordinary considering the impunity with which slaves and free blacks commanded the city's streets during daylight hours. The Swedish visitor Fredrika Bremer described Charleston's urban landscape by day: "Negroes swarm in the streets. Two thirds of the people whom one sees out in the town are negroes or mulattoes." During the day, black Charlestonians, free and enslaved, appropriated the public and civic spaces of the city.[12] In these spaces slaves ran errands, bought and sold goods, and generally made work. They also visited with one another and passed the time of day. Walking the city streets became so disagreeable to some white citizens that the city built a segregated park at the southernmost point of the peninsula. Constructed at great effort and expense by extending the Battery and filling the low ground, White Point Gardens was guarded by city police and afforded the only outdoor public space that whites could enjoy away from the "swarm" of "negroes or mulattoes" in the streets.[13]

Confined to their houses and comfortable promenading only in a guarded park, white citizens sought to secure the city streets by establishing a City Guard. The Guard House, designed to resemble a classical fortress, was located at Broad and Meeting Streets, the symbolic center of the city. On the four corners were located City Hall, the courthouse, St. Michael's Church, and, after 1838, the city's Guard House. Faced on each street with a monolithic Doric colonnade that extended over the sidewalk, the Guard House literally sheltered the public realm. The massive Doric portico was in keeping with the classical visual vocabulary that white Charlestonians had long employed in their public and private buildings as symbols of their ties to an exclusive past reaching back not only to Greece and Rome but to European centers of culture and the heritage of slaveholding.

The Guard House went beyond symbolic claims to aesthetic heritage. The building's scale dominated the civic square and the relentless rhythm of the monolithic Doric colonnade dwarfed the blacks who "swarmed" around them with a Piranesean-like psychological force that was reassuring to the white observer. Whereas the Doric porch of St. Michael's would be perceived as sheltering the white body, the Guard House would be perceived as dominating the black body. The lofty porch of St. Michaels added dignity and stateliness to the white body; the massively scaled colonnade of the Guard House put blacks in a visual perspective, dwarfing them in a scene of authority. In fact, the building committee, upon first seeing plans for the portico of the Guard House, had asked for the columns to be made higher, wider, and more imposing.[14]

The City Guard accounted for an average of 10 percent of the city's annual budget, which indicates that securing the public realm was a major priority for white Charlestonians. Although it seems that many enslaved people moved through the dark city with forged permissions or without them at all, the guard made few arrests. In his annual report of 1837, Mayor Robert Y. Hayne stated that only 573 slaves were "arrested for being out at night without tickets." That number was less than .5 percent of the entire slave population, which suggests that the City Guard was either extremely effective or incompetent in performing its duties. Mayor Hayne thought it to be the former. He considered the guard so well-organized and vigilante that he declared, "Nothing but the most culpable negligence, could expose us to any danger from domestic insurrection." Still, white Charlestonians complained.[15]

Religious services, for example, provided slaves with a reason to be abroad during the night, and chagrined masters were loath to deprive their slaves of the opportunity to worship. One master complained, "Almost every night there is a meeting of these noisy, frantic worshippers. . . . Midnight! Is that the season for religious convocation? Even allowing that these meetings were conducted with propriety, is that the accepted time?" Funerals drew the largest crowds. In 1835, for example, a Charleston resident wrote,

> Negro funerals are also most always held at night. There are sometimes every evening in the week funerals of Negroes accompanied by three or four hundred Negroes and a tumultuous crowd of other slaves who disturb all the . . . inhabitants in the neighborhood of [the] burying grounds. . . . It appears to be a jubilee for every slave in the city. They are seen eagerly pressing to the place from all quarters, and such is [the] frequency [of] the crowd and noise made by them that carriages cannot safely be driven.

If the number of mourners described in this account is accurate, they outnumbered the entire night guard by four to one. Most likely, the guard, which traveled in groups of twenty, declined trying to police so large a crowd, focusing instead on individuals or smaller groups of slaves they found in the streets.[16] Clearly, the somewhat condoned movement of blacks at night rattled white Charlestonians. The noise that accompanied such movement pierced the night and permeated temporal and spatial enclaves constructed by white Charlestonians.

If an account by a free black from New York City is accurate, the behavior of a City Guardsman might explain the few slave arrests that were reported in the records. Using the pseudonym "A Colored American," the author wrote,

> I recollect seeing him shoot down dead a colored man, who did not give him the slightest offence, in Bull street.... The man whom he shot was in some difficulty with his wife, and the Captain passing by at the time, ordered him to surrender; but the man declining to obey his order, was shot, and fell into the arms of death for his temerity. I never heard of his being called to account for his noble deed, except it be his re-election to the captaincy, a snug sinecure of the City Guard, for many years in succession.[17]

In addition to bells and drums, nightfall brought the occasional sound of gunfire. The threat of such swift and arbitrary punishment might have kept slaves off the streets after curfew, as intended.

DOMESTIC SPACE

Following the Vesey scare, increased security for whites became an issue not only in public places but also on private property. As noted earlier, Charlestonians employed distinct architectural arrangements to protect themselves. In Charleston, most white slave owners housed their slaves in compact urban compounds within close proximity to main houses. Elite domestic lots comprised imposing dwellings behind which stood kitchens, laundries, stables, carriage houses, privies, gardens, and yards. While high walls—sometimes topped with iron spikes or broken glass—gates, and fences separated public streets from the domestic lots, yards, fences, gardens, and walkways subdivided elite residential property. Typically, a white visitor or resident would enter the domestic lot

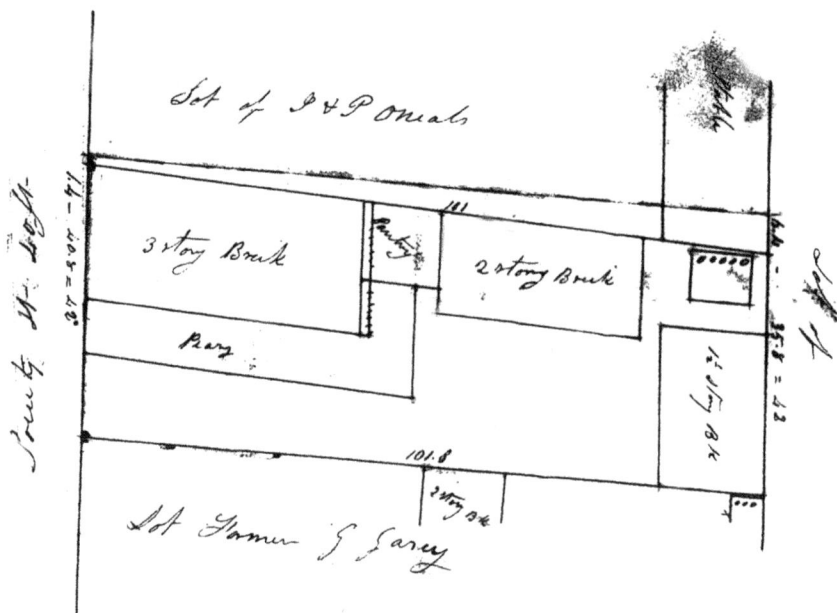

Figure 2. Plat depicting pantry, Society Street, July 1843. (Courtesy McCrady Plat Collection, no. 3464, Register of Means and Conveyance for the County of Charleston)

through a main door or gate facing or embedded in the principal house facade. Enslaved and free people typically entered the domestic lot through a gate or door located to the side of the main house and on axis with the service buildings and spaces known as the backlot or, in nineteenth-century Charleston, the "yard."[18]

While these buildings were separate, architectural fieldwork and the examination of over two hundred city plats confirm that during the antebellum period elite Charlestonians constructed small pantries between the main dwelling and kitchen. Such rear additions made back buildings look as if they were seamless extensions of the main house, and in city plats they appear as unified masses within the lots (figs. 2, 3). Despite this illusion of cohesion, the standpoints of experience—shaped by physical and nonphysical environments— were in constant flux as architectural and social hierarchies were enforced and contested.

GINA HANEY

Figure 3. Exterior of main house and back buildings, Pinckney House, Pitt Street. (Copyright William Struhs)

LANDSCAPES OF SENSES

From the eyes of slaveholders, backlots and back buildings were organized so that the movements of slaves could be observed from the main dwelling. Slaves needed to be close by to answer summonses, whether by bell or voice, yet far enough way as not to impose on masters. By the 1820s, Charleston slaveholders favored a kitchen plan that emphasized the connection between this service building and the yard. In most cases, backlot workspaces such as kitchens and stables also served as dwelling space for enslaved people; rarely were such buildings constructed exclusively as quarters. In this plan, the lobby entry, with its own door to the yard, forced visitors, including enslaved people and free blacks, to enter the yard where they might be seen from the main house (fig. 4). Subtle, yet conscious, decisions such as these reinforced some measure of visual—and thus physical and psychological—control within the domestic lot.[19]

Enslaved people, however, found ways of undercutting slaveholders' efforts to control the backlot, just as they undercut white control of the larger urban

Figure 4. Interior of kitchen-laundry, Miles Brewton House, King Street. (Copyright William Struhs)

landscape. As a result of living and working in the backlot, many slaves adopted proprietary attitudes toward these spaces. For example, the enslaved residents living in Thomas Heyward's backlot made crude locking systems for their quarters above stairs in the kitchen-laundry (fig. 5). Heyward's slaves drilled diagonal holes into the jambs of the chamber doors into which they wedged a stick, preventing the door from opening while the occupants were inside. This simple and effective locking system provided security and privacy.[20]

Another piece of evidence suggesting that slaves adopted proprietary attitudes is Susan L. Buck's analysis of outbuilding quarters at the Aiken-Rhett House. Buck maintains that these spaces were painted with vibrant colors including bright greens and oranges. Furthermore, analysis reveals that each space was different and indicates that each was redecorated frequently. Such frequency and variation suggests that enslaved residents of these spaces may have made choices. For those slaves confined by alarm bells to the backlot, the cloak of darkness, along with the backlot's architectural features of high walls

GINA HANEY

Figure 5. Exterior of kitchen-laundry, Heyward-Washington House, Church Street. (Copyright William Struhs)

and separate working and living spaces from their masters, allowed enslaved people to assert their own will. In 1835, a visitor to Charleston noted "a merry, or busy, or idle group may be seen in almost every kitchen, between ten and one o'clock at night. This is the negro's holiday" (fig. 6).[21]

The Denmark Vesey trials publicly recorded the actions of enslaved people after dark, and these accounts by slaves themselves profoundly changed white Charlestonians' perceptions of safety in the private and public realm. In the wake of the aborted insurrection, Thomas Pinckney maintained that "house servants . . . are . . . the most dangerous." Elias Horry's transcribed interrogation of his former waiting man, an accused accomplice to Denmark Vesey, reveals the incongruity of paternalism and fear. Horry asked, "Tell me you are guilty? For I cannot believe unless I hear you say so. . . . What were your intentions?" The slave replied, "To kill you, rip open your belly, and throw your guts in your face." Although evidence proved otherwise, the city's official report to the

Figure 6. Interior of kitchen-laundry, Pinckney House, Pitt Street. (Copyright William Struhs)

South Carolina Senate and House of Representatives claimed that "slaves who are kept in the yards of their masters, are immediately under their eyes. . . . They cannot, therefore, act in concert, and 'concert is the very life of a conspiracy.'"[22]

In the accounts of white women we find evidence that nighttime on these properties belonged to the enslaved residents. Charlestonian Margaret Izard Manigault articulated her fears of "les villains Noirs" when she wrote, "These horrible ideas [obsess me] at night when nothing interrupts them, [and] I almost envy those who have already died peaceably in their beds." Manigault's fear was rooted deep, both in the collective southern memories of slave insurrections and of unknown plots like Vesey's.[23]

An entry from Elizabeth Waites Allston's Charleston diary, dated July 1861, describes in detail a series of nocturnal interactions between mistress and male slave. With many of the Allston men away at war, the women were in close contact with their uncle, Henry Allston, who on this night was expected to call at the house. Such callers, especially after dark, would require the enslaved footman, Nelson, to light the entry of the house and unlock the front door as well as the gate that led from the street into the compound. Nelson's actions that night caused commotion and fear within the household. Elizabeth recounted in her diary: "Last night we had a dreadful time[.] Nelson was quite drunk. . . . [He] came & locked the gate & door without heeding at all the ringing of the bell when he came upstairs I noticed that his clothes were all muddy just as tho he had fallen on his side in the Street[.] Mamma told him not to put out the light in the entry."[24]

Nelson, however, extinguished the entry light and then absented himself entirely from service for the rest of the evening. When Uncle Henry returned, he "rang and rang but no one came." Elizabeth's mother was forced to bring a light to the entry and unlock the house and gate for Uncle Henry. After he left, Mrs. Allston "locked the gate and bolted the door." Nelson's drunken condition caused more than inconvenience for the female Allstons, as Elizabeth further described in her diary:

[Mrs. Allston] then went into the pantry to look for Nelson she found him fast asleep in the back door, she tried to wake him up called, & [at] last took and stick a pushed him but all in vain. Then as there was no one to be sum[moned] Mamma wanted to put out all the lights herself and leave him there, but I am ashamed to say I was very much scared and so Lella and I woke up Nannie & sent her to call Joe she went [to him and] had to wake him up and told him to shut up [the house and gate] & so we went to bed it was dreadful felt so miserable.[25]

The behaviors of the whites and blacks, women and men, within the Allston household, conditioned by the sound and timing of the bells, is illustrative of an aural landscape that existed within an otherwise conventional architectural setting. In the main dwelling, call bells were used to summon enslaved people to white spaces. After emancipation, slave masters and mistresses grew nostalgic for all they had lost and many fondly remembered the "sweet" tone of such bells. But the bell in a domestic setting had different meanings for those who heard it. The psychological effect of these bells—both call and alarm— could be chilling to slaveholders. To a company of white slaveholders having dinner in one of the great townhouses of Charleston, the remote sound of a bell might bring with it associations of aromatic food and drink, physical sensations of whetted appetites, and convivial conversation among good company. That same bell, rung later in the night after guests had departed, could take on a sinister, menacing silence were it not answered promptly. Spaces took on added significance or an entirely different meaning when the sound of bells was introduced.[26]

Drunk and/or choosing to not obey the bells, Nelson failed to attend his duties—which included extinguishing lights and generally securing the main house and lot—leaving them to the mistress of the house. Direct contact with other male slaves living in the backlot was not an option during the night. Yet the prospect of leaving the house to shut the lot provoked trepidation, so much so that Elizabeth considered it a "dreadful" and "miserable" night. Afraid to enter the backlot themselves, the white women woke Nannie, a female slave who probably slept in the house. So it was Nannie who left the house, entered the backlot, and fetched Joe, another Allston slave. The backlot took on another very different aspect after dark. Bells, which were meant to regulate movement and behavior among the enslaved household, fell on deaf or unwilling ears, and darkness changed the nature of the domestic compound. The absence of light—natural or artificial—and the unanswered bell left sinister voids in the psyche of the Allston women, and the otherwise genteel and secure spaces they inhabited suddenly became vulnerable. The slaveholders' narrower standpoint often left them in a weak psychological position when trying to fathom sometimes harmless events or phenomenon.

Despite nineteenth-century security systems, civic regulations, and imposing public buildings, Charlestonians lived in anything but a tranquil and secure environment. Enslaved people were feared collectively in the larger urban landscape and individually working and living in the backlots of slave owners. In the public realm bells and drums were used to make enslaved people disappear; in the private realm bells, if properly hung, summoned slaves or alerted slave owners of their unannounced presence. While nighttime provoked anxiety in the white population, it allowed slaves to exert some autonomy within and without the domestic lot. In either case, it was white Charlestonians who attempted to establish, constrict, and control space—whether through architecture or the bodily senses. Such notions were central to slaveholding and resistance.

GINA HANEY

Research for this paper was made possible by the Beehive-Mills Lane Architectural Fellowship and the Historic Charleston Foundation. Many thanks to my editors, Clifton Ellis and Rebecca Ginsburg, for helping to shape these ideas into an essay, and to William Struhs for his time.

1. *Charleston Courier,* October 16, 1804.

2. Dell Upton, "The City as Material Culture," in *The Art and Mystery of Historical Archaeology: Essays in Honor of James Deetz,* ed. Anne Elizabeth Yentsch and Mary C. Beaudry (Boca Raton, Fla.: CRC Press, 1992). More recently, Bernard L. Herman has explored these ideas in his book *Town House: Architecture and Material Life in the Early American City, 1780–1830* (Chapel Hill: University of North Carolina Press, 2005). Stephanie M. H. Camp, in *Closer to Freedom: Enslaved Women and Everyday Resistance in the Plantation South,* maintains that the control of slave movement was an important issue in the early nineteenth-century South, surpassing plotting rebellions, manumission, sale, inheritance, and taxation (Chapel Hill: University of North Carolina Press, 2004), 15.

3. For more on temporal landscapes, see Mark M. Smith, *Mastered by the Clock: Time, Slavery, and Freedom in the American South* (Chapel Hill: University of North Carolina Press, 1997), and Camp, *Closer to Freedom,* chap. 1.

4. Alicia Hopton Middleton, *Life in Carolina and New England during the Nineteenth Century* (Bristol: N.p., 1929), 100.

5. See Sandra Harding, *Whose Science? Whose Knowledge? Thinking from Women's Lives* (Ithaca, N.Y.: Cornell University Press, 1991); Alison Wylie, "Why Standpoint Matters," in *The Feminist Standpoint Theory Reader,* ed. Sandra Harding (New York: Routledge, 2003), 339–51; Patricia Hill Collins, *Black Feminist Thought: Knowledge, Consciousness, and the Politics of Empowerment* (Boston: Unwin Hyman, 1991).

6. On the Stono Rebellion, see Mark M. Smith, ed., *Stono: Documenting and Interpreting a Southern Slave Revolt* (Columbia: University of South Carolina Press, 2005). On the Denmark Vesey uprising, see Douglas R. Egerton, *He Shall Go out Free: The Lives of Denmark Vesey,* rev. ed. (1999; Lanham, Md.: Rowman and Littlefield, 2004), and John Lofton, *Denmark Vesey's Revolt* (Kent, Ohio: Kent State University Press, 1983). On the Haitian Revolution, see David Patrick Greggus, *Haitian Revolutionary Studies* (Bloomington: Indiana University Press, 2002), 5.

7. The Negro Seaman's Act was suspended the following year when a federal court deemed it unconstitutional, yet in 1823 similar legislation passed. Census data is from Peter A. Coclanis, *The Shadow of a Dream: Economic Life and Death in the South Carolina Low Country, 1670–1920* (Oxford: Oxford University Press, Inc., 1989), 115.

8. David Robertson, *Denmark Vesey* (New York: Knopf, 1999), 36–40. Robertson provides excellent descriptions of the myriad Africans, and their associated languages and religions, who filled Charleston. This fear of those black, scarred, or speaking other tongues

is a form of sociological othering, a way of attempting to establish unacceptability by differentiating from what critical social theorist Audre Lord calls the mythological norm—the average white male. Lorde, *Sister Outsider* (Berkeley, Calif.: Crossing, 1984), 116.

9. *Charleston Courier*, September 23, 1845, quoted in Maurie D. McInnis, *The Politics of Taste in Antebellum Charleston* (Chapel Hill: University of North Carolina Press, 2005), 181.

10. J. Benwell, *An Englishman's Travels in America: His Observations of Life and Manners in the Free and Slave States* (London: Binns and Goodwin, 1853), 185, quoted in McInnis, *The Politics of Taste*, 85. Several other ordinances further restricted the actions of blacks. An ordinance of 1813 prohibited blacks from swearing, smoking, walking with a cane, or making a joyful celebration. An 1848 ordinance excluded blacks from public parks. J. S. Glennie, *The United States in 1810–1811: The Original Manuscript Journal of a Tour through the Atlantic States*, DeCoppet Collection, Firestone Library, Princeton University, Princeton, N.J.; Bernard Karl, Duke of Saxe-Weimar Eisenach, *Travels through North America during the Years 1825 and 1826* (Philadelphia: Carey, Lea, and Carey, 1828), quoted in George C. Rogers, Jr., *Charleston in the Age of the Pinckneys* (Columbia: University of South Carolina Press, 1980), 147; Frederick Law Olmsted, *A Journey in the Seaboard Slave States: With Remarks on Their Economy* (New York: Dix and Edwards, 1856), 404, in *Documenting the American South* (Chapel Hill: University of North Carolina, 2000), http://docsouth.unc.edu/nc/olmsted/olmsted.html#p404.

11. Francis Ann Kemble, ed., *Journal of a Residence on a George Plantation, 1838–1839* (New York: Harper, 1961), 39, quoted in Charles Fraser, *Charleston! Charleston!* (Columbia: University of South Carolina Press, 1991), 206.

12. Black Charlestonians succeeded in creating a "rival geography," what postcolonial theorist Edward Said notes constituted alternative ways of knowing and using space that conflicted with the prescribed ideals and uses. Said, *Culture and Imperialism* (New York: Knopf, 1993), 266.

13. Fredrika Bremer, *The Homes of the New World: Impressions of the America* (New York: Harper and Brothers, 1853), 1:264, quoted in McInnis, *The Politics of Taste*, 84.

14. The idea for a more imposing colonnade was later discarded. McInnis, *The Politics of Taste*, 86, provides an overview of this discussion.

15. Robert Y. Hayne, *Report of the Proceedings of the City Authorities of Charleston, during the Past Year, Ending September 1st, 1837; with Suggestions for the Improvement of the City* (Charleston: A. E. Miller, 1837), quoted in H. M. Henry, *Police Control of the Slave in South Carolina* (New York: Negro Universities Press, 1914), 49.

16. Henry, *Police Control*, 141, 144.

17. *The Late Contemplated Insurrection in Charleston, SC* (New York: N.p., 1850), 8, quoted in *Exploring Amistad at Mystic Seaport* (Mystic, Conn.: Mystic Seaport, 1997), http://amistad.mysticseaport.org/library/misc/1850.charlestn.insur.html.

18. Other buildings are noted on plats, but these are the dominant buildings. Quarters

are rarely, if at all, noted on antebellum plats. These urban service buildings ranged from clapboarded frame to multistoried brick structures yet, generally speaking, they were more substantial than slave dwellings found on plantations. Gina Haney, *In Complete Order: Social Control and Architectural Organization in the Charleston Back Lot* (M.A. thesis, University of Virginia, 1996). Numerous primary sources for nineteenth-century Charleston use the term "yard" to describe the backlot.

19. Both a white and black space, the pantry acted as a buffer between dwellings of the slave owner and enslaved. This space allowed the slave owner to interface with the slave in a somewhat neutral setting—not in the main house or in enslaved work/living areas. Herman, *Town House,* 134, 126–27.

20. This architectural analysis is based on observations made by Edward Chappell, director of architectural research, Colonial Williamsburg Foundation, and the author in 1997. Chappell reports that the locking mechanism in the jamb securing the east door was drilled with a pointed bit system dating after the 1790s.

21. Susan L. Buck, "Paint Discoveries in the Aiken-Rhett House Outbuildings," paper presented at the Vernacular Architecture Forum, Newport, Rhode Island, 2001; "Charleston Drum Beat," *Southern Rose Bud,* May 2, 1835, 141, quoted in McInnis, *The Politics of Taste,* 264. Saidiya V. Hartman, in *Scenes of Subjection: Terror, Slavery, and Self-Making in Nineteenth-Century America,* examines what slaveholders deemed "the negro's holiday" within the larger scope of antebellum power relations (Oxford: Oxford University Press, 1997), 59–61. She maintains that the sense of the black community expressed by merry-making was dependent on connections forged not by race or status but made "in the context of disrupted affiliations, sociality amid the constant threat of separation, and shifting sets of identification particular to site, location, and action" (60). Community existed not because of sameness but, rather, because of the common desire to escape enslavement. Resistance existed in the establishment community which was made visible and existed outside of temporal zones set by slaveholders.

22. Robertson, *Denmark Vesey,* 79; "Memorial of the Citizens of Charleston to the Senate and House of Representatives of South Carolina," 1822, quoted in Robert S. Starobin, *Denmark Vesey: The Slave Conspiracy of 1822* (Englewood Cliffs, N.J.: Prentice-Hall, 1970), 144–46.

23. Quoted in Jeffrey Young, *Domesticating Slavery: The Ideological Formation of the Master Class in the Deep South, from Colonization to 1837* (Ph.D. diss., Emory University, 1996), 165.

24. Elizabeth Waites Allston, diary, July 16, 1861, Allston-Pringle-Hill Collections, South Carolina Historical Society, Charleston.

25. Ibid.

26. Ellen Parker, "Memories of 128 Tradd Street," Ellen Parker Papers, South Carolina Historical Society, quoted in McInnis, *The Politics of Taste,* 260.

URBAN SITES OF SLAVERY IN ANTEBELLUM TEXAS

KENNETH HAFERTEPE

When Anglo-Americans began to settle in the Mexican state of Coahuila y Tejas in the 1820s, they brought with them a system of enslaved labor. So fundamental was the peculiar institution to Anglo settlers that historian Randolph B. Campbell has characterized antebellum Texas as "an empire for slavery." Yet the landscape of slavery in Texas has been little studied, due in part to the paucity of resources that have survived into the twenty-first century. John Michael Vlach has analyzed the Robertson Ranch in Salado as a "plantation landscape ensemble," but there has been no interpretive analysis of urban dwellings in antebellum Texas similar to Bernard L. Herman's article on "Slave and Servant Housing in Charleston." Herman had in Charleston an environment in which scores of properties had retained their antebellum spatial arrangements, including not only spaces within the houses but also spaces of the distinctive backlot. In addition, much of Charleston's antebellum urban fabric remained intact.[1]

Although none of Texas's cities can claim such a rich and telling legacy, there is enough evidence from eight households in four Texas cities in order to allow us to draw some conclusions. Sanborn Fire Insurance Maps, which recorded the footprint and materials for main buildings and outbuildings, and Bird's Eye Views, lithographs in which artists created an aerial view of a city, map-like but also panoramic, reveal long-lost slave spaces and a variety of urban forms used in response to the exigencies of slavery. When an analysis of these spaces is combined with a deep reading of the few letters and memoirs left by both Anglo-Americans and African Americans, we begin to understand some of the ways in which slaveholding households in Texas towns differed from others in the South. In his article on slave housing in Charleston, for example, Herman analyzes the veranda of the Charleston single house as a point from which masters could scrutinize the movements of their slaves, concluding that the urban domestic compound of Charleston was organized to ensure surveillance and security. In Texas, however, urban domestic compounds were seemingly arranged more for convenience of service to the white owners, and enslaved workers moved with relative freedom in and out of the compound. Whether Texans drew from urban examples in New Orleans or Charleston, or adapted older Hispanic houses to meet the needs of slaveholders, slaves in these raw new Texas cities moved through a landscape that was, in spatial terms, more open and porous than the densely packed urban fabric of older southern cities. Identifying these differences is important because they demonstrate the insidious nature of slavery—the ability of its perpetrators to adapt and establish this institution to virtually any circumstance.

The institution of slavery in Texas was overwhelmingly rural; only 6 percent of enslaved Texans lived in one of the four largest towns, all of them much smaller than the older cities of the South. In 1860, all four cities combined had fewer residents than Charleston (40,000) or Richmond (38,000), themselves dwarfed by New Orleans (168,675). In 1860, San Antonio, with a population of 8,200, was the largest city in Texas but had far fewer slaves than Galveston, Houston, or Austin. San Antonio's small slave population has been attributed to the antislavery leanings of the Mexican and German populations of San Antonio, but others have suggested that poorer Mexicans and Germans were willing to do the work often done by slaves in other southern cities. Enslaved workers were a higher percentage of Austin's population, but in real numbers Houston and Galveston counted more slaves.[2]

Much of the work performed by enslaved servants in urban settings was little different from plantation work. Female slaves cooked, cleaned house, did laundry, and cared for the children of their masters, as well as their own. Female slaves could also "work out" at hotels such as the Tremont House in Galveston. Male slaves were expected to fill a variety of roles: raising food crops, tending horses and other livestock, working in the house, and driving their masters around town or cross-country. Many urban slaves developed additional skills in manufacturing and building trades. In Houston, Thomas S. Lubbock most certainly worked some of his forty-one slaves at his cotton press, and F. M. Anderson no doubt trained some of his forty-two slaves to work at his brick kiln. In Austin, the master builder Abner Cook, who was responsible for the Governor's Mansion and other Greek Revival houses, probably trained some of his seven slaves in the building trades. Some slaves are known to us by name through public records. In Galveston, James Moreau Brown's slave Aleck was a brick mason who worked on commercial and residential buildings, including Brown's imposing Italianate residence, known as Ashton Villa. In Houston, J. J. Cain's slave Richard Allen was a carpenter and contractor both before and after freedom came.[3]

The slave schedule of the 1860 U.S. Census provides useful information for analyzing urban slave housing. Austin, Galveston, and San Antonio were quite consistent in averaging 3.5 slaves per slave household. However, many urban masters allowed their slaves to "live out," which provided these relatively independent slaves with the opportunity to acquire their own living quarters. Many slaves who lived out built their own dwelling places, making an unmistakable mark on the urban fabric of the city. This practice drew the ire of a committee of the Galveston City Council; from their point of view these spaces were little more than "wretched hovels or huts," but from the point of view of enslaved workers, these spaces provided a remarkable freedom from the prying eyes of masters. Not surprisingly, many masters were disturbed at the drinking, dancing, gambling, and other activities that took place on the margins of cities and in the backrooms of the town.[4]

Although we have anecdotal descriptions of "hovels" and "huts," the interstitial spaces of slaves who lived out are lost to history and cannot be analyzed for what they might reveal about the lives of urban slaves. The living conditions and spaces of slaves who lived in the households of their master or mistress are better documented. While some slaveholding households adapted local building customs and spatial arrangements, others imported Anglo models of spatial configurations.

In San Antonio, founded in 1718 by Spanish missionaries and presidial sol-

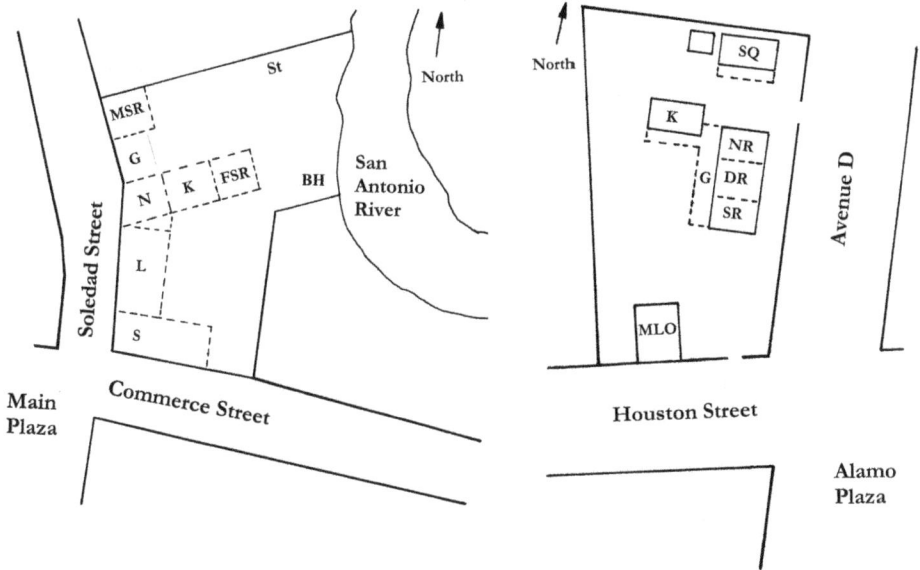

Figure 1. Sam and Mary Maverick houses on the Main Plaza (1839) and Alamo Plaza (1850), San Antonio. Abbreviations for rooms in the Main Plaza house (as identified in Mary Maverick's memoirs) include **S** (Storeroom), **L** (Long-room), **N** (North Room), **K** (Kitchen), **FSR** (Female Servants Room), **G** (Gateway or zaguan), **MSR** (Male Servants Room), **St** (approximate site of Stable), and **BH** (approximate site of Bath House); those in the Alamo Plaza house include **MLO** (Maverick Land Office), **K** (Kitchen), **G** (Gallery or verandah), **NR** (North Room), **DR** (Dining Room), **SR** (Sitting Room), and **SQ** (Slave Quarter). (Floor plans by the author based on Sanborn Fire Insurance Maps)

diers, Anglo-Americans sometimes adapted Spanish colonial house types to suit their needs. For example, in 1839, Samuel A. Maverick, a native of South Carolina, and his wife, Mary Adams Maverick, from Alabama, purchased an older house of three stone rooms and an adobe kitchen located at the northeast corner of the Main Plaza (S/L/N/K in fig. 1). They promptly enlarged the house, adding an adobe room to the kitchen for their cook, Jinny Anderson; her children; and other female servants (FSR), and another adobe room for the male servants Griffin and Granville (MSR), which was at the north end of the complex, separated from the main house by a zaguan (G), a covered passage from street to patio. The placement of Jinny's quarters next to the kitchen was a blunt reminder of the work that the Mavericks demanded of her. The place-

Figure 2. Sam and Mary Maverick House, Alamo Plaza, San Antonio. Built 1850. Photograph ca. 1870 showing the big house and quarter for male slaves. (Courtesy San Antonio Conservation Society, the Raba Collection)

ment of the male servants' quarter directly on the street suggests that Griffin and Granville served as gatekeepers and guards for the complex. This should not be surprising, given that slaves frequently had to run errands. It made no sense to create barriers to their mobility or to keep them away from an entrance, especially a work entrance.[5]

A decade later, the Mavericks built a new house on the Alamo Plaza, about a mile east of the Main Plaza (figs. 1 and 2). This new stone house, built by immigrant German masons, was remarkably similar to the single houses of Charleston, so familiar to a South Carolinian like Maverick. The two-story main block (SR/DR/NR) presented a single room to Houston Street and had a two-story veranda (G) on the west side, which faced away from the plaza. This veranda connected the main house with a two-story kitchen-laundry (K) unit, the second floor of which presumably contained quarters for Jinny and other servants. As with their previous house, the new one was at the corner of a plaza, and a one-story unit for male slaves (SQ) was at the opposite end from the plaza. And again the male servants' quarter adjoined the entry from the side street, placing the male servants in the role of guards. The placement of the buildings made two discrete yards; presumably the larger side yard was for the pleasure of the family, while the rear yard was for the work of the servants. The veranda provided a covered passageway from the kitchen to the dining room table, and also provided a view to the garden on the west side of the house. It allowed a view to the kitchen-laundry block but not to the male slave quarter or the work space that it fronted. Moreover, the slaves would be expected to use the side exit onto Avenue D. Although the layout of the complex recalled those of Charleston, the veranda was of limited use as an observation post.[6]

In Texas cities with no established building tradition, Anglo styles and building types quickly prevailed. In Austin, for example, master builder Abner Cook used details from northern pattern book authors Asher Benjamin and Minard Lafever, but finished products like the Texas Governor's Mansion (1854–56) were nevertheless adapted for the needs of a slaveholding society. Although the grounds of the Governor's Mansion were spacious enough to accommodate freestanding outbuildings such as a kitchen, laundry, and slave quarters, the plan of the mansion featured an attached service wing (fig. 3). The chairman of the building committee—and first governor to occupy the house—was Elisha Marshall Pease, a native of Connecticut. His wife, Lucadia, and sister-in-law Juliet had previously been critical of freestanding outbuildings. In 1853, Juliet observed that a friend of theirs in Brazoria, Texas, was adding on to her house, and that "her new room is separate from the house Texas fashion, in spite of some suggestions of [Lucadia's] and mine to join it to the main house."[7]

Pease family members clearly considered the New England use of attached ells to be a much more rational and practical solution as a means to facilitate service. The New England ell was a house form with which the Peases' were more familiar and comfortable, but nevertheless a form that was eminently adaptable to the needs of a slave household. The configuration of slave spaces for working and sleeping, combined with the segregated circulation afforded by the service stairs of an ell, offered the Pease family convenience as well as privacy from their "black family." Although the ell was a common feature in both northern and southern cities by the 1850s, southerners were just as likely to arrange their deep urban lots as they did their plantations, constructing detached buildings in which their slaves would work and live. Whether the ell of the Governor's Mansion was the idea of Abner Cook or of Marshall and

Figure 3. Governor's Mansion, Austin. Built 1854–56. West elevation showing the kitchen ell. Detail of photograph taken in 1912 as demolition began. (Courtesy Center for American History, University of Texas at Austin)

Lucadia Pease, it is another adaptation of an existing form to the desires of a slaveholding household.

The ell consisted of three rooms: a service stair against the main block of the house, the kitchen in the middle, and the laundry at the rear. The service stair provided access not only to second floor quarters but into the chambers of the big house, so that dirty clothes and linens could be taken to the laundry. A covered gallery connected the kitchen to the dining room at the southwest corner of the main block. The stable was at the northwestern corner of the lot, as far away from the big house as was possible. Yet it was also quite visible, with the second story serving as another quarter.[8]

Unfortunately, there is little documentation for living arrangements of the Pease family slaves. When Sam Houston became governor late in 1859, the brick ell was certainly home to Eliza, the Houston cook, and other Houston slaves. There is no reason to think that any money was expended to ornament the interior of the spaces in the kitchen ell, but the sturdy brick walls, tidily whitewashed, made it the nicest accommodations Eliza ever had. At least one of Houston's slaves lived in the big house. Nineteen-year-old Jeff Hamilton slept

KENNETH HAFERTEPE

on a pallet in the upper hall, just outside the governor's bedroom. Hamilton's sleeping arrangement was no token of favoritism but rather work-related: he was "on call" as a family servant. The sleeping place closest to status and luxury was also most closely related to menial labor. Thus, when white families made provisions for the living and sleeping arrangements of their slaves, segregation was not always the intended result. Circumstances or needs often determined the segregation or integration of slaves into the house itself. In the case of Hamilton, he was integrated, albeit in the hallway.[9]

The kitchen wing at the Governor's Mansion was replaced by a more modern one in 1912, and its material evidence is now lost. However, a similar two-story limestone outbuilding survives at the house of Washington and Mary Hill, now known as the Neill-Cochran House. In the northwest corner of the ground-floor room is a set kettle for doing laundry and related chores. Above was a single room that might have housed servants, with whitewashed limestone rubble walls, two windows, and an opening into the chimney that received the flue of a cast-iron stove. Again, a hierarchy among second-floor spaces is implicit: the owners of the house would sleep in a chamber located directly above a refined public space of the house like a parlor, dining room, or study; the servants would sleep in rooms above utilitarian spaces, which they tended during the day, like a kitchen, laundry, or carriage house.[10]

However, not all of an urban slave's life could be spent behind the big house: cleaning and other work required their presence in the formal rooms. After the first party in the Governor's Mansion in 1856, Governor Pease wrote to Lucadia, who was visiting family in Connecticut, that "at least five hundred persons" attended the party and that "over three hundred staid to supper." He further reported, "it was an awful sight the morning after the party, it almost made me sick to look at it." He did not report the feelings of Emily, Sam, Tom, and Dave, who had to deal with the party's aftermath, but after his slaves had cleaned for two days Pease noted that "it looks quite decent."[11]

The Austin residence of Alexander Gregg, the first Episcopal bishop of Texas, straddled the boundary between townhouse and suburban plantation (fig. 4). When he moved from South Carolina in 1860, Gregg brought some twenty-seven slaves to Texas. His small frame house was just outside the original city limits but faced West Avenue, the western boundary of the town. Behind

Figure 4. Bishop Alexander Gregg house, Austin. Built 1860. Detail from *Austin, State Capital of Texas*, by Augustus Koch, 1887. (Courtesy Austin History Center, Austin Public Library)

the main house was a freestanding kitchen or carriage house, as in most town-houses, but the lot extended down the hill and over Shoal Creek. Just on the other side of the creek were the quarters for his slaves. Gregg reported six slave houses on the slave schedule of the 1860 census, and the 1887 Bird's Eye View shows five houses lined up in a neat row. Gregg's linear arrangement was quite unusual for an urban or suburban context in Texas. However, the north–south linear arrangement made it easier for Gregg to keep watch over his slaves from atop the hill, or at least to reassure himself that he could keep watch from his rather distant perch if necessary. Gregg's enslaved servants may have occasionally enjoyed the creek-front housing but were probably acutely aware that they were situated in a floodplain.[12]

Another example of a southern urban arrangement of big house and quarters was the Houston house of Hester and William R. Baker. A native of New York, Baker made his fortune in real estate, while Hester was a native of Mississippi; the couple owned twenty-two slaves. Their house was built in 1858 for E. A. Palmer, a native of Virginia, but quickly sold to the Bakers. Given that the master builder, C. J. Grainger, owned four slaves, two of them males, this might be another house erected in part by black hands. The house had an imposing Greek Revival portico, a central passage plan, and an attached ell. Even more striking was the fact that the house occupied an entire city block and had a work courtyard at a rear corner of the property. A two-story stable and four other single-story outbuildings, which certainly included two or three houses for some of the servants, formed a courtyard for work and living. In addition, house slaves may well have lived in the ell over the kitchen, as at the Governor's Mansion in Austin. The Baker house slave quarter was an emphatic endorsement of spatial segregation within a townhouse.[13]

In Galveston a two-block area was home to twenty-six slaves in three different households: four in the household of Rebecca Stoddart and James Moreau Brown, ten in the household of Ephraim McLean, and twelve in the household of Margaret Stone and Ebenezer Nichols. The Nichols and Brown houses faced Broadway, which was then emerging as the elite residential address in Galveston and, indeed, Texas; the McLean house backed up to the Brown house on the north. This concentration of slaves along the alley must have allowed for a sense of community among the slaves beyond the individual households they served, and after freedom many African Americans continued to live in small and often substandard alley houses.[14]

The Nichols house, built around 1850, was a frame temple-form structure, presumably with a central passage plan. The brick kitchen was not freestanding but rather attached to the rear of the west flank. A covered gallery led from the kitchen to the big house. A Sanborn map records a variety of smaller frame outbuildings, and the kitchen block was not as close to the alley as the Bird's Eye View of 1871 would suggest. At the northwestern corner was another two-story building, which contained a stable on the first floor and additional slave quarters on the second. Across the street from the Nichols place was Ashton Villa, the home of James Moreau Brown; his wife, Rebecca Stoddart Brown; and their children. Their three-story Italianate house followed Philadelphia fashion as epitomized by the architect and author Samuel Sloan, but their kitchen-laundry unit departed from Sloan's designs to follow southern fashion by removing to a separate building the working and living spaces of the household's enslaved workers. White Texans, fresh from cities, farms, and plantations in both the North and South, used various architectural forms, whether familiar, adapted, or adopted, not only for their convenience to service but sometimes as the means by which they separated themselves from their slaves.[15]

The Bird's Eye Views of Austin and Houston, along with the watercolor of

Figure 5. *George Allen's Residence, Houston, Texas, 1845*, by Friedrich Rothaas. Watercolor. (Courtesy Center for American History, University of Texas at Austin)

the George Allen house in Houston (fig. 5), show cities and properties that seem more suburban in character than urban, and this is a distinctive feature of the early Texas city. Houston residences are located in a neighborhood laid out as a grid with broad streets and large blocks bisected by straight alleys. The city plan is regular and practical and offers a spaciousness unknown to older cities in the South like Charleston or New Orleans. Similarly, the Austin residence of Bishop Gregg, located at the outskirts of town, has none of the confining architectural features expected of an urban environment. George Allen's house in Houston is set within a garden and defined as distinct from the rest of the city only by a picket fence. Unlike the Charleston single house in Herman's study, the porch of the Allen house seems to be oriented toward the garden paths for pleasure, with little concern for monitoring slave movement along those paths.

All of these images depict urban landscapes that have little to do with confining or observing an enslaved population, and more to do with practical conveniences of service. Yet the racial barriers were present. No doubt, as the population of enslaved workers grew in these Texas cities, the urban environment would become more restrictive, even defensive as in Charleston. Yet, as Gina Haney has shown in her study of that city in this volume, such restrictions were a response to a powerful people who were enslaved. As the system of slavery spread over the continent, adapting to new conditions each step of the way, enslaved African Americans consistently appropriated space for themselves in new environments. Indeed, they not only appropriated spaces but also marked them as their own. Slaves of course owned no real estate, but they nevertheless had a keen sense of possession, which they often asserted to the chagrin of white people.[16]

Former slaves in Galveston, for example, declared their attachment to their homes, and a few even took legal action to preserve their right to live in the city. When Betsy Webster's master—with whom she had apparently had a common-law relationship—died in 1856, she was freed under the terms of his will. Webster hired lawyer William Pitt Ballinger not only to defend the terms of the will but also to attack Texas laws that required free blacks to leave the state or revert to an enslaved condition. Ballinger told the court that Webster was determined "not to abandon the home where all her attachments centered. She has lived many years in this city in a home of comfort and taste—a white cottage embowered amid flowers and orange trees. All her affections clung to this island home, where she had lived with her former master, sustaining perhaps, relations to him not sanctioned by law, but sanctified by all the sentiments of her nature." Ballinger was successful in defending Betsy Webster's right to her home—and to possession of her own body—but the prevailing attitude of Texans in the years leading up to the Civil War made the life of a free black difficult indeed.[17]

Attorney Ballinger had difficulties with one of his own enslaved servants, Dave, who was also passionate about living in an urban area. After the outbreak of the Civil War, Ballinger sent his six slaves to a plantation to protect his investment. However, Aaron Coffee, the owner of the plantation, wrote to Ballinger that Dave "has sworned not to work on any plantation & says he will not live out of a city or town." Although his master insisted that he work in the country, Dave continued to run away and return to his home in Galveston. Apparently Dave was not alone in his dislike of rural life: though Coffee insisted that he had supplied the other Ballinger slaves with decent clothes, they would return to Galveston wearing rags. Coffee wrote somewhat defensively that "your negroes hate a farm or plantation so much they go to you in the condition you state in order that you will retain them in town." While returning to a master's townhouse might seem an odd form of resistance, it is not hard to imagine why Dave was so attached to his life in town, given his awareness of opportunities to make his own money, as well as a preference for house chores to fieldwork. For Dave, running away from something meant running toward something else, toward a place where he felt a better chance to realize his freedom.[18]

Slaveholding Texans like Ballinger who lived in towns built complex relationships that allowed enslaved workers enough freedom to perform their assigned labors while at the same time maintaining traditional social and racial hierarchies. In the towns of Galveston, Austin, Houston, and San Antonio, the spatial arrangement of slaveholding households varied, depending on the experiences of the slaveholder with the institution of slavery. Some urban compounds were closed, others were open. Some slave spaces meant for work and sleeping were dispersed throughout a compound, while others were attached as an ell to the main house. Unlike such older cities as Charleston, New Orleans, or Richmond, which had, in response to the requirements of slavery, long since settled into distinctive urban forms, Texas towns developed a remarkable variety of forms that answered the needs of urban slaveholders. Slaveholding Texans had immigrated from both the North and the South, from towns and cities, and from farms and plantations. They brought with them their own notions of how a household should be served by enslaved workers, and these notions were translated into built forms, like the compounds of Bishop Alexander Gregg or George Allen, which were as open and free-ranging as the big landscape of Texas itself. Texas towns were shaped from a variety of models that had been tested elsewhere, and slaveholding Texans discovered that these models were eminently adaptable to their needs: the New England ell used by the Pease family at the Governor's Mansion; the Maverick's enclosed compound in San Antonio, reminiscent of the Charleston gated yard; Gregg's carefully arranged row of slave houses. All of these arrangements created a landscape that seemed more open and permeable, less confining to a slave like Dave. With the recovery of instances of slave resistance like that of Dave, or the assertion of a legal principle in favor of a slave, as in the case of Betsy Webster, it is tempting to celebrate the resilience of the enslaved community in the face of subjugation. Such resistance should indeed be commemorated as courageous, life-affirming acts, but care must be taken to remember that for every Dave and Betsy for whom we have a record, there were scores of enslaved African Americans who remained trapped in hopeless subjugation.[19]

In reality the remarkable variety of forms found in Texas's antebellum towns is a testament to the many ways that the system of enslaved labor could insinuate itself into any context. Despite such a multiplicity of forms, there was nothing different or unique about the slaveholding households of Texas towns, and, in fact, it is the "sameness" of these forms, various as they might be in Texas, that is so remarkable. Slaves were not bound to their masters by confined space but rather by an entire society dedicated to maintaining the institution of slavery. A telling example of that dedication to maintenance is found at the highest level of government in antebellum Texas. On March 14, 1861, the dining room of the Governor's Mansion was the scene of a remarkable meeting of the Sam Houston family. Texas had just seceded from the Union, and the secession convention demanded that Governor Houston take an oath to support the Confederate states. After the Houston family had dinner and the servants had cleared the table, Margaret Houston placed the family Bible before her husband at the head of the table. Daughter Nancy recalled that "the Negroes brought in their raw hide bottom chairs from the kitchen and the servant's quarters and arranged them along the back wall of the dining room. The General then read a chapter from the Bible, and they all knelt in family prayer as was the usual custom."[20]

Although slaves were ubiquitous in the dining room, evening prayers changed, for just a few minutes, the nature of the space. In the minds of the Houstons, an open Bible and the invocation of the Holy Spirit made them and their slaves one family, united in the eyes of a benevolent God who had ordained their stations in life. Yet the Houstons gathered around the dining table while their slaves sat in a row against the wall. The Houstons remained seated in their usual, comfortably padded set of matching dining chairs while the slaves settled on rawhide-bottom chairs brought in for this unique occasion. And when Sam Houston closed the Bible, his enslaved servants removed their chairs and themselves from the dining room, returning to "the kitchen and the servants' quarters." This "usual custom" of the Houstons and their slaves united in prayer is indicative of the complex and contradictory interactions between master and slave, and serves as a reminder that the ease with which slaves moved through Texas towns belied the reality of their true confines.[21]

NOTES

1. The standard work on slavery in Texas is Randolph B. Campbell, *An Empire for Slavery: The Peculiar Institution in Texas, 1821–1865* (Baton Rouge: Louisiana State University Press, 1989). On the architecture of plantation slavery, see John Michael Vlach, *Back of the Big House: The Architecture of Plantation Slavery* (Chapel Hill: University of North Carolina Press, 1993), and Larry McKee, "The Ideals and Realities behind the Design and Use of 19th Century Virginia Slave Cabins," in *The Art and Mystery of Historical Archaeology: Essays in Honor of James Deetz*, ed. Anne Elizabeth Yentsch and Mary C. Beaudry (Boca Raton, Fla.: CRC Press, 1992), 195–213. For urban slave quarters, see Vlach, "'Without Recourse to Owners': The Architecture of Urban Slavery in the Antebellum South," *Perspectives in Vernacular Architecture,* vol. 6, *Shaping Communities,* ed. Carter L. Hudgins and Elizabeth Collins Cromley (Knoxville: University of Tennessee Press, 1997), 150–60, and Bernard L. Herman, "Slave and Servant Housing in Charleston, 1770–1820," *Historical Archaeology* 33, no. 3 (1999): 88–101.

2. 1860 U.S. Census, Texas, Slave Schedule, Bexar, Galveston Harris, and Travis Counties.

3. On Cook's slaves, see Kenneth Hafertepe, *Abner Cook: Master Builder on the Texas Frontier* (Austin: Texas State Historical Association, 1992), 35–36, 54. On Aleck, see Hafertepe, *A History of Ashton Villa: A Family and Its House in Victorian Galveston, Texas* (Austin: Texas State Historical Association, 1991), 8, 17. On Richard Allen, see Ann Patton Malone, "Matt Gaines: Reconstruction Politician," in *Black Leaders: Texans for Their Times*, ed. Alwyn Barr and Robert A. Calvert (Austin: Texas State Historical Association, 1981), 56, 57, 66, 76n29; "Richard Allen," in Alwyn Barr and Cary D. Wintz, Handbook of Texas Online, http://www.tsha.utexas.edu/handbook/online/articles/view/AA/fal24.html; J. Mason Brewer, *Negro Legislatures of Texas and Their Descendants,* 2nd ed. (1935; Austin: Jenkins, 1970), 53–54; and Paul Casdorph, *A History of the Republican Party in Texas, 1865–1965* (Austin: Pemberton Press, 1965), 39.

4. Paul D. Lack, "Urban Slavery in the Southwest," *Red River Valley Historical Review* 4, no. 2 (Spring 1981): 13.

5. On the Mavericks, see Paula Mitchell Marks, *Turn Your Eyes toward Texas: Pioneers Sam and Mary Maverick* (College Station: Texas A&M University Press, 1989). On their house on the Main Plaza, see Kenneth Hafertepe, "The Texas Homes of Sam and Mary Maverick," *Southwestern Historical Quarterly* 109 (July 2005): especially 4–10.

6. Hafertepe, "The Texas Homes," 15–27.

7. On Cook, see Hafertepe, *Abner Cook*. The quotation from Juliet Niles's letter of January 5, 1853, can be found in Katherine Hart and Elisabeth Kemp, *Lucadia Pease and the Governor: Letters, 1850–1857* (Austin, Tex.: Encino Press, 1974), 93. Elizabeth C. Cromley, "Transforming the Food Axis: Houses, Tools, Modes of Analysis," *Material History Review* 44 (Fall 1996): 8–22. Cromley notes that "by the mid-nineteenth century, middle class urban and suburban houses were conceived according to zones of use: the social zone . . . [and] the service zone" (8). For an interpretation of the ell's significance to a slave society, see Clifton Ellis, "The Mansion House at Berry Hill Plantation: Architecture and the Changing Nature of Slavery in Antebellum Virginia," *Perspectives in Vernacular Architecture* 1 (Fall 2006): 22–48.

8. The evidence for the arrangement of the original ell consists of the Sanborn Fire Insurance Map of 1894 [sheet 6] and a photograph of the rear of the mansion taken just as demolition of the ell was starting in 1912. The Sanborn Map is in the Geography and Map Division of the Library of Congress, Washington, D.C. The photograph is in the collection of the Dolph Briscoe Center for American History, the University of Texas at Austin.

9. The Houston family servants are some of the best-documented in the Texas. On Joshua Houston, the senior slave in the Houston household, see Patricia Smith Prather and Jane Clements Monday, *From Slave to Statesman: The Legacy of Joshua Houston, Servant to Sam Houston* (Denton: University of North Texas Press, 1993), 9, 12, 25n32. Eliza was first given a full treatment in William Seale, *Sam Houston's Wife: A Biography of Margaret Lea Houston* (Norman: University of Oklahoma Press, 1970); her epitaph is on p. 263. She also figures in Madge Thornall Roberts, *Star of Destiny: The Private Life of Sam and Margaret Houston* (Denton: University of North Texas Press, 1993). Roberts, a descendant of Sam and Margaret Houston, provided five of Eliza's recipes, including those for Cedar Point Gumbo and Apple Crisp, for inclusion in the Study Club of Huntsville, Huntsville, Texas, *Tastes and Traditions: The Sam Houston Heritage Cookbook* (Kearney, Neb.: Morris Press, 1992). The youngest, Jeff Hamilton, wrote an autobiography: Jeff Hamilton (as told to Lenoir Hunt), *My Master: The Inside Story of Sam Houston and His Times,* reprint ed. (1940; Austin, Tex.: State House Press, 1992); on Jeff's sleeping arrangements, see pp. 47–48.

10. On the Hill-Neill-Cochran House, see Hafertepe, *Abner Cook,* 112–20.

11. Hart and Kemp, *Pease and the Governor,* 292–93.

12. Wilson Gregg, *Alexander Gregg, First Bishop of Texas* (Sewanee, Tenn.: University of the South, 1912), 64–65, 73; Travis County Deed Records, O, 162, 167; Q, 696, Travis County Courthouse, Austin, Tex.; Augustus Koch, Bird's Eye View of Austin, 1887, Austin History Center, Austin Public Library. In the 1861 Travis County property tax records, now at the Austin History Center, Gregg valued his 27 slaves at $10,800. His two lots in Division Z, which included his house, were worth $2,000.

13. Dorothy Houghton et al., *Houston's Forgotten Heritage: Landscape, Houses, Interiors, 1824–1914* (College Station: Texas A&M University Press, 2014), 114.

14. See Ellen Beasley, *The Alleys and Back Buildings of Galveston: An Architectural and Social History* (College Station: Texas A&M University Press, 1996).

15. The arrangement of service spaces and slave quarters at the Nichols house is preserved in Camille N. Drie, *Bird's Eye View of the City of Galveston, Texas,* 1871, and the Sanborn Fire Insurance Map of 1889, sheet 27, both Dolph Briscoe Center for American History. On Ebenezer and Margaret Nichols, see Charles W. Hayes, *History of the Island and the City of Galveston,* reprint ed. (1879; Austin, Tex.: Jenkins, 1974), 2:855–60, and Annie Doom Pickrell, *Pioneer Women in Texas,* reprint ed. (1929; Austin, Tex.: Jenkins, 1970), 270–73. See also Barbara J. Rozek, "Galveston Slavery," *Houston Review* 15, no. 2 (1993): 67–101.

16. Dylan C. Penningroth, *The Claims of Kinfolk: African American Property and Community in the Nineteenth-Century South* (Chapel Hill: University of North Carolina Press, 2003).

17. John Anthony Moretta, *William Pitt Ballinger: Texas Lawyer, Southern Statesman, 1825–1888* (Austin: Texas State Historical Association, 2000), 113–16.

18. Paul D. Lack, "Dave: A Rebellious Slave," in Barr and Calvert, eds., *Black Leaders,* 1–18; Lack, "Urban Slavery in the Southwest," 11–12.

19. Two works reexamine and emphasize the effects of racialization, the process by which slaveholders subjugated African and African American slaves through a variety of cultural (e.g., religious) and economic (e.g., capitalistic) devices. See James Oliver Horton and Lois Horton, *Slavery and the Making of America* (New York: Oxford University Press, 2005), and Saidiya V. Hartman, *Scenes of Subjection: Terror, Slavery, and Self-Making in Nineteenth-Century America* (New York: Oxford University Press, 1997).

20. Quoted in Llerena Friend, *Sam Houston: The Great Designer* (Austin: University of Texas Press, 1954), 338.

21. According to Saidiya Hartman, dancing, singing, and other means of amusement that slaves might employ for their enjoyment could be turned in an instant into forms of ritualized subjugation, such as having slaves sing or dance on the auction block. Hartman might interpret the prayer scene in the Houston dining room as an example of a ritualized act of submission on the part of the slaves to the authority of God and to the authority of Texas law, which defined them as chattel. In this instance, however, there is no documentary evidence to hint that kneeling in "family prayer as was the usual custom" was an act of subjugation. Nevertheless, Hartman gives insight into some of the coercive mechanisms inherent in slave systems. See Hartman, *Scenes of Subjection,* 17–49. The chairs in the room were listed in the H. W. Raglin inventory of November 8, 1861; see Jean Houston Daniel, Price Daniel, and Dorothy Blodgett, *The Texas Governor's Mansion: A History of the House and Its Occupants* (Austin: Texas State Library and Archives Commission, 1984), 320.

SLAVERY IN KNOXVILLE, TENNESSEE

In, but Not Entirely of, the South

CHARLES H. FAULKNER

Of that "peculiar" institution, as slavery was called in the United States during the nineteenth century, nothing was more peculiar according to some historians than slavery in southern urban centers. Cities were seen as the embodiment of American technological progress and intellectual achievement, certainly no place for such an archaic and evil institution to persist. But it is this persistence of enslavement in southern cities that some historians believe helped fan the flames of resistance among both the enslaved and free blacks alike at the eve of the Civil War and further expose its evils to white Americans.

Studies of urban slavery have recorded a general decline in the slave population of many southern cities during the nineteenth century, especially during the decade before the Civil War.[1] For example, statistics on nine cities with populations between 20,000 and 100,000 in 1860 indicate only two showed a steady increase in slave population between 1820 and 1860.[2] While the cause of this decline has been hotly debated by social historians, most researchers agree that slaves were generally able to exercise more freedom in the urban setting, thereby influencing fundamental changes in social control and local economies. An example of the freedom that slaves exercised in some cities such as Wilmington, North Carolina, was an opportunity to engage in more skilled or semiskilled jobs in a commercial and industrial milieu that was rapidly expanding within southern urban centers by the mid-nineteenth century. While both rural and urban bondspersons could be hired out, it was usually in the cities that hired slaves were allowed to live apart from their masters. Hiring out meant financial gain for masters, but it also presented the risk that their slaves might associate with free blacks, whom whites believed encouraged yearnings for freedom and harbored runaways. Free blacks sometimes taught slaves how to read and write, which was almost universally prohibited in the South. Urban slavery also had an impact on postbellum skill levels among freedmen. While trades were cut off to northern blacks because of a larger number of foreign immigrants and emerging unions, the South offered greater opportunities to blacks after emancipation, especially since many had been trained in special skills or trades.[3] It might be expected, then, that the percentage of skilled and semiskilled blacks would have increased in southern cities immediately after the Civil War, although this could have been checked by an influx of skilled European immigrants.[4]

Although the development of black residential patterns in many southern cities after the Civil War remains relatively obscure, it is known that many of the older cities had integrated neighborhoods since masters wanted to keep tight reins on their servants and workers, and these mixed neighborhoods often remained intact. Newer cities, which experienced their greatest growth spurt after the war, had little antebellum heritage of mixed neighborhoods and developed segregated residential patterns more rapidly than the older cities. In both types of cities, however, as blacks began to exercise greater freedom of residential choice, they were restrained by discrimination and low income to less desirable areas of the urban periphery.[5] Demographic studies of the enslaved in the older deep-South cities indicate they constituted a fairly large percentage of the total population, with about equal numbers of female and male slaves, and large numbers of skilled or semiskilled male slaves. This contrasted with the slave demography of border cities, which had smaller black populations, an increasing female-to-male ratio, and an older-than-average mean age among slaves.[6]

SLAVERY IN KNOXVILLE, TENNESSEE

Knoxville, Tennessee, located in the southern Appalachian region, is not an old, deep-South city, having been settled in the 1780s by white pioneers, largely from North Carolina and Virginia. To underscore this point, East Tennessee and its urban center, Knoxville, had from early on been a maverick compared to Middle and West Tennessee, the latter two areas sharing more social and political institutions with their neighbors to the south. On the eve of the Civil War, the absence of large plantations in Knoxville's countryside, and the small-scale craft and trade composition of its economy, distinguished it from many southern cities. More importantly, it was the urban center for the mountainous region of western North Carolina, East Tennessee, and northern Georgia, which favored the Union in the face of national division. In February 1861, Knox County voted ten to one against considering secession; however, Knoxville proper favored the southern cause by more than two to one.[7] This allegiance to the Confederacy was largely economic rather than social since Knoxville's commerce was directed south down the Great Valley. Although Knoxville was transformed from a sleepy craft and trade center into a vigorous manufacturing and commercial center by the end of the nineteenth century, it continued to remain unlike other southern cities in her predominantly white majority and Republican politics.[8]

Chase Mooney in his book *Slavery in Tennessee* proposes that since no large plantations were found in East Tennessee, and the slave population was smaller than that found in the middle and western parts of the state, slaves worked more closely with their masters in the absence of overseers and therefore were treated more humanely and given more freedom.[9] This myth that East Tennessee and Knoxville slaves had a better life is echoed by almost every historian who has written about antebellum life in this region. Knox County historian Mary U. Rothrock believed that since most Knoxville slaves probably worked as domestics, "This contact not only made for more kindly relations between master and slave, but gave to the slaves opportunities to gain a certain degree of culture."[10] A popular history of Knoxville proudly proclaimed the humane treatment of blacks and abolitionist sentiments by such prominent Knoxvillians as Reverend Thomas W. Humes, who opened a school for free black children before the Civil War, and Perez Dickinson, one of Knoxville's leading businessman, who was praised as an abolitionist and purportedly had a tunnel constructed from his house to the Tennessee riverbank for aiding runaway slaves.[11] Such praise was supposedly supported by the idea that Tennessee was before 1830 one of the most antislavery states in the Union, and the Knoxville area was described as the "most thoroughly anti-slavery part of the South."[12] That a greater humanitarianism prevailed in Knoxville is more myth than reality, however, is underscored by the fact that the above prominent citizens with supposed abolitionist credentials, Thomas Hughes and Perez Dickinson, owned four and six slaves, respectively. Census and deed records indicate Dickinson also bought and sold slaves.[13]

Knoxville also passed ordinances to control slaves in addition to the stringent state laws already on the books, which reveal increasing hostility toward free blacks with the registration system of 1806, the Exclusion Act of 1831, and disenfranchisement in 1834. Under the registration system, free blacks had to be registered by the county clerk for their right to freedom. One of the laws of the Exclusion Act of 1831 required that blacks emancipated in Tennessee must leave the state and post bond to guarantee their removal. These were part of the broader grouping of laws called slave codes throughout the slave states.[14] As early as 1802, slaves were prohibited from assembling on streets, in kitchens, or in uninhabited houses at nights or on Sundays.[15] An ordinance for the "Regulation of Slaves," passed in 1817, provided that no slave could live in the city unless in the service of a white inhabitant, liquor retailers could not give liquor to slaves except their own, and residents could not hire slaves belonging to a nonresident.[16] Punishment for breaking these laws was administered by the whip.

SLAVE AND FREE BLACK DEMOGRAPHY IN KNOXVILLE

In 1820, there were 434 blacks in a population of 1,406 (30.8%) and in 1850, there were 598 blacks in a population of 2,076 (28.8%), a slight decline, following the general population decline during this period cited earlier.[17] The number of black residents in Knoxville quadrupled between 1860 and 1880.[18] This reflects the presence of so-called contraband camps after the Union Army captured the city in 1863. These camps were occupied by rural migrants seeking freedom during the war and employment in Tennessee cities after emancipation.[19] A consequence of the population decline recorded in 1850 could have meant slave living space remained relatively unchanged before emancipation, with conditions such as crowding and more stringent segregation appearing after the Civil War.

A comparison of the black population of Knoxville to that of Nashville and Memphis between 1820 and 1870 indicates similar trends in demography. In Nashville, blacks constituted 33 percent of the population in 1820, and their numbers hovered between 33 and 36 percent until 1850, when they dropped to 25 percent of the population.[20] There was a continued decrease to 23 percent in 1860 and then a marked jump up to 38 percent of the total in 1870.[21] A more precipitous drop in the black population between 1850 and 1860 is seen in Memphis, where the percentage of blacks fell from 28 percent in 1850 to 17 percent in 1860.[22] Like Nashville, the black population of Memphis increased significantly by 1870 to 39 percent of the population, fueled by fleeing freed or enslaved refugees during the war and rural migrants after the conflict. While population trends of blacks in the three Tennessee cities are similar, the numbers of free blacks in these cities in the decade before the Civil War reveal a difference in Knoxville, which witnessed an increase in free blacks from 23 to 35 percent of the black population.[23] In contrast, during the same decade, free blacks actually decreased from 20 to 18 percent of the Nashville black population and stayed at only 17 percent of the black population in Memphis.[24]

SLAVES IN KNOXVILLE

Enslaved African Americans resided in Knoxville from the time of earliest settlement. Slaves accompanied James White, founder of Knoxville who built a fort in the future city in 1786; likewise, Governor William Blount, who established the capital of the territory south of the Ohio River there in 1792, had ten slaves in his household.[25] Based on a study of Knoxville tax records, Amy Lambeck Young suggests that in 1806, 62 of the 86 enslaved persons, and in 1828, 157 of 206 enslaved individuals may have resided on farms surrounding Knoxville since most of their owners owned land in rural areas.[26] Both James White and William Blount had "plantations" near Knoxville, suggesting that there was considerable interaction between the urban and rural enslaved in this area. For example, a trust deed in 1797 lists twenty-seven slaves owned by the governor, too many to have been housed in town and undoubtedly living on his nearby farm.[27]

By 1860, eighty-five Knoxvillians owned between one and twenty slaves, averaging five slaves per master. Female slaves outnumbered male slaves by a ratio of 54 to 45 percent, about the same as the female-male ratio in Nashville and lower than the ratio in the five southern border cities studied by Claudia D. Goldin.[28] A further study of the 1860 Knoxville enslaved population reveals that of those masters owning more than one slave, 55 percent housed family units of adults and children. These tentative families could be further broken down into one (40%), two (30%), and three nuclear family (2%) groups of spouses and children, and families with only adult males (12%) or females (15%) and children. Of the remaining 45 percent of the households, a majority (78%) were female-headed.[29] While females constituted a significant social force in slave social organization, if the above figures are correct, they suggest a relatively strong nuclear family orientation. What is missing from the documents is the occupations of the Knoxville slaves. Fortunately, an 1860 census-taker in the upper East Tennessee town of Jonesboro recorded the full names and occupations of enslaved persons there, later discovering his "error" and lightly scratching out this information.[30] While Jonesboro was a smaller urban center than Knoxville, it was also a craft and trade center, and the occupations of the enslaved there may have been similar to what was found in Knoxville. A comparison of the 1860 free black workforce in Knoxville and Jonesboro indicates that 10 percent of the Jonesboro enslaved and 20 percent of the free blacks were skilled, compared to 30 percent skilled free blacks in Knoxville. These figures might suggest a higher percentage of skilled slaves residing in the latter city. This may also be expected because Knoxville was a larger, more "metropolitan" town. Only four skilled occupations are found in Jonesboro as compared to eleven in Knoxville. On the other side of the coin, it may be significant that so few railroad workers are found in Knoxville; although not an industrial town in 1860, it was a major railroad center for the East Tennessee and Georgia and the East Tennessee and Virginia lines. Perhaps certain skilled positions were more restricted here for both free and enslaved blacks. This also appears to have been the case in Nashville, where slaves composed only a small proportion of the skilled trades.[31]

Using the 1860 Knox County slave schedule and the 1859 Knoxville city directory, the approximate location of the slave owners' houses in Knoxville has been plotted (fig. 1). They were widely distributed throughout the central part

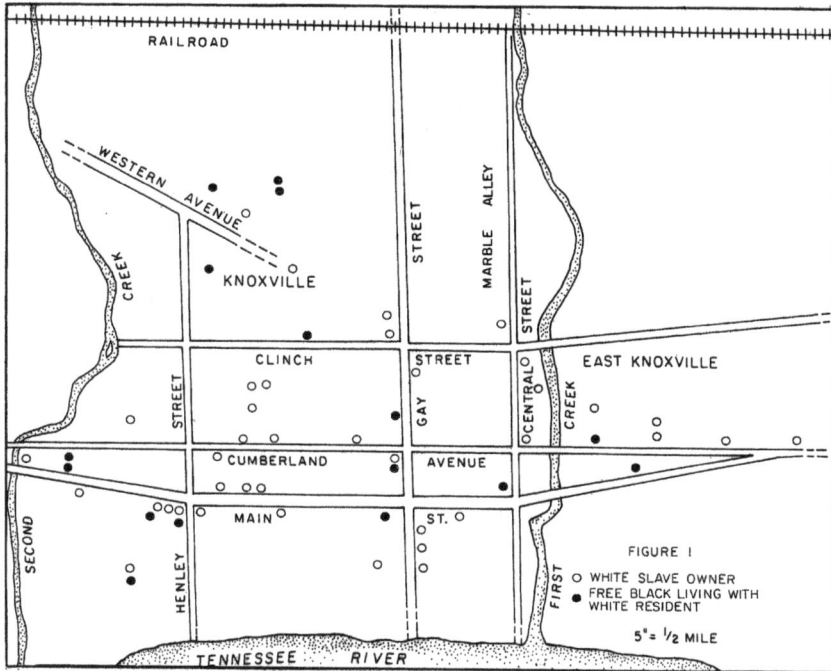

Figure 1. Map of Knoxville with residences of white slave owners and free blacks living with residents, 1860. (Drawn by Terry Faulkner)

of town between Henley, Clinch, and Central Streets and the river, especially along the major thoroughfares such as Gay and West Main Streets. Based on the 1817 law, one can assume that slaves also lived at these locations. There is evidence from other areas of Tennessee that slaves often lived within the homes of their masters.[32] Unfortunately, of the antebellum houses still standing within the 1860 Knoxville city limits, only two, the Park and Mabry-Hazen houses, have evidence of possible slave quarters in their cellars. As in Wilmington and Charleston, the enslaved, especially what appear to be family groups, seemed to have been usually housed in separate quarters. Sixty-five Knoxville slave owners (76%) were listed on the 1860 slave schedule as having from one to three slave houses. The archaeological excavation of two of these quarters provides a glimpse of the daily lifeways of the enslaved in Knoxville.

The late eighteenth-century slave quarters location at Blount Mansion, home of Governor William Blount, was tested by the author from 1991–97 with an archaeological field school from the University of Tennessee. These excavations revealed the remains of a timber-frame structure measuring 12 by 30 feet with a roughly dressed limestone foundation and fireplace at the west gable end. A 1992 architectural study of Blount Mansion established that the west wing of the mansion was the quarters that had been moved and attached to the west end of the house. The study of this wing revealed a timber-frame, cladded building with doorways in the north and east elevation and glazed windows on the north, east, and south elevations.[33] Domestic refuse in the crawlspace under the original building site indicated access to this area via a trapdoor in the floor. Archaeological remains reveal the structure was moved in the 1830s, the new quarters being another frame structure with a central chimney that can be seen in an 1865 panoramic photograph of the city.[34] One edge of the root cellar was visible under these latter quarters.[35] Root cellars have been excavated under two rural slave house sites near Knoxville. Two cellars were found under a double house at the Mabry site, a large early to mid-nineteenth-century farm,[36] and two were found under a single pen slave house on the late eighteenth- or early nineteenth-century farm of John Sevier, first governor of Tennessee.[37]

The Perez Dickinson slave quarters was revealed during salvage excavations at a bank construction site in 1988. One end of this two-room frame structure (approximately 20 by 12 feet) with a brick foundation and brick end chimneys was hastily excavated before it was destroyed by earth-moving equipment.[38] No evidence of an escape tunnel was observed on the site. While the two antebellum slave quarters in Knoxville constitute too small a sample for meaningful comparisons, the variation in construction is similar to that noted in a study of standing slave quarters in East Tennessee.[39] Seven standing quarters include buildings of brick, frame, and log construction, ranging from single-room dwellings to multi-room dormitory-style buildings. There is no indication that one single model prevailed in the city and rural areas for slave quarters construction.

The salvage excavation of the Perez Dickinson slave quarters did not produce enough domestic artifacts to reveal the lifeways of the enslaved there. However, the excavation of the Blount Mansion quarters produced hundreds of artifacts that provide a glimpse of the foodways, dress, and leisure activities of the enslaved residents.

No written record of slave diet in Knoxville is known to exist. However, the Blount Mansion ceramics and faunal remains offer a clue about the type of food consumed and the way it was prepared and consumed. While the Blount enslaved ate the same kinds of meat as people in the mansion, the cuts of beef and pork were of lesser quality. Most noticeable in the faunal assemblage was the larger quantity of wild animal foods, especially fish.[40] Supplementing the diet with wild animals is also a characteristic of the enslaved at the rural Mabry house and Marble Springs sites.[41] Ceramic frequencies reveal a small number of food preparation and storage vessels, suggesting meals were largely prepared in the nearby kitchen, a pattern also seen at the Marble Springs site. Another noticeable difference in vessel frequency is the high percentage of refined ceramic cups and saucers from the Blount quarters.[42] It is not known, however, if this means the Blount slaves were participating in the popular "tea ceremony" or were preparing herbal and medicinal teas. While no definite charred medicinal plants were found in the Blount quarters that may have been used in African American folk medicine, charcoal from several of these plants were present at the Mabry and Marble Springs farms.[43]

Clothing of enslaved Knoxvillians is described for runaways in numerous advertisements in the late eighteenth-century *Knoxville Gazette*. All of these ads are for enslaved men and denote European dress. The numerous buttons found in the Blount quarters also suggest European American garb, and that both adult men and women lived in this building. One distinctive pattern in the Blount clothing assemblage and also found at rural East Tennessee slave quarters but rarely on local European American sites is a large number of glass beads.[44] Historical archaeologists have noted that glass beads are typical finds at African American sites.[45] An unusual bead suggesting trade or exchange found in the Blount quarters is a "bubble shell" from the Atlantic Coast between North Carolina and Florida.[46] Does the wearing of beaded necklaces constitute what has often been called a retention of "Africanisms," that is, a custom handed down through the generations, or is it also a defiant symbol of personality?

Perhaps such transformations of function and/or meaning might also be illustrated by the stone marbles found in the Blount quarters, Mabry house, and Marble Springs.[47] At this time it is unclear if marbles were used like Europeans in adult men's leisure activity or had an entirely different function and meaning to enslaved African Americans.

FREE BLACKS IN KNOXVILLE

In addition to a population increase of free blacks in Knox County not witnessed in Nashville and Memphis, the location of earlier free black neighborhoods in Knoxville shows a pattern that still affects modern racial demography in the city. While it is difficult to determine exactly where free blacks were living before the Civil War since they are not listed in the 1859 city directory, the 1850 and 1860 censuses suggest they were located in mixed neighborhoods similar to the population distribution of Knoxville's enslaved (see fig. 1). The 1869 city directory and the 1870 Knox County census show that most blacks were now living around the periphery of the central city in what has been called "marginal" land.[48] Knoxville has unusual natural and cultural features that affected the settlement of its lower-income citizens—both black and white. On the south, east, and west sides of the central city are low floodplains of the Tennessee River, First Creek, and Second Creek, respectively, and on the north was the east–west railroad yards. Ten years after the Civil War blacks were concentrated in all of these less desirable areas of the city, with an especially large number living along First Creek and adjacent East Knoxville, is still the case today (fig. 2). The former neighborhood abutted the downtown area along Crozier Street (now Central) and Marble Alley. A smaller black neighborhood was on the west side of town on Second Creek. A focal building in each area was a church, the congregation on Patton Street in East Knoxville being listed in the 1859 city directory. Black businesses were concentrated along Gay Street, but at the north end closer to the railroad on the edge of town and the densely population Marble Alley neighborhood.

Based on census data, the settlement pattern of pre– and immediate post–Civil War blacks in Knoxville is unlike that in Nashville, which was more like northern cities with large concentrations of blacks in a few segregated neighbor-

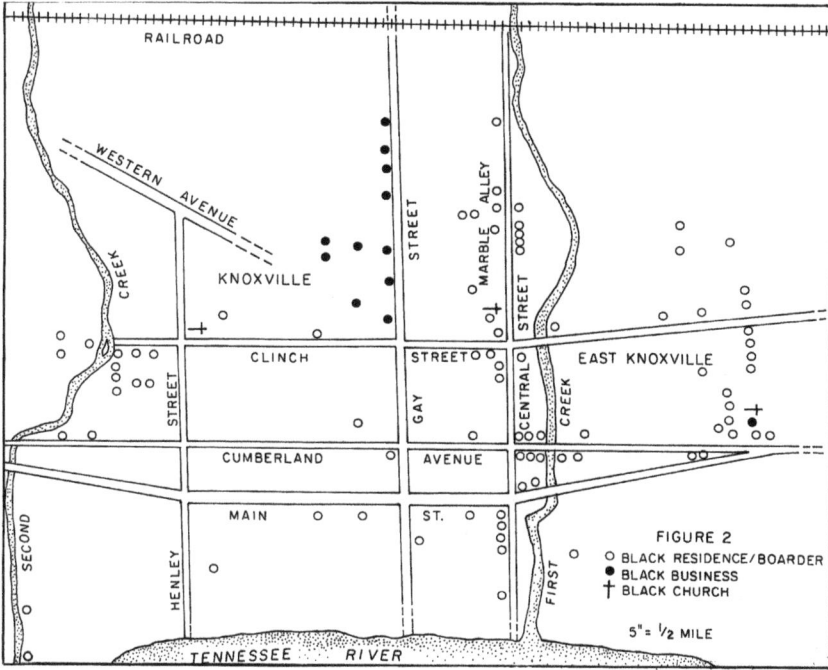

Figure 2. Map of Knoxville showing black residences, businesses, and churches, 1860. (Drawn by Terry Faulkner)

hoods. In the First and Second Creek areas of Knoxville, working-class blacks and whites were interspersed or concentrated on one or both sides of certain streets in the last decades of the nineteenth century. The Marble Alley neighborhood was an overcrowded and apparently red-light district by the 1880s, but at the same time a west side neighborhood between Henley Street and Second Creek had larger and more widely spaced houses and higher-income blue- and white-collar working-class families. When the demography and family structure of Knoxville's free blacks is examined, an interesting change in the family structure is seen between 1850 and 1860. The male/female ratio is very similar in 1850 and 1860: 41 to 59 percent in 1850 and 45 to 55 percent in 1860. Regarding family makeup, of the thirty-one groups of adults and children living together, 45 percent were nuclear families with the male listed as head of household and

48 percent were female-headed households. This family composition changes in the 1860 census with only 38 percent of the thirty-seven groups being male-headed nuclear families and 51 percent being female-headed households. Similar to Knoxville slave society in 1860, free black families had become more matrifocal. This may also be reflected by the highest employment of washers, domestics, and nurses, the majority being women.

The Knoxville free black population between 1850 and 1860 also appears to have been fairly transitory. Of the fifty-three and fifty-seven surnames of free black individuals or families found in the 1850 and 1860 censuses, respectively, only eleven names were shared on these records and only one individual found on the 1850 census could be definitely identified ten years later.

While no archaeological study has been conducted on free black domestic sites in Knoxville, we can still discern what may be African American patterns in the later nineteenth century. Since some free blacks owned their houses and two were listed as carpenters in the 1850 census, they were probably building their own houses by this time. Shotgun houses, believed by some research to be an African style, were present in the Marble Alley neighborhood as early as 1884.[49] In that year there were at least twenty-six black carpenters living in Knoxville.[50] An 1865 panoramic view of Knoxville suggests these houses were present as early as the mid-nineteenth century, but how this housing style came to Knoxville is unknown.[51]

Another earlier African cultural pattern in Knoxville might be represented by a black grave in a Knoxville cemetery. A late nineteenth-century African American grave has been found in a South Knoxville cemetery that had numerous artifacts and mussel shells on the grave.[52] The placement of artifacts and shells on African American graves is believed to be a retention of an African American funerary pattern.[53]

CONCLUSIONS

One theory on the genesis of early African American culture is that it did not result from imitating or internalizing the world of the slaveholders but was rooted in the memories and social relations of the slave community.[54] David Goldfield has compared plantation slavery to the African American experience in the urban ghetto, or what he calls the urban slave quarters, where blacks found the same group solidarity that slaves also forged on the plantation.[55] While a smaller black population in Knoxville before the Civil War may have impacted group solidarity in some instances, the apparent interaction between the urban slave community and the farms surrounding the town would have insured the maintenance of broad lines of communication. Additionally, unlike her sister cities of Nashville and Memphis, Knoxville had an increase in free blacks in the decade before the Civil War, bringing new ideas to the slave community. Interestingly, this population influx does not appear to have resulted in an increase in skilled trades within the black community until the post–Civil War industrialization of Knoxville.[56]

The bicultural model was also at work where the enslaved were alternately pulled and pushed by the dominant white culture as well as their own subservient one.[57] While the earlier notion that these smaller groups working closely with their masters received more humane and permissive treatment is highly questionable, this closer association possibly resulted in greater adoption and use of material culture from the dominant group, such as the fine tableware and European clothing styles evident at the Blount Mansion and Perez Dickinson sites. What is unclear, however, is if the functions of the white material culture remained the same in the slave cultural milieu. We also have no records of hiring out in Knoxville so we do not know how this practice affected master-slave relationships. What the population figures tell us, however, is that a spatial distance existed between white masters and black slaves since three-quarters of the Knoxville slave owners maintained slave houses. The census records also indicate over half of the slave families lived in their own quarters where they could maintain and share their own cultural traditions, away from the spying eyes of their masters. The popularity of beads and grave offerings seem to be examples of these continuing traditions.

J. W. Joseph has stated that "southern cities were the crucibles of African American culture."[58] Applying this concept to the study of slavery in Knoxville, I believe that every city can be its own "melting pot." While each city shared certain ingredients in an antebellum cultural mix, they also added their own distinctive features based on innumerable social and economic factors. The principal question in this study is, did a "border" city like Knoxville have distinctive characteristics of enslavement? Although no excavations have been done on domestic slave sites in Nashville or Memphis that can be compared to Knoxville, documents indicate that except for a larger population of free blacks, Knoxville shared several population statistics with her sister cities before the Civil War. Based on the data at hand, some possible distinctive social and economic characteristics of Knoxville were a common spatial separation of master and slave in housing, the absence of large plantations in the surrounding countryside, and the small scale craft and trade composition of its economy. Unfortunately, the absence of documentary data on slave crafts and trade, the practice of hiring out, and the intensive archaeological excavation of only one site, Blount Mansion, prevents a clear understanding of what these patterns meant to slave life in Knoxville at this time. However, it is encouraging that Knoxville, like many southern cities, has become increasingly aware of the historic importance of the so-called invisible people in its antebellum past: blue-collar workers, women, and especially enslaved Africans. Hopefully such budding enlightenment will result in more intensive archaeological studies of slavery within this city.

NOTES

I wish to thank Laurie Baradat and Donna Griffin, who typed several drafts of this paper, and Terry Faulkner, Faye Harrison, Gerald Schroedl, and Amy Lambeck Young, who provided valued opinions, insights, and incisive criticism in their reviews of this work. Also thanks to my wife Terry who drew the two figures. Any omissions or errors in this paper are the author's responsibility.

1. Clement Eaton, "Slave Hiring in the Upper South: A Step toward Freedom," *Mississippi Valley Historical Review* 46, no. 4 (1960): 663–78; Claudia D. Goldin, *Urban Slavery in the American South, 1820–1860* (Chicago: University of Chicago Press, 1976); Richard Wade, *Slavery in the Cities* (New York: Oxford University Press, 1964).

2. Goldin, *Urban Slavery in the American South,* table 13.

3. Charles H. Wesley, *Negro Labor in the United States* (New York: Vanguard Press, 1927).

4. Ira Berlin and Herbert G. Gutman, "Natives and Immigrants, Free Men and Slaves: Urban Workingmen in the Antebellum American South," *American Historical Review* 88, no. 5 (1983): 1175–1200.

5. Paul A. Groves and Edward K. Muller, "The Evolution of Black Residential Areas in Late Nineteenth Century Cities," *Journal of Historical Geography* 1, no. 2 (1975): 169–71.

CHARLES H. FAULKNER

6. Goldin, *Urban Slavery in the American South,* 114, 113.

7. William J. McArthur, "Knoxville's History: An Interpretation," in *Heart of the Valley: A History of Knoxville, Tennessee,* ed. Lucile Deaderick (Knoxville: East Tennessee Historical Society, 1976), 23.

8. Michael J. McDonald and William Bruce Wheeler, *Knoxville, Tennessee: Continuity and Change in an Appalachian City* (Knoxville: University of Tennessee Press, 1983).

9. Chase Mooney, *Slavery in Tennessee* (Bloomington: Indiana University Press, 1957).

10. Mary U. Rothrock, ed., *The French Broad—Holston Country: A History of Knox County, Tennessee* (Knoxville: East Tennessee Historical Society, 1946), 308–9.

11. Betsy B. Creekmore, *Knoxville* (Knoxville: University of Tennessee Press, 1976).

12. W. Freeman Galpin, ed., "Letters of an East Tennessee Abolitionist," *East Tennessee Historical Societies Publications* 3 (1932): 134–49, 138 (quotation).

13. Timothy E. Baumann, "Questioning Popular History: Knoxville's Perez Dickinson—Abolitionist or Slave Owner," *Ohio Valley Historical Archaeology* 11 (1996): 6–18.

14. Caleb P. Patterson, *The Negro in Tennessee, 1790–1865* (New York: Negro Universities Press, 1968).

15. Alred J. Gray and Susan F. Adams, "Government," in Deaderick, ed., *Heart of the Valley,* 72.

16. Rothrock, ed., *The French Broad—Holston Country,* 310.

17. McArthur, "Knoxville's History," 74; Rothrock, ed., *The French Broad—Holston Country,* 308.

18. McDonald and Wheeler, *Knoxville, Tennessee,* 19.

19. William C. Harris, "East Tennessee's Civil War Refugees and the Impact of the War on Civilians," *Journal of East Tennessee History* 75 (2003): 62–75.

20. Anita Goodstein, *Nashville, 1780–1860: From Frontier to City* (Gainesville: University Press of Florida, 1989), 205, appendix, table 1.

21. Don H. Doyle, *Nashville in the New South, 1880–1930* (Knoxville: University of Tennessee Press, 1985), 235, appendix A.

22. Gerald M. Capers, Jr., *The Biography of a River Town, Memphis: Its Heroic Age* (New Orleans: G. M. Capers, Jr., 1966), 164, table 9.

23. U.S. Census, Tennessee, Knoxville, 1st District, 1860.

24. Goodstein, *Nashville,* appendix, table 1; Capers, *The Biography of a River Town,* table 9.

25. Anna Lisa N. Oakley, "Interpreting the Frontier Slave Experience: Slavery at Blount Mansion, Knoxville, Tennessee, 1792–1800" (M.A. thesis, Middle Tennessee State University, 1966).

26. Amy Lambeck Young, "Developing Town Life in the South: Archaeological Investigations at Blount Mansion," in *Archaeology of Southern Urban Landscapes,* ed. Amy Lambeck Young (Tuscaloosa: University of Alabama Press, 2000), 157–58.

27. Oakley, "Interpreting the Frontier Slave Experience," 42.

28. Goodstein, *Nashville,* appendix, table 3; Goldin, *Urban Slavery in the American South,* table 20.

29. U.S. Census, Slave Schedule, Tennessee, Knoxville, 1860.

30. U.S. Census, Tennessee, Washington County, 1860.

31. Berlin and Gutman, "Natives and Immigrants, Free Men and Slaves," 1187.

32. Michael Strutt, "An Architectural Survey of Slave Houses in Tennessee," unpublished report, 2002, Tennessee Historical Commission, Nashville.

33. Michael Emrick and George Fore, "Historic Structures Report: Blount Mansion, Knoxville Tenn.," report to Blount Mansion Association, 1992.

34. Charles H. Faulkner, "Moved Buildings: A Hidden Factor in the Archaeology of the Built Environment," *Historical Archaeology* 38, no. 2 (2004): 55–67.

35. Charles H. Faulkner, "Archaeology at Blount Mansion: Architectural Metamorphosis of a Frontier Landmark," paper presented at the 11th Symposium, Ohio Valley Urban and Historical Archaeology, Giant City State Park, Ill., 1993.

36. Henry S. McKelway, "Slaves and Master in the Upland South—Data Recovery at the Mabry Site (40KN86)," research report for the Tennessee Department of Transportation, University of Tennessee Transportation Center, Knoxville, 1994.

37. Tanya A. Faberson and Charles H. Faulkner, eds., "Archaeological Excavations at Marble Springs, Summer 2003," unpublished research report, Tennessee Historical Commission, Department of Anthropology, University of Tennessee, Knoxville, 2005.

38. Baumann, "Questioning Popular History."

39. Deborah L. German, "Seven Old Houses: A Preliminary Inventory of Possible Slave Quarters in East Tennessee," manuscript on file, Department of Anthropology, University of Tennessee, Knoxville, 1992.

40. Cary Coxe, "Urban Slave Diet in Early Knoxville: Faunal Remains from Blount Mansion, Knoxville, Tennessee" (M.A. thesis, University of Tennessee, Knoxville, 1993).

41. Amy Lynne Young, "Slave Subsistence at the Upper South Mabry Site, East Tennessee: Regional Variability in Plantation Diet of the Southeastern United States" (M.A. thesis, University of Tennessee, Knoxville, 1997); Jessie Duncan, "Faunal Analysis," in Faberson and Faulkner, eds., "Archaeological Excavations at Marble Springs."

42. E. Brooke Hamby, "An Archaeological and Historical Investigation of the Blount Mansion Slave Quarters" (M.A. thesis, University of Tennessee, Knoxville, 1999).

43. E. Brooke Hamby, "The Roots of Healing: Archaeological and Historical Investigations of African-American Herbal Medicine" (Ph.D. diss., University of Tennessee, Knoxville, 2004).

44. Charles H. Faulkner, *Life at Swan Pond: The Archaeology and History of an East Tennessee Farm* (Knoxville: University of Tennessee Press, 2008)

45. Linda France Stein, Melanie A. Cabak, and Mark D. Grover, "Blue Beads as African-American Symbols," *Historical Archaeology* 30, no. 3 (1996): 49–75.

46. Hamby, "An Archaeological and Historical Investigation of the Blount Mansion Slave Quarters," 46–49.

47. Ibid., 49–51; McKelway, "Slaves and Master in the Upland South," 172; Faberson and Faulkner, eds., "Archaeological Excavations at Marble Springs," 34.

48. J. W. Joseph, "Archaeology and the African-American Experience in the Urban South," in Young, ed., *Archaeology of Southern Urban Landscapes,* 112.

49. John M. Vlach, "The Shotgun House: An African Architectural Legacy," in *Common Places: Readings in American Vernacular Architecture,* ed. Dell Upton and John M. Vlach (Athens: University of Georgia Press, 1986), 58–78; Sanborn Insurance Company, Map of Knoxville, Tennessee, December 1884 (New York: Sanborn Map Company, 1884).

50. Charles H. Faulkner, "Knoxville's Hidden Architecture: The Shotgun House," *Knoxville Heritage, Inc., Newsnotes* (1991): 1–2.

51. Dagmar VonToal, "The Shotgun House in Knoxville, Tennessee" (M.A. thesis, University of Tennessee, Knoxville, 1998).

52. Christine M. Haynak, "Investigations at the Cunningham-Flenniken Cemetery, Knoxville, Tennessee," *Journal of the Symposium of the Ohio Valley Urban and Historic Archaeology* 14 (1999): 51–57.

53. John D. Combes, "Ethnography, Archaeology, and Burial Practices among Coastal South Carolina Blacks," *Conference on Historic Site Archaeology Papers* 7 (1972): 52–61; John M. Vlach, "Graveyards and Afro-American Art," *Southern Exposure* 5 (1977): 162–65.

54. George P. Rawick, "Some Notes on a Social Analysis of Slavery: A Critique and Assessment of the 'The Slave Community,'" in *Revisiting Blassingame's* The Slave Community: *The Scholars Respond,* ed. Al-Tony Gilmore (Westport, Conn.: Greenwood Press, 1978), 227–28.

55. David Goldfield, "Review of Blassingame's *The Slave Community," Agricultural History* 47, no. 3 (1973): 227–28.

56. McDonald and Wheeler, *Knoxville, Tennessee.*

57. Charles A. Valentine, "Deficit, Difference, and Bicultural Models of Afro-American Behavior," *Harvard Educational Review* 41 (1971): 137–57.

58. Joseph, "Archaeology and the African-American Experience," 123.

HENRY, A SLAVE, V. STATE OF TENNESSEE

The Public and Private Space of Slaves in a Small Town

LISA TOLBERT

The moon shone very bright on Main Street in Franklin, Tennessee, on Sunday night, February 24, 1850. Most of the town's 1,500 or so residents were at home asleep, but sometime between ten and eleven o'clock, the quiet street filled with people. A prayer meeting had just ended at the home of Hannah Henderson, a free black woman who lived on Indigo Street. The slaves who had worshipped there walked leisurely toward their various places of residence, chatting in small groups spread out along Main Street. The tranquil scene changed abruptly when the moonlight revealed three men—two white and one black—wrestling in the street up ahead, near the Presbyterian church corner. Someone cried, "Look there, they are about to take that negro." But the "scuffle" took a deadly turn. Before they could cry out for help, both white men lay dead in the street as the black man disappeared up the Columbia Turnpike, pursued only by the barking of dogs.[1]

The victims, William P. Barham and John G. Eelbeck, described as "respectable citizens" of Franklin, had both been stabbed in the heart.[2] Beside the bodies lay four slabs of bacon that the murderer had dropped during the fight. It appeared that Barham and Eelbeck had attempted a citizen's arrest of a black man they accused of stealing the meat. Barham's heart had been "laid open, a piece cut off," along with one of his ribs. Doctors Ewing, Cliffe, and Morton all examined the bodies and determined that they must have been murdered by a powerful and skillful man, one who "had knowledge where the vital organs lay." Investigation of the crime scene and the search for the murderer continued through the night and into Monday morning. Sometime after breakfast on Monday, authorities arrested Henry, whose job at the local tannery and previous experience as a butcher made him a likely suspect. "After a patient hearing of all the evidence and the able argument of counsel, the jury . . . returned a verdict of guilty."[3] Henry was convicted primarily on circumstantial evidence. Only one eyewitness, a slave named Oney, identified him by name after repeated questioning. Even Oney insisted that she "could not say positively" that Henry was the man she saw run up the Columbia Turnpike on the night of the murders. Henry, who did not testify during the trial, declared his innocence on the gallows to a crowd estimated at about four thousand spectators, "a great portion being negroes."[4]

The testimony at Henry's trial might be studied with interest as a dramatic murder mystery. But the trial transcript ultimately reveals a deeper mystery with broader historical implications than a simple whodunit tale. As the slave witnesses told what they had seen on that fateful Sunday night, they also exposed some of the mysteries of their own lives. Testimony at Henry's trial offers a rare glimpse of the everyday world of small-town slavery from the slave's perspective. The fact that the murders took place in a small town mattered.

Given their widespread distribution in the region, small towns remain surprisingly peripheral in the prevailing history of the antebellum South. Historians have learned much about the nature of rural and urban life in the antebellum South, but the regional landscape has been drawn largely as a map of contrasting extremes. Widely dispersed plantations and yeoman farmsteads composed the agrarian center,[5] while on the periphery, a few major cities, largely riverine or coastal ports, emerged.[6] Elizabeth Fox-Genovese represents the prevailing consensus that even though small towns and villages were "ubiquitous" in the region, "southern towns primarily reflected the countryside."[7] The small-town South remains obscure, on one hand subsumed by an undifferentiated rural countryside, and on the other assumed to be nothing more than an urban microcosm.

Small towns appear only incidentally in this landscape as a setting for social, political, and economic interactions among planters.[8] Yet slaves constituted nearly half of the population of Franklin in 1850.[9] The testimony at Henry's trial reveals the outlines of a system with its own unique characteristics—a type of slavery that was qualitatively different compared to urban or rural forms of the institution. Furthermore, hearing this story from the perspective of slaves enables us to see more fully how slaves were active participants in town life.

Henry's routine on that fateful weekend in February reveals some of the patterns of work and leisure in a small town, where streets and shop floors rather than farm fields were the routine sites of action. Henry worked for Samuel Tenneswood at the local tanyard. Before sundown on Sunday evening, February 24, Henry walked over as usual to Mrs. Doyle's house to get his employer's supper, which consisted of "a coffeepot and a plate of battercakes." Earlier in the day he had played a card game at Ragsdale's shop. According to trial testimony, Henry "was in the habit of staying at night" with Susan in the kitchen of her owner, Peter McConnell, a tobacconist from Pennsylvania. Early Monday morning Henry rose before daylight and put on a clean white homespun shirt and his grey roundabout coat with its red flannel lining. His first task was to cut the firewood Susan would need for cooking and laundry that day. He made the fire in the McConnell kitchen, slung the ax over his shoulder, and proceeded to his next job—sweeping the floor at King's grocery on the Square. James King, who also lived in the store, had hired Jake Childress "to make fires for him." Jake had in turn employed Henry. For the past two or three weeks Henry had walked up Main Street early every morning to clean King's room, sweep out the store, and chop the firewood. Henry was accustomed to seeing Jeff, slave of Hugh Duff, who started his work early at Short's stone yard near the grocery. Town slaves began their workday before sunrise, so Henry and Jeff were among the first town residents to appear on the public square on Monday morning. Henry finished sweeping out the grocery just after daybreak, and once again slung the ax over his shoulder and walked back up Main Street to his job at the tanyard on Columbia Turnpike.[10]

These circumstantial details of Henry's life are insignificant by themselves, but taken as a whole these ordinary activities and encounters begin to outline the contours of small-town slavery. From hard and bloody labor in the tanyard, to odd jobs and errands, to casual conversations and card games, Henry came

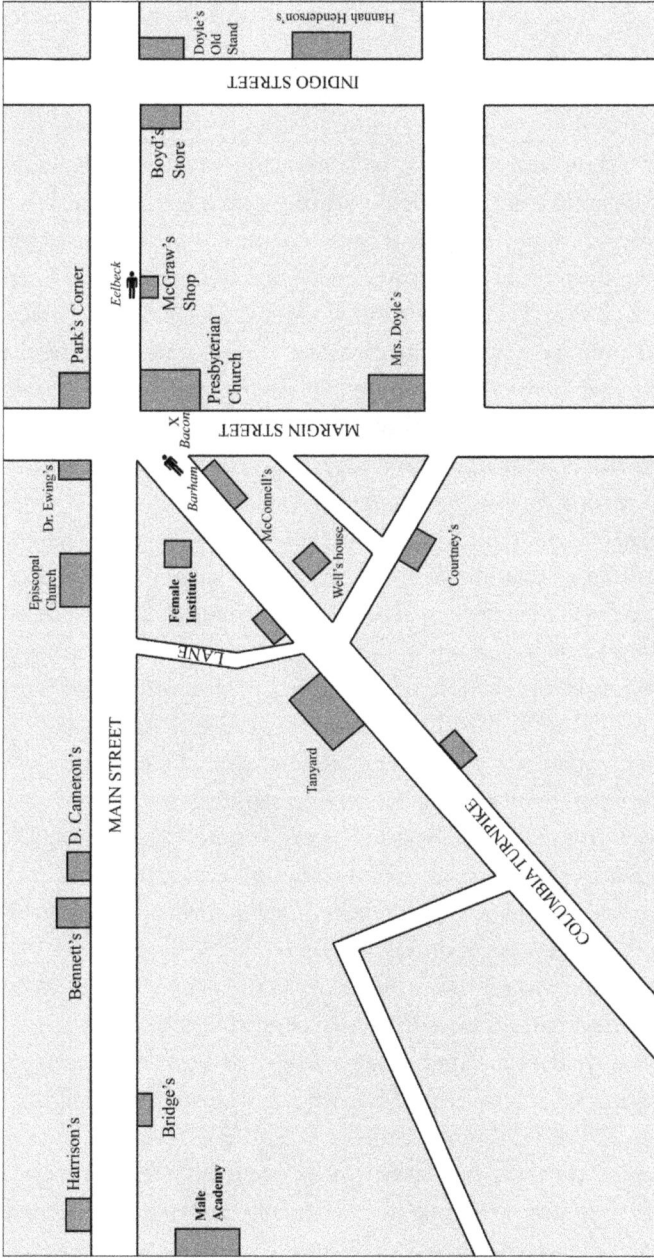

Figure 1. Map showing Henry's movement through Franklin, Tennessee, February 1850. (Source: Trial transcript, *Henry, A Slave, v. State of Tennessee*)

into contact with other slaves more often than with white residents. Besides Susan, there was the neighbor Isabella; Jake, who exchanged chores with Henry; Jeff, who worked across the square from one of Henry's early morning jobs; Mourning, who cooked supper for his employer; Tom, a church sexton; card players at Ragsdale's shop; and many others. Whether Henry took his walks in the pursuit of a particular work duty or as part of his own leisure time, town streets offered numerous opportunities for casual conversations with slaves and others he met along the way. Through such interactions, Henry exerted a certain amount of flexibility and control over his work routine. Small-town streets were full of slaves running errands for their masters or employers who took the same opportunities that Henry did to choose their own routes and stop to talk to friends and acquaintances along the way.

Although most slaves were household servants—cooks, washerwomen, stable hands, dining room servants—Henry was one of the numerous slaves whose work took them beyond individual households. His story suggests some of the ways that slaves used small-town hiring practices to shape their own lives. Samuel Tenneswood was Henry's employer, not his owner. A farmer named John Bennett, whose house stood on Main Street, actually owned Henry and eleven other slaves. But Henry's actions on that February weekend in 1850 show that he neither lived in the Bennett household nor worked as a fieldhand for Bennett. Indeed, in the last few years, Henry had performed a variety of jobs including butcher, wood-hauler, and meat vendor, selling game he hunted in the vicinity of town. This pattern of localized hiring was more typical than the long-range hiring practices of some antebellum cities, where business was brisk enough to support hiring agents who connected slaves or their masters with potential employers. Hired slaves in the small town tended to have masters who lived in the town or county where they worked. Slaves themselves often took an active part in hiring negotiations in a small-town context.[11]

Henry's work and residential experience fits larger patterns of slave experience in Franklin. In 1850, 68 percent of households in town owned slaves.[12] Franklin's slaveholders certainly included the wealthiest town residents— merchants, physicians, lawyers—but slave owners occupied a broad range of social and economic positions in the small-town hierarchy. For example, there was John Burch, a shoemaker who owned a twelve-year-old boy; John Short, a stonecutter who owned a twenty-year-old woman; and Elijah Porter, a mulatto laborer who owned a thirty-year-old woman, a four-year-old girl, and a two-year-old girl. Most Franklin slaveholders owned only one or two slaves.[13] But as Henry's story demonstrates, actual slave ownership was only part of the story of town slavery. Many householders not counted among slave owners nevertheless hired cooks, laundresses, and stable hands. Thus, widespread slave ownership and hiring practices distributed the slave population evenly across the townscape. African Americans lived and worked throughout the county seat, from the public square to the railroad depot, from Italianate townhouses to middle-class cottages and even a few laborers' cabins.

Deciphering the context of slave experience in Franklin suggests that small towns cannot be understood simply as urban microcosms. One of the most striking differences was the contrast between slaves and free black residents. The number of free black residents remained insignificant in county seats throughout the first half of the nineteenth century. Only twenty-three free black men and women lived in Franklin in 1850, about 1 percent of the town's population.[14] Thus black residents were much more likely to be slaves than freemen. In contrast, on the eve of the Civil War, the largest population of free blacks in Tennessee resided in the city of Nashville and surrounding Davidson County.[15] Seventy-two percent of free blacks lived together near the waterfront and public square, in the second and fourth wards of the city.[16] There were no separate racial neighborhoods in the county seat to compare with the density of free black residents on the waterfront in Nashville. The defining characteristic of slave experience in the small town was living dispersed among white households.[17]

The spatial configuration of small-town slavery was also significantly different from rural patterns of the institution. Southern plantations were often described as town-like by observers searching for a metaphor to encompass the many buildings that composed the plantation landscape—from the master's dwelling to the barns and service buildings to the slave quarters.[18] Although the clustered buildings suggest a town-like appearance, the racial configuration of the plantation, where the dwelling of one white family was outnumbered by the dwellings of multiple slave families, was quite different from the racial integration of small-town Franklin, Tennessee. Likewise, small-town slavery was also distinct from rural neighborhoods where slaves lived widely scattered on smaller farms. Just as slave experience shows that small towns were more than urban microcosms, so it also demonstrates that the small town should not be subsumed seamlessly into the rural landscape.

One of the most striking aspects of town slavery was the apparent freedom of movement and broad access to town space that was an everyday part of the work slaves performed. Much to the slaveholders' dismay, however, slaves extended the broad access to town streets that was customary to their work routines into their leisure hours. Unlike rural farm labor, town business depended less on long agricultural cycles and more on a weekly routine that left many slaves with spare time, especially after business on Saturday night until work began again on Monday morning. Slave owners attempted to establish a temporal boundary in the small town. The same streets that thronged with slave messengers and draymen during the day were forbidden territory after dark, when slaves presumably would be engaged in something other than their masters' business. The slave who murdered Barham and Eelbeck appeared to confirm the worst nightmares of white residents.

Yet evidence presented at the murder trial demonstrates the fluidity or capriciousness of temporal boundaries in a slave town. Testimony revealed that the accused murderer was not the only potential criminal in attendance. The slave witnesses themselves were guilty of breaking several laws of the town. For example, it was illegal for Hannah Henderson, a free black woman, to "entertain any slave in . . . her house or residence on Sunday, or between sunset and sunrise of any day."[19] Nevertheless, slaves testified that "there was a house full of negroes at prayer meeting that night."[20] Furthermore, it was illegal for these slaves to "be found from home after 10 o'clock at night" without written permission from an "owner or manager."[21] They risked arrest, not only by the watchmen but by any "citizen" of the town. This explains the reaction of Oney, the slave who saw the "scuffle" between the three men on her way home from the prayer meeting. Believing that "white men were whipping negro for being out so late . . . she pushed on home."[22] From the slaves' perspective, white residents could not be trusted to let them walk the streets in peace. Vulnerable to the arbitrary decisions of white residents, slaves might be punished for breaking curfew—or not.

In fact, despite these flagrant curfew violations, the trial testimony suggests an almost casual disregard on the part of Franklin slave owners for enforcing the letter of the law. They expressed no surprise or dismay about the prayer meeting at Hannah Henderson's, which seems to have been a routine gathering for the slaves in attendance. Although laws regarding slaves convey an impression that social control in the county seat was rigid and absolute, town officials were never willing or able to enforce strict compliance from either white or black residents. Custom was frequently at odds with the law in the antebellum town, a situation that becomes more understandable when viewed in the larger context of small-town slavery.

The demographics of the antebellum county seat reassured white residents that any black person within town limits was almost certainly a slave. Widespread slave ownership and hiring practices among white residents fostered an enlarged sense of ownership that extended to African American town residents in general. Lax enforcement and casual disregard for the letter of the law demonstrate that white residents rarely felt any concerted threat from the slave community. Efforts to regulate time and space in the townscape of slavery were, ultimately, contradictory. On one hand, repressive legislation set clear racial boundaries that circumscribed the movements of slave residents. On the other hand, whites were confident that racial dominance was secured by more effective means than legislation and found it more convenient in practice to disregard the letter of the law. White residents, whether they actually owned slaves or not, were authorized to exert substantial power over slave residents. For example, even though they were not officially deputized, Barham and Eelbeck had the authority to stop and take into custody the slave they had suspected of stealing hams. In effect, small-town slaves had multiple masters.

Given the distinctiveness of small-town slavery it is no coincidence then that the antebellum southerner who drew the clearest distinctions among urban, rural, and small-town life was a slave. We can only speculate about Henry's thoughts and attitudes, but the remarkable autobiography of one small-town slave opens a window onto the particular experience of slave residents in a small town. Harriet Jacobs, who grew up in Edenton, North Carolina, defined herself explicitly as a small-town slave. "How often did I rejoice that I lived in a town where all the inhabitants knew each other!" she declared. "If I had been on a remote plantation, or lost among the multitude of a crowded city, I should not be a living woman at this day."[23]

The essential distinction of town life, Jacobs felt, was spatial and social intimacy—a strong contrast to isolation or anonymity. Jacobs exploited the social dynamic of the small town to her advantage when she rejected the unwanted advances of her master, Dr. James Norcum. She reasoned that she was protected by her abusive owner's concern for his own good name as a wealthy doctor and plantation owner in Edenton. "It was lucky for me that I did not live on a distant plantation," she carefully explained, "but in a town not so large that the inhabitants were ignorant of each other's affairs. Bad as are the laws and customs in a slaveholding community, the doctor, as a professional man, deemed it prudent to keep up some outward show of decency."[24]

But Norcum's public image was not the only reputation that mattered. Jacobs's grandmother Molly Horniblow cultivated a powerful one of her own. Horniblow had secured personal freedom in 1828 and operated a bakery in the heart of town. "Her presence in the neighborhood was some protection to me," Jacobs argued. The doctor "dreaded her scorching rebukes," but more importantly, "she was known and patronized by many people; and he did not wish to have his villainy made public."[25] The interactions of James Norcum, Molly Horniblow, and her influential white clientele illuminate the complex racial dynamic that distinguished southern towns. It was the spatial and social proximity of mixed-race households that made small-town servitude distinctive.

Henry, who was ultimately executed for murder, might have come to a different conclusion about the protective possibilities of living in a small town where everybody knew each other. His daily movements were widely known. His occupation as a butcher and tanner of hides made him a handy murder suspect. He lived with Susan in the McConnell kitchen along the murderer's getaway route.

Harriet Jacobs herself was victimized by small-town intimacy. When she became a fugitive, her escape was threatened by myriad possibilities of discovery. For a while, she was unable even to send her grandmother a message because "every one who went in or out of her house was closely watched."[26] For better or worse, the lives of white and black were intimately intertwined in a small town. Slaves managed to turn this situation to their own advantage whenever possible—negotiating employment and housing arrangements, for example—but communal intimacy brought its own dangers and limitations for small-town slaves.

Some historians have emphasized the possibilities for community building on plantations where African American slaves were often the majority of residents.[27] Similarly, historians of urban slavery have found that free blacks and slaves who lived in antebellum cities were able to accumulate property, maintain separate households, form social organizations, and build independent churches—in short, to create autonomous African American communities.[28] In small towns, by contrast, slaves did not have the opportunity to create physically segregated black communities. Nevertheless, antebellum town space was racially configured, its communities separated by powerful social customs. Yet Jacobs expressed her preference for town life as a slave, despite the seemingly limited opportunities for building communal autonomy in a place "where all the inhabitants knew each other."

The testimony presented at Henry's trial confirms Jacobs's assertion that the small-town South must be understood on its own terms. Above all town slavery had the potential to produce extremely complex living and working arrangements, which slaves themselves played an influential role in formulating. Compared to urban and rural population patterns, small towns composed a distinctive racial configuration of space. In the antebellum county seat black and white residents lived closer together than they did in the countryside or in cities. Scattered throughout town, slaves became architects of communal intimacy as they hauled water, delivered messages, and ran errands for white employers. But forced dispersal constrained the slaves' ability to create their own communal institutions. Still, in casual exchanges on the street, card games in the backrooms of storehouses, and the neighborly sharing of household duties across unfenced back lots, slaves managed to create a kind of community. The story of Henry reveals the vital role slaves played in the construction of small-town society. Indeed, it is impossible to understand the distinctive dynamic of small-town life in the antebellum South without taking into account the influence of slaves like Henry.

NOTES

This essay is based on the article previously published as "Murder in Franklin: The Mysteries of Small-Town Slavery," *Tennessee Historical Quarterly* 57, no. 4 (December 1998): 203–17.

1. Quotations are from the trial transcript, *Henry, A Slave, v. State of Tennessee*, Middle Tennessee Supreme Court, box 92A, Tennessee State Library and Archives, Nashville.

2. A Nashville newspaper described William Barham as a member of the Oddfellows and John Eelbeck as "a Mason and a Son of Temperance." See Nashville *Daily Centre-State American,* March 2, 1850. Eelbeck was the son of a prosperous carriage maker in Franklin, and Barham's family owned a grocery store near the public square.

3. Franklin, Tenn., *Western Weekly Review,* November 29, 1850.

4. For coverage of the execution, see Nashville *Daily American,* February 22, 1851 (quotation); *Nashville Daily True Whig,* February 22, 1851; and *Nashville True Whig and Weekly Commercial Register,* February 28, 1851.

5. See, for example, W. J. Cash, *The Mind of the South* (New York: Vintage Books, 1991); William R. Taylor, *Cavalier and Yankee: The Old South and American National Character* (New York: George Braziller, 1961); Eugene Genovese, *Roll, Jordan, Roll: The World the Slaves Made* (New York: Pantheon, 1994); James Oakes, *The Ruling Race: A History of American Slaveholders* (New York: Knopf, 1982); and Elizabeth Fox-Genovese, *Within the Plantation Household: Black and White Women of the Old South* (Chapel Hill: University of North Carolina Press, 1988). While these scholars construct very different arguments about the nature of southern society, they all assume the centrality of the plantation. For two exceptions to this rule, see Robert C. Kenzer, *Kinship and Neighborhood in a Southern Community* (Knoxville: University of Tennessee Press, 1987), which develops the concept of distinctive plantation neighborhoods in Orange County, North Carolina, and Orville Burton, *In My Father's House Are Many Mansions: Family and Community in Edgefield, South Carolina* (Chapel Hill: University of North Carolina Press, 1985), which examines town and country in one district of South Carolina.

6. See, for example, David R. Goldfield, *Cotton Fields and Skyscrapers: Southern City and Region, 1607–1980* (Baton Rouge: Louisiana State University Press, 1982); David R. Goldfield and Blaine Brownell, eds., *The City in Southern History: The Growth of Urban Civilization in the South* (New York: Kennikat Press, 1977); Claudia Goldin, *Urban Slavery in the American South, 1820–1860: A Quantitative History* (Chicago: University of Chicago Press, 1977); Joseph A. Ernst and H. Roy Merrens, "'Camden's Turrets Pierce the Skies!': The Urban Process in the Southern Colonies during the Eighteenth Century Turrets," *William and Mary Quarterly,* 3rd ser., 30, no. 4 (October 1973): 549–74; Leonard P. Curry, "Urbanization and Urbanism in the Old South: A Comparative View," *Journal of Southern History* 40, no. 1 (February 1974): 43–60; and Lyle W. Dorsett and Arthur H. Shaffer, "Was the Antebellum South Anti-Urban? A Suggestion," *Journal of Southern History* 38, no. 1 (February 1972): 93–100.

7. Fox-Genovese, *Within the Plantation Household,* 5, 74.

8. For example, Elizabeth Fox-Genovese admits that small towns "constituted the focus of the lives of so many slaveholders, including planters." Ibid., 5–6. And James Oakes has acknowledged that small towns were the primary stage for slaveholders' social, legal, political, and religious activity. Oakes, *The Ruling Race,* 92.

9. Forty-two percent of Franklin residents were slaves, as calculated from the 1850 U.S.

Census for Williamson County. The proportion of slave residents in antebellum Franklin was comparable to other Middle Tennessee county seats of the period.

10. Henry's activities are reconstructed from testimony provided in *Henry, A Slave, v. State of Tennessee.*

11. Lisa C. Tolbert, *Constructing Townscapes: Space and Society in Antebellum Tennessee* (Chapel Hill: University of North Carolina Press, 1999), especially chapter 6, "Small-Town Slaves."

12. This included 176 total households, 119 slaveholding households. Calculated from the 1850 U.S. Census. Franklin's slaveholding patterns were comparable to other Middle Tennessee county seats of the period. For example, in Murfreesboro (Rutherford County), 77% of households owned slaves (163 total households, 125 slaveholding households); in Columbia (Maury County), 52% of households owned slaves (297 total households, 155 slaveholding households); and in Shelbyville (Bedford County), 51% of households owned slaves (174 total households, 89 slaveholding households). In *Middle Tennessee Society Transformed, 1860–1870: War and Peace in the Upper South* (Baton Rouge: Louisiana State University Press, 1988), Stephen Ash estimated that 76% of "town families" in Middle Tennessee owned no slaves in 1860. During the 1850s, the slave population increased, although at a slower rate than the white population. In Murfreesboro, slaves had dropped to 41% of the population by 1860. Nevertheless, it seems unlikely that the proportion of slave owners should have declined as dramatically as Ash's figures suggest. Ash's calculations were based on a random sample that included residents of towns other than county seats. He used a quantitative definition of town population with no reference to the landscape or actual town boundaries. It is possible that slaveholding was more widespread in these four towns because the counties surrounding Nashville were the wealthiest in the region.

13. In Franklin, 42% of slaveholders owned only 1 or 2 slaves as calculated from the 1850 U.S. Census. Compare this to other county seats in the region: Murfreesboro, 28% of slaveholders owned only 1 or 2 slaves; Columbia, 31% of slaveholders owned only 1 or 2 slaves; and Shelbyville, 33% of slaveholders owned only 1 or 2 slaves.

14. Population statistics were calculated from the 1850 manuscript census returns. Free blacks in Franklin included twelve women and sixteen men. The same pattern holds true for other county seats in the region. The small free black presence in Middle Tennessee county seats is consistent with population patterns described by Ira Berlin. He found that in the Lower South free blacks gravitated toward cities, while in the Upper South, free blacks remained primarily rural peasants. See Berlin, *Slaves without Masters: The Free Negro in the Antebellum South* (New York: Pantheon Books, 1974), 181.

15. Nashville had 1,209 free black residents or 17% of free blacks in the state. As much as 18% of the total black population of Nashville was free in 1860. Anita Shafer Goodstein, *Nashville, 1780–1960: From Frontier to City* (Gainesville: University Press of Florida, 1989), 137. See also Loren Schweninger, ed., *From Tennessee Slave to Entrepreneur: The Autobiog-*

raphy of James Thomas (Columbia: University of Missouri Press, 1984), for a free black's perspective on antebellum Nashville.

16. Goodstein, *Nashville*, 141. Ira Berlin notes that southern cities lagged far behind northern cities in the development of residential segregation. Although free blacks increasingly chose, or were compelled, to live in racially segregated districts within cities, there were few urban counterparts in the South to Boston's "Nigger Hill," Pittsburgh's "Hayti," and Cincinnati's "Little Africa." Berlin, *Slaves without Masters*, 255.

17. "An Ordinance in Relation to Slaves," published in the Shelbyville *Western Freeman*, December 17, 1833, suggests that some slaves may have been living in separate households, unsupervised by whites. According to section 2 of the ordinance, "It shall not, hereafter, be lawful for any slave or slaves to occupy or reside in any house or houses within said corporation, unless he, she or they shall have been actually hired by and be then in the bonafide employ of some white person or persons within the corporation aforesaid."

18. John Michael Vlach, *Back of the Big House: The Architecture of Plantation Slavery* (Chapel Hill: University of North Carolina Press, 1993), 12.

19. *By-Laws of the Town of Franklin: Together with the Acts of Incorporation* (Franklin, Tenn.: Henry Van Pelt, 1838).

20. *Henry, A Slave, v. State of Tennessee.*

21. *By-Laws of the Town of Franklin.*

22. *Henry, A Slave, v. State of Tennessee.*

23. Harriet Jacobs, *Incidents in the Life of a Slave Girl: Written by Herself*, ed. Jean Fagan Yellin (Cambridge, Mass.: Harvard University Press, 1987), 35.

24. Ibid., 29.

25. Ibid.

26. Ibid., 97.

27. Vlach, *Back of the Big House;* Genovese, *Roll Jordan, Roll.* Rhys Isaac argues that the communal ethos slave quarter presented a sharp contrast by the end of the eighteenth century to the increasingly privatized dwellings of slave owners; see Isaac, *The Transformation of Virginia, 1740–1790* (Chapel Hill: University of North Carolina Press, 1982).

28. Elsa Brown and Gregg D. Kimball, "Mapping the Terrain of Black Richmond," *Journal of Urban History* 3, no. 21 (1995): 296–346; David R. Goldfield, "Black Life in Old South Cities," in *Before Freedom Came: African-American Life in the Antebellum South*, ed. Edward Campbell and Kym Rice (Charlottesville: University Press of Virginia, 1991), 123–53; Mary Tyler-McGraw and Gregg D. Kimball, *In Bondage and Freedom: Antebellum Black Life in Richmond, Virginia* (Richmond, Va.: Valentine Museum, 1988); Berlin, *Slaves without Masters*; Richard C. Wade, *Slavery in the Cities: The South, 1820–1860* (New York: Oxford University Press, 1964); Robert S. Starobin, *Industrial Slavery in the Old South* (New York: Oxford University Press, 1970).

CONCLUSION

Directions for Future Studies of North American Slavery

This volume's authors show that the study of urban slavery offers many possibilities for theoretical and methodological inquiry, and they demonstrate a variety of profitable approaches to the topic. As a group, they share a commitment to fieldwork as a methodology. Vernacularists have long believed that fieldwork—the investigation and documentation of actual buildings and landscapes—is the starting point for any analysis of sociocultural practices. Significantly, these authors have turned as well to other disciplines for theoretical paradigms that bring breadth and depth to their interpretations of the conditions they discovered in the course of their fieldwork. Such disciplines as African American studies, black studies, American studies, feminist studies, and others employ analytical models that greatly aid our efforts to reinterpret the experiences of slavery.

More than forty years ago, cultural geographer Henry Glassie led the way with his groundbreaking study *Folk Housing in Middle Virginia: A Structural Analysis of Artifacts* (1976). Drawing on work in linguistics, Glassie's structuralist approach to the study of early Virginia domestic architecture set a new standard for architectural historians, challenging that discipline to look beyond the limiting methods of connoisseurship.[1] Slowly, the study of architectural history began to change, and its practitioners enlarged their vision of what the

study of architecture had to offer. Today, architectural historians join archaeologists, cultural geographers, landscape historians, and others in a dynamic
dialogue that seeks sophisticated, nuanced understanding of specific historical
contexts and, more generally, better intellectual tools for making sense of how
individuals and communities operate within their material worlds. Although
each discipline remains distinct, all have gained richer understanding of their
unique potentials and the value of interdisciplinarity.

Historian Lisa Tolbert, for example, has augmented fieldwork with firsthand
accounts and court records in her examination of the landscape of a small
southern town from the perspective of a slave accused of murder.[2] Architectural
historians such as Clifton Ellis explore the rich possibilities offered by critical
theories such as postprocessual archaeological theory. Gina Haney examines
slavery in Charleston through the lens of standpoint theory, an approach developed by feminists scholars, who themselves drew on Karl Marx's analysis of the
proletariat. Intersectionality, as developed most prominently by Patricia Hill
Collins, should be seriously considered in future studies of space and slavery.[3]
It posits that race, gender, class, religion, and other dimensions of social identity
interact on multiple, intersecting levels to form the structures that individuals
must navigate, and holds promise for raising important questions about racialization, gender, and space, among others.

As this volume demonstrates, sites of enslavement can be found in many
contexts. Slavery on the great plantation still looms large in the popular imagination. Yet slaveholders with more than ninety-nine slaves comprised only
0.1 percent of the slaveholding population. In 1860, about 24 percent of households owned slaves, and among them, 17.2 percent owned between one and
nine slaves. Large plantations using forced labor certainly dominated the slave
economy, but it was on the farm that slavery was statistically more common.[4]

Although many large plantation sites still exist, it is rare to find the extant resources that would help interpret slavery at such places. Farms are even less well
documented. Yet a more holistic and truer picture of the landscape of slavery
in North America requires better understanding of the enactment of slavery on
farms, and the conditions on these places for enslaved individuals.

If farms offer few resources for studying slavery, cities offer fewer. Slavery in
the larger southern cities was a dynamic, integral part of the urban economy. By

1860, more than 140,000 bondsmen lived in southern cities. Half of these slaves lived in the region's ten largest cities, and the three largest had the greatest slave populations: Charleston counted 13,909 slaves, New Orleans 13,385, and Richmond 11,699. In the ten largest southern cities, slaves counted for 8.3 percent of the population and free blacks counted for 7.1 percent. The slave population for all southern cities in 1860 was 14.5 percent and the free black population was 6.8 percent.[5]

This was a dramatic decrease from the 1840 populations, which were 26.3 and 13.3 percent, respectively. This decrease is accounted for by the increase in cotton prices, which had a corresponding increase in the need for plantation laborers; planters hesitated to hire out their slaves to city dwellers when larger profits could be made by keeping them on the plantation. Despite the decline in urban slavery, by 1860 enslaved and free black inhabitants of southern cities accounted for one-fifth of their populations.[6]

Slavery was an integral part of the South's urban economy; half of the 900 workers at Richmond's Tredegar Iron Works were enslaved, for example.[7] The body of solid works on urban slavery is growing, and we welcome this renewed interest, long overdue. Yet we need more case studies in order to piece together the larger narrative of slavery sites in urban America. Granted, the extant resources of urban sites are very few, but one case study by Maurie McInnis is an excellent example of the way that architectural historians might approach a spatial analysis of urban sites that have long since disappeared and now lay beneath layers of new urban conditions. McInnis's work also reminds us that the South's urban economy was not necessarily based in industry. The selling and buying of human beings was a business that linked cities all over the region. A quarter of a million enslaved men, women, and children passed through Richmond and its slave pens. Reconstructing the commerce of slavery itself is another way to make the history of urban slavery a palpable reality.[8]

Akin to the slave market was the slave ship, and we need more studies that focus on these twin horrors of enslavement. The studies of historians Marcus Rediker, Stephanie E. Smallwood, and Walter Johnson are good examples of how we can recover the spatial relations and material culture associated with the business of enslavement.[9] With their examples before us, more historians, geographers, archaeologists, and others can contribute to our understanding of slavery as a series of interlocking landscape systems that stretched from the interior of the African continent to towns and farms in the American South, and beyond.

Slavery was legal in northern states as late as 1846, the year that New Jersey abolished it. However, as John Michael Vlach explains in this volume, the spaces of northern slavery remain largely unexplored. Slavery also existed, of course, beyond the United States. Another important future direction for the field of slavery studies is to broaden our studies beyond that country. For example, slavery was legal in Mexico until 1829, yet we were unable to find a single essay in English that addressed the landscapes of Mexican slavery or a scholar working on the subject. More studies of slavery in the Caribbean and South America focusing on the spatial relations of slavery would bring a new understanding of how these locales were connected by space and material culture through politics, travel, and trade. Just as we need more studies that look closely at the multiple forces that shaped the settings of slavery at the local level, we also need studies that consider these inextricable relationships among sites — for example, the Carolinas and the Caribbean or the Southwest and Mexico.

We should remember that slavery was legal in Cuba until 1886 and in Brazil until 1888, and there is promise of enough extant resources for the profitable study of spaces of slavery. Our understanding of the spaces of slavery are more complete when we consider the larger forces that affected the shaping and reshaping of landscapes in the Americas.

Atlantic slavery, of course, extended well beyond the Americas, involving the entire Atlantic world. We are reminded by such works as William St. Clair's *The Door of No Return: The History of Cape Coast Castle and the Atlantic Slave Trade* (2007) that the "slave forts" that Europeans and Americans established along Africa's west coast can be a rich source of study.[10] Captives carried with them memories and skills from their homelands and used these to refashion the environments in which they found themselves. We must try to understand the experience of slavery in these spaces from the perspective of those enslaved individuals who were forced to occupy them.

Some scholars have with great success written about the African slave trade from the perspective of the African societies involved in it. The work of Patrick Manning, Paul E. Lovejoy, Sylviane Diouf, Robin Law, David Northrop, and

Martin Klein offer paradigms for scholars who seek to examine specific building types, landscapes, and larger-scale sites that formed part of those workings.[11] Other exemplary work in these areas include *West Africa during the Atlantic Slave Trade: Archaeological Perspectives,* edited by Christopher R. DeCorse (2001), Anne C. Bailey's *African Voices of the Atlantic Slave Trade: Beyond the Silence and the Shame* (2005), and Saidiya Hartman's *Lose Your Mother: A Journey along the Atlantic Slave Route* (2007).[12]

Needless to say, and considering the excellent works to which we refer above, *Slavery in the City: Architecture and Landscapes of Urban Slavery in North America,* is not the definitive collection on the topic of the landscapes of slavery. It is a contribution, and we hope for more research and publications from a new generation of scholars who use methods and theories imaginatively to study spaces of slavery on all scales. There is great value in studying slavery within its material, spatial contexts, and we urge scholars in our discipline to boldly apply methods and theories from other fields to architectural history. We also encourage those from other disciplines to incorporate the methods and sensibilities of architectural history.

Lastly, we hope that while reading the essays in the volume, the general reader will have a palpable understanding of the conditions and experiences of enslaved peoples, slaveholders, and their contemporaries in such disparate locales as Jamaica, New Jersey, and Tennessee. Studying the built environment provides a uniquely powerful and effective way to challenge stereotypical images of slavery as unchanging and tame. The essays in this book allow us to imagine real individuals who, in their own places and times, were forced to adopt historically specific strategies that allowed them to negotiate a pernicious system. By studying closely the material settings of slavery that they had to navigate, we can engage their experiences with imaginative and critical sympathy, and—we hope—a commitment to telling a more complete account of slavery in the Americas.

NOTES

1. Henry Glassie, *Folk Housing in Middle Virginia: A Structural Analysis of Artifacts* (Knoxville: University of Tennessee Press, 1976).

2. Michael Ann William, *Homeplace: The Social Use and Meaning of the Folk Dwelling in*

Southwestern North Carolina (Athens: University of Georgia Press, 1991), provides an even stronger example of a vernacular study that employs oral historical methodology.

3. See, for example, Patricia Hill Collins, *Black Feminist Thought: Knowledge, Consciousness, and the Politics of Empowerment* (Boston: Unwin Hyman, 1991), and Collins and Sirma Bilge, *Intersectionality* (Boston: Polity, 2016).

4. See John B. Boles, *Black Southerners, 1619–1869* (Lexington: University Press of Kentucky, 1984), 75.

5. See Boles, *Black Southerners,* 124–26.

6. Ibid.

7. Ronald L. Lewis, "Ironworkers," in *Dictionary of Afro-American Slavery,* ed. Randall M. Miller and John David Smith (Westport, Conn.: Greenwood, 1997), 368–69.

8. Maurie McInnis, *Slaves Waiting for Sale: Abolitionist Art and the American Slave Trade* (Chicago: University of Chicago Press, 2011).

9. Marcus Rediker, *The Slave Ship: A Human History* (New York: Viking, 2007); Stephanie E. Smallwood, *Saltwater Slavery: A Middle Passage from Africa to American Diaspora* (Cambridge, Mass.: Harvard University Press, 2007); Walter Johnson, *Soul by Soul: Life inside the Antebellum Slave Market* (Cambridge, Mass.: Harvard University Press, 1999).

10. William St. Clair, *The Door of No Return: The History of Cape Coast Castle and the Atlantic Slave Trade* (New York: BlueBridge, 2007).

11. See, for example, Patrick Manning, *Slavery and African Life: Occidental, Oriental, and African Slave Trades* (Cambridge: Cambridge University Press, 1990); Paul E. Lovejoy, *Transformations in Slavery: A History of Slavery in Africa,* 3rd ed. (Cambridge: Cambridge University Press, 2011); Sylviane Diouf, *Fighting the Slave Trade: West African Strategies* (Athens: Ohio University Press, 2003), and Diouf, *Slavery's Exiles: The Story of the American Maroons* (New York: New York University Press, 2016); Robin Law, *Ouidah: Social History of a West African Slavery Port, 1727–1892* (Athens: Ohio University Press, 2004); David Northrop, *Africa's Discovery of Europe,* 3rd ed. (Oxford: Oxford University Press, 2013); and Martin Klein, *Slavery and Colonial Rule in French West Africa* (Cambridge: Cambridge University Press, 1998).

12. Christopher R. DeCorse, ed., *West Africa during the Atlantic Slave Trade: Archaeological Perspectives* (London: Leicester University Press, 2001); Anne C. Bailey, *African Voices of the Atlantic Slave Trade: Beyond the Silence and the Shame* (Boston: Beacon Press, 2005); Saidiya Hartman, *Lose Your Mother: A Journey along the Atlantic Slave Route* (New York: Farrar, Straus, and Giroux, 2007).

SELECTED BIBLIOGRAPHY

Ash, Stephen. *Middle Tennessee Society Transformed, 1860–1870: War and Peace in the Upper South*. Baton Rouge: Louisiana State University Press, 1988.

Bailey, Rosalie Fellows. *Pre-Revolutionary Dutch Houses and Families in Northern New Jersey and Southern New York*. New York: William Morrow, 1936.

Baumann, Timothy E. "Questioning Popular History: Knoxville's Perez Dickinson— Abolitionist or Slave Owner." *Ohio Valley Historical Archaeology* 11 (1996): 6–18.

Baumgarten, Linda. *What Clothes Reveal*. Williamsburg, Va.: Colonial Williamsburg Foundation, 2002.

Beasley, Ellen. *The Alleys and Back Buildings of Galveston: An Architectural and Social History*. College Station: Texas A&M University Press, 1996.

Berlin, Ira. *Many Thousands Gone: The First Two Centuries of Slavery in North America*. Cambridge, Mass.: Harvard University Press, 1998.

———. *Slaves without Masters: The Free Negro in the Antebellum South*. New York: Pantheon, 1974.

———. "Time, Space, and the Evolution of Afro-American Society on British Mainland North America." *American Historical Review* 85 (February 1980): 57–59.

Berlin, Ira, and Herbert G. Gutman. "Natives and Immigrants, Free Men and Slaves: Urban Workingmen in the Antebellum American South." *American Historical Review* 88, no. 5 (1983): 1175–1200.

Berlin, Ira, and Leslie M. Harris, eds. *Slavery in New York*. New York: New Press, 2005.

Bill, Alfred Hoyt. *A House Called Morven*. Princeton, N.J.: Princeton University Press, 1954.

Bishir, Catherine W. "Urban Slavery at Work: The Bellamy Mansion Compound, Wilmington, North Carolina." *Buildings and Landscapes: Journal of the Vernacular Architecture Forum* 17, no. 2 (Fall 2010): 13–32.

Boles, John B. *Black Southerners, 1619–1869.* Lexington: University Press of Kentucky, 1984.

Boyd, John T., Jr. "Some Early Dutch Houses in New Jersey." *Architectural Record* 36 (1914): 31–48.

Brewer, J. Mason. *Negro Legislatures of Texas and Their Descendants.* Austin, Tex.: Jenkins, 1970.

Brown, Elsa, and Gregg D. Kimball. "Mapping the Terrain of Black Richmond." *Journal of Urban History* 3, no. 21 (1995): 296–346.

Burnard, Trevor. *Mastery, Tyranny, and Desire: Thomas Thistlewood and His Slaves in the Anglo-Jamaican World.* Chapel Hill: University of North Carolina Press, 2004.

Burton, Orville. *In My Father's House Are Many Mansions: Family and Community in Edgefield, South Carolina.* Chapel Hill: University of North Carolina Press, 1985.

Butler, Joseph T. *Van Cortlandt Manor.* Tarrytown, N.Y.: Sleepy Hollow Restorations, 1978.

By-Laws of the Town of Franklin: Together with the Acts of Incorporation. Franklin, Tenn.: Henry Van Pelt, 1838.

Camp, Stephanie M. H. *Closer to Freedom: Enslaved Women and Everyday Resistance in the Plantation South.* Chapel Hill: University of North Carolina Press, 2004.

Campbell, Randolph B. *An Empire for Slavery: The Peculiar Institution in Texas, 1821–1865.* Baton Rouge: Louisiana State University Press, 1989.

Capers, Gerald M., Jr. *The Biography of a River Town, Memphis: Its Heroic Age.* New Orleans: G. M. Capers, Jr., 1966.

Carson, Cary. "Doing History with Material Culture." In *Material Culture and the Study of American Life,* edited by Ian M. G. Quimby, 47–64. New York: Norton, 1978.

Casdorph, Paul. *A History of the Republican Party in Texas, 1865–1965.* Austin, Tex.: Pemberton Press, 1965.

Cash, W. J. *The Mind of the South.* New York: Vintage Books, 1991.

Chappell, Edward A. "Housing a Nation: The Transformation of Living Standards in Early America." In *Of Consuming Interests: The Style of Life in the Eighteenth Century,* edited by Cary Carson, Ronald Hoffman, and Peter J. Albert, 167–232. Charlottesville: University Press of Virginia, 1994.

Coclanis, Peter A. *The Shadow of a Dream: Economic Life and Death in the South Carolina Low Country, 1670–1920.* Oxford: Oxford University Press, 1989.

Collins, Patricia Hill. *Black Feminist Thought: Knowledge, Consciousness, and the Politics of Empowerment.* Boston: Unwin Hyman, 1991.

Collins, Patricia Hill, and Sirma Bilge. *Intersectionality.* Boston: Polity, 2016.

Combes, John D. "Ethnography, Archaeology, and Burial Practices among Coastal South Carolina Blacks." *Conference on Historic Site Archaeology Papers* 7 (1972): 52–61.

Conn, Steven, and Max Page, eds. *Building the Nation: Americans Write about Their Archi-*

tecture, Their Cities, and Their Landscape. Philadelphia: University of Pennsylvania Press, 2003.

Connolley, Ivor C., and James Parrent. "Land Deeds That Tell the Story of the Birth of Falmouth." *Jamaica Historical Society Bulletin* 11 (2005): 383–409.

Cousins, Frank, and Phil M. Riley. *The Colonial Architecture of Philadelphia.* Boston: Little, Brown, 1920.

Coxe, Cary. "Urban Slave Diet in Early Knoxville: Faunal Remains from Blount Mansion, Knoxville, Tennessee." M.A. thesis, University of Tennessee, Knoxville, 1993.

Creekmore, Betsy B. *Knoxville.* Knoxville: University of Tennessee Press, 1976.

Cromley, Elizabeth C. "Transforming the Food Axis: Houses, Tools, Modes of Analysis." *Material History Review* 44 (Fall 1996): 8–22.

Curry, Leonard P. "Urbanization and Urbanism in the Old South: A Comparative View." *Journal of Southern History* 40, no. 1 (February 1974): 43–60.

Daniel, Jean Houston, Price Daniel, and Dorothy Blodgett. *The Texas Governor's Mansion: A History of the House and Its Occupants.* Austin: Texas State Library and Archives Commission, 1984.

Diouf, Sylviane. *Fighting the Slave Trade: West African Strategies.* Athens: Ohio University Press, 2003.

———. *Slavery's Exiles: The Story of the American Maroons.* New York: New York University Press, 2014.

Ditmas, Charles Andrew. *Historic Homesteads of Kings County.* Brooklyn, N.Y.: C. A. Ditmas, 1909.

Dorsett, Lyle W., and Arthur H. Shaffer. "Was the Antebellum South Anti-Urban? A Suggestion." *Journal of Southern History* 38, no. 1 (February 1972): 93–100.

Doyle, Don H. *Nashville in the New South, 1880–1930.* Knoxville: University of Tennessee Press, 1985.

Eaton, Clement. "Slave Hiring in the Upper South: A Step toward Freedom." *Mississippi Valley Historical Review* 46, no. 4 (1960): 663–78.

Egerton, Douglas R. *He Shall Go out Free: The Lives of Denmark Vesey.* Revised ed. Lanham, Md.: Rowman and Littlefield, 2004.

Ellis, Clifton. "The Mansion House at Berry Hill Plantation: Architecture and the Changing Nature of Slavery in Antebellum Virginia." *Perspectives in Vernacular Architecture* 1 (Fall 2006): 22–48.

Ernst, Joseph A., and H. Roy Merrens. "'Camden's Turrets Pierce the Skies!': The Urban Process in the Southern Colonies during the Eighteenth Century Turrets." *William and Mary Quarterly,* 3rd series, 30, no. 4 (October 1973): 549–74.

Fabend, Firth Haring. *A Dutch Family in the Middle Colonies, 1600–1800.* New Brunswick, N.J.: Rutgers University Press, 1991.

Faulkner, Charles H. *Life at Swan Pond: The Archaeology and History of an East Tennessee Farm.* Knoxville: University of Tennessee Press, 2008.

———. "Moved Buildings: A Hidden Factor in the Archaeology of the Built Environment." *Historical Archaeology* 38, no. 2 (2004): 55–67.

Fazio, Michael W., and Patrick A. Snadon. *The Domestic Architecture of Benjamin Henry Latrobe*. Baltimore: Johns Hopkins University Press, 2006.

Fields, Barbara Jeanne. *Slavery and Freedom on the Middle Ground: Maryland during the Nineteenth Century*. New Haven, Conn.: Yale University Press, 1985.

Fithian, Philip Vickers. *Journal and Letters of Philip Vickers Fithian*. Ed. Hunter Dickinson Farish. Williamsburg, Va.: Colonial Williamsburg, 1943.

Fitts, Robert K. "The Landscapes of Northern Bondage." *Historical Archaeology* 30, no. 2 (1996): 53–73.

Fogarty, Catherine, John E. O'Connor, and Charles F. Cummings. *Bergen County: A Pictorial History*. Norfolk, Va.: Donning, 1985.

Fox-Genovese, Elizabeth. *Within the Plantation Household: Black and White Women of the Old South*. Chapel Hill: University of North Carolina Press, 1988.

Fraser, Charles. *Charleston! Charleston!* Columbia: University of South Carolina Press, 1991.

Friend, Llerena. *Sam Houston: The Great Designer*. Austin: University of Texas Press, 1954.

Galpin, W. Freeman, ed. "Letters of an East Tennessee Abolitionist." *East Tennessee Historical Societies Publications* 3 (1932): 134–49.

Genovese, Eugene. *Roll, Jordan, Roll: The World the Slaves Made*. New York: Pantheon, 1994.

Glassie, Henry. *Folk Housing in Middle Virginia: A Structural Analysis of Artifacts*. Knoxville: University of Tennessee Press, 1976.

———. *Pattern in the Material Folk Culture of the Eastern United States*. Philadelphia: University of Pennsylvania Press, 1968.

Goldfield, David R. "Black Life in Old South Cities." In *Before Freedom Came: African-American Life in the Antebellum South,* edited by Edward Campbell and Kym Rice, 123–53. Charlottesville: University Press of Virginia, 1991.

———. *Cotton Fields and Skyscrapers: Southern City and Region, 1607–1980*. Baton Rouge: Louisiana State University Press, 1982.

———. "Review of Blassingame's *The Slave Community*." *Agricultural History* 47, no 3 (1973): 227–28.

Goldfield, David R., and Blaine Brownell, eds. *The City in Southern History: The Growth of Urban Civilization in the South*. New York: Kennikat Press, 1977.

Goldin, Claudia Dale. *Urban Slavery in the American South, 1820–1860: A Quantitative History*. Chicago: University of Chicago Press, 1976.

Goodstein, Anita Shafer. *Nashville, 1780–1960: From Frontier to City*. Gainesville: University Press of Florida, 1989.

Gray, Alfred J., and Susan F. Adams. "Government." In *Heart of the Valley: History of Knoxville, Tennessee,* edited by Lucile Deaderick, 91–93. Knoxville: East Tennessee Historical Society, 1976.

Greggus, David Patrick. *Haitian Revolutionary Studies.* Bloomington: Indiana University Press, 2002.

Griggs, Susan Jewett. *Early Homesteads of Pomfret and Hampton.* Abingdon, Conn.: N.p., 1950.

Grover, Kathryn. *Make a Way Somehow: African-American Life in Northern Community, 1790–1965.* Syracuse, N.Y.: Syracuse University Press, 1994.

Groves, Paul A., and Edward K. Muller. "The Evolution of Black Residential Areas in Late Nineteenth Century Cities." *Journal of Historical Geography* 1, no. 2 (1975): 169–91.

Hafertepe, Kenneth. *Abner Cook: Master Builder on the Texas Frontier.* Austin: Texas State Historical Association, 1992.

———. *A History of Ashton Villa: A Family and Its House in Victorian Galveston, Texas.* Austin: Texas State Historical Association, 1991.

———. "The Texas Homes of Sam and Mary Maverick." *Southwestern Historical Quarterly* 109 (July 2005): 1–29.

Hamby, E. Brooke. "An Archaeological and Historical Investigation of the Blount Mansion Slave Quarters." M.A. thesis, University of Tennessee, Knoxville, 1999.

———. "The Roots of Healing: Archaeological and Historical Investigations of African-American Herbal Medicine." Ph.D. diss., University of Tennessee, Knoxville, 2004.

Haney, Gina. "In Complete Order: Social Control and Architectural Organization in the Charleston Back Lot." M.A. thesis, University of Virginia, 1996.

Harding, Sandra. *Whose Science? Whose Knowledge? Thinking from Women's Lives.* Ithaca, N.Y.: Cornell University Press, 1991.

Harris, William C. "East Tennessee's Civil War Refugees and the Impact of the War on Civilians." *Journal of East Tennessee History* 75 (2003): 62–75.

Harrower, John. *The Journal of John Harrower, an Indentured Servant in the Colony of Virginia, 1773–1776.* Ed. Edward Miles Riley. Williamsburg, Va.: Colonial Williamsburg, 1963.

Hart, Katherine, and Elisabeth Kemp. *Lucadia Pease and the Governor: Letters, 1850–1857.* Austin, Tex.: Encino Press, 1974.

Hartman, Saidiya V. *Scenes of Subjection: Terror, Slavery, and Self-Making in Nineteenth-Century America.* Oxford: Oxford University Press, 1997.

Hayes, Charles W. *History of the Island and the City of Galveston.* Cincinnati: N.p., 1879.

Henry, H. M. *Police Control of the Slave in South Carolina.* New York: Negro Universities Press, 1914.

Herman, Bernard L. "Slave and Servant Housing in Charleston, 1770–1820." *Historical Archaeology* 33, no. 3 (1999): 88–101.

———. "Slave Quarters in Virginia: The Persona behind Historic Artifacts." In *The Scope of Historical Archaeology,* edited by David G. Orr and Daniel G. Crozier, 253–83. Philadelphia: Laboratory of Anthropology, Temple University, 1984.

———. *Town House: Architecture and Material Life in the Early American City, 1780–1830.* Chapel Hill: University of North Carolina Press, 2005.

Higman, B. W. *Jamaica Surveyed*. Kingston: Institute of Jamaica, 1988.

Hodges, Graham Russell. *Root and Branch: African Americans in New York and East Jersey*. Chapel Hill: University of North Carolina Press, 1999.

———. *Slavery and Freedom in the Rural North: African Americans in Monmouth County, New Jersey*. Madison, Wis.: Madison House, 1997.

Hodges, Graham Russell, and Alan Edward Brown, eds. *"Pretends to Be Free": Runaway Slave Advertisements from Colonial and Revolutionary New York and New Jersey*. New York: Garland, 1994.

Horton, James Oliver, and Lois Horton. *Slavery and the Making of America*. New York: Oxford University Press, 2005.

Houghton, Dorothy, et al. *Houston's Forgotten Heritage: Landscape, Houses, Interiors, 1824–1914*. College Station: Texas A&M University Press, 2014.

Isaac, Rhys. *Landon Carter's Uneasy Kingdom: Revolution and Rebellion on a Virginia Plantation*. Oxford: Oxford University Press, 2004.

———. *The Transformation of Virginia, 1740–1790*. Chapel Hill: University of North Carolina Press, 1982.

Jacobs, Harriet. *Incidents in the Life of a Slave Girl: Written by Herself*. Ed. Jean Fagan Yellin. Cambridge, Mass.: Harvard University Press, 1987.

Johnson, Walter. *River of Dark Dreams: Slavery and Empire in the Cotton Kingdom*. Cambridge, Mass.: Harvard University Press, 2013.

———. *Soul by Soul: Life inside the Antebellum Slave Market*. Cambridge, Mass.: Harvard University Press, 1999.

Jones, Rhett S. "Plantation Slavery in the Narragansett Country of Rhodes Island, 1690–1790: A Preliminary Study." *Plantation Society* 2 (1986): 157–70.

Joseph, J. W. "Archaeology and the African-American Experience in the Urban South." In *Archaeology of Southern Urban Landscapes*, edited by Amy Lambeck Young, 109–26. Tuscaloosa: University of Alabama Press, 2000.

Kenzer, Robert C. *Kinship and Neighborhood in a Southern Community*. Knoxville: University of Tennessee Press, 1987.

Klein, Martin. *Slavery and Colonial Rule in French West Africa*. Cambridge: Cambridge University Press, 1998.

Lack, Paul D. "Urban Slavery in the Southwest." *Red River Valley Historical Review* 4, no. 2 (Spring 1981): 8–27.

Law, Robin. *Ouidah: Social History of a West African Slavery Port, 1727–1892*. Athens: Ohio University Press, 2004.

Leone, Mark P., and Silas D. Hurry. "Seeing: The Power of Town Planning in the Chesapeake." *Historical Archaeology* 32, no. 4 (1998): 34–62.

Leveen, Lois, "Dwelling in the House of Oppression: The Spatial, Racial, and Textual Dynamics of Harriet Wilson's *Our Nig*," *African American Review* 35, no. 4 (Winter 2001): 561–80.

Levy, Andrew. *The First Emancipator.* New York: Random House, 2005.

Litwack, Leon F. *North of Slavery: The Negro in the Free States, 1790–1860.* Chicago: University of Chicago Press, 1961.

Lofton, John. *Denmark Vesey's Revolt.* Kent, Ohio: Kent State University Press, 1983.

Lovejoy, Paul E. *Transformations in Slavery: A History of Slavery in Africa.* 3rd ed. Cambridge: Cambridge University Press, 2011.

Mair, Lucille Matharin. *A Historical Study of Women in Jamaica, 1655–1844.* Mona, Jamaica: University of West Indies Press, 2006.

Malone, Ann Patton. "Matt Gaines: Reconstruction Politician." In *Black Leaders: Texans for Their Times,* edited by Alwyn Barr and Robert A. Calvert, 49–81. Austin: Texas State Historical Association, 1981.

Manca, Joseph. *George Washington's Eye: Landscape, Architecture, and Design at Mount Vernon.* Baltimore: Johns Hopkins University Press, 2012.

Manning, Patrick. *Slavery and African Life: Occidental, Oriental, and African Slave Trades.* Cambridge: Cambridge University Press, 1990.

Marks, Paula Mitchell. *Turn Your Eyes toward Texas: Pioneers Sam and Mary Maverick.* College Station: Texas A&M University Press, 1989.

McArthur, William J. "Knoxville's History: An Interpretation." In *Heart of the Valley: A History of Knoxville, Tennessee,* edited by Lucile Deaderick, 46–52. Knoxville: East Tennessee Historical Society, 1976.

McDonald, Michael J., and William Bruce Wheeler. *Knoxville, Tennessee: Continuity and Change in an Appalachian City.* Knoxville: University of Tennessee Press, 1983.

McInnis, Maurie D. *The Politics of Taste in Antebellum Charleston.* Chapel Hill: University of North Carolina Press, 2005.

———. *Waiting for Sale: Abolitionist Art and the American Slave Trade.* Chicago: University of Chicago Press, 2013.

McKee, Larry. "The Ideals and Realities behind the Design and Use of 19th Century Virginia Slave Cabins." In *The Art and Mystery of Historical Archaeology: Essays in Honor of James Deetz,* edited by Anne Elizabeth Yentsch and Mary C. Beaudry, 195–214. Boca Raton, Fla.: CRC Press, 1992.

Middleton, Alicia Hopton. *Life in Carolina and New England during the Nineteenth Century.* Bristol: N.p., 1929.

Miller, William Davis. "The Narragansett Planters." *Proceedings of the American Antiquarian Society* 43 (1933): 49–115.

Mooney, Barbara Burlison. "Racial Boundaries in a Frontier Town: St. Louis on the Eve of the American Civil War." In *Identities in Space: Contested Terrains in the Western City since 1850,* edited by Simon Gunn and Robert J. Morris, 82–99. Aldershot, Eng.: Ashgate, 2001.

Mooney, Chase. *Slavery in Tennessee.* Bloomington: Indiana University Press, 1957.

Moorehead, Singleton P. "Tazewell Hall: A Report on Its Eighteenth-Century Appearance." *Journal of the Society of Architectural Historians* 14, no. 1 (March 1955): 14–17.

Moretta, John Anthony. *William Pitt Ballinger: Texas Lawyer, Southern Statesman, 1825–1888*. Austin: Texas State Historical Association, 2000.

Morgan, Almyra. *The Catskill Turnpike*. Cayuga, N.Y.: Daughters of the American Revolution, 1929.

Moss, Richard Shannon. *Slavery on Long Island: A Study in Local Institutional and Early African-American Communal Life*. New York: Garland, 1993.

Nash, Gary B. *Forging Freedom: The Formation of Philadelphia's Black Community, 1720–1840*. Cambridge, Mass.: Harvard University Press, 1988.

Nash, Gary B., and Jean R. Soderlund. *Freedom by Degrees: Emancipation in Pennsylvania and Its Aftermath*. New York: Oxford University Press 1991.

Neiman, Frazier D. *The "Manner House" before Stratford*. Stratford, Va.: A Stratford Handbook, 1980.

Nelson, Louis P., and Edward A. Chappell, eds. *Falmouth, Jamaica: Architecture as History*. Kingston, Jamaica: University of West Indies Press, 2014.

Newman, Paul Douglas. *Fries's Rebellion: The Enduring Struggle for the American Revolution*. Philadelphia: University of Pennsylvania Press, 2004.

Northrop, David. *Africa's Discovery of Europe*. 3rd ed. Oxford: Oxford University Press, 2013.

Oakes, James. *The Ruling Race: A History of American Slaveholders*. New York: Knopf, 1982.

Oakley, Anna Lisa N. "Interpreting the Frontier Slave Experience: Slavery at Blount Mansion, Knoxville, Tennessee, 1792–1800." M.A. thesis, Middle Tennessee State University, 1966.

O'Leary, Elizabeth L. *At Beck and Call: The Representation of Domestic Servants in Nineteenth-Century American Painting*. Washington, D.C.: Smithsonian Institution Press, 1996.

Olmsted, Frederick Law. *A Journey in the Seaboard Slave States: With Remarks on Their Economy*. New York: Dix and Edwards, 1856.

Olson, Edwin. "Negro Slavery in New York, 1626–1827." Ph.D. diss., Columbia University, 1938.

Omi, Michael, and Howard Winant. *Racial Formation in the United States: From the 1960s to the 1980s*. New York: Routledge, 1987.

Painter, Jacob. *Reminiscence: Gleanings and Thoughts*. Vol. 1, nos. 1–2. N.p.: N.p., 1871.

Patterson, Caleb P. *The Negro in Tennessee, 1790–1865*. New York: Negro Universities Press, 1968.

Penningroth, Dylan C. *The Claims of Kinfolk: African American Property and Community in the Nineteenth-Century South*. Chapel Hill: University of North Carolina Press, 2003.

Phillips, Ulrich B. "The Slave Labor Problem in Charleston District." In *Plantation, Town and Country: Essays on the Local History of American Slave Society,* edited by Elinor Miller and Eugene Genovese, 7–28. Urbana: University of Illinois Press, 1974.

Pickrell, Annie Doom. *Pioneer Women in Texas*. Austin, Tex.: Jenkins, 1970.

Piersen, William D. *Black Yankees: The Development of an Afro-American Subculture in Eighteenth-Century New England*. Amherst: University of Massachusetts Press, 1988.

Pogue, Dennis J. *King's Reach and 17th-Century Plantation Life.* Annapolis: Maryland Historical and Cultural Publications, 1990.

Prather, Patricia Smith, and Jane Clements Monday. *From Slave to Statesman: The Legacy of Joshua Houston, Servant to Sam Houston.* Denton: University of North Texas Press, 1993.

Preston, Howard W. "Godfrey Malbone's Connecticut Investment." *Rhode Island History* (October 1923): 115–20.

Rawick, George P. "Some Notes on a Social Analysis of Slavery: A Critique and Assessment of the 'The Slave Community.'" In *Revisiting Blassingame's* The Slave Community: *The Scholars Respond,* edited by Al-Tony Gilmore, 22–24. Westport, Conn.: Greenwood Press, 1978.

Rediker, Marcus. *The Slave Ship: A Human History.* New York: Viking, 2007.

Reynolds, Helen Wilkinson. *Dutch Houses in the Hudson Valley before 1776.* New York: Holland Society, 1929.

Ridout, Orlando V. "Reediting the Architectural Past: A Comparison of Surviving Physical and Documentary Evidence on Maryland's Eastern Shore." *Buildings and Landscapes: Journal of the Vernacular Architecture Forum* 21, no. 2 (Fall 2014): 88–112.

Roberts, Madge Thornall. *Star of Destiny: The Private Life of Sam and Margaret Houston.* Denton: University of North Texas Press, 1993.

Robertson, David. *Denmark Vesey.* New York: Knopf, 1999.

Rogers, George C., Jr. *Charleston in the Age of the Pinckneys.* Columbia: University of South Carolina Press, 1980.

Rothrock, Mary U., ed. *The French Broad—Holston Country: A History of Knox County, Tennessee.* Knoxville: East Tennessee Historical Society, 1946.

Rozek, Barbara J. "Galveston Slavery." *Houston Review* 15, no. 2 (1993): 67–101.

St. Clair, William. *The Door of No Return: The History of Cape Coast Castle and the Atlantic Slave Trade.* New York: BlueBridge, 2007.

Scarupa, Harriet Jackson. "Learning from Ancestral Bones: New York's Exhumed African Past." *American Visions* 9, no. 1 (1994): 18–21.

Schweninger, Loren, ed. *From Tennessee Slave to Entrepreneur: The Autobiography of James Thomas.* Columbia: University of Missouri Press, 1984.

Scott, James C. *Weapons of the Weak: Everyday Forms of Peasant Resistance.* New Haven, Conn.: Yale University Press, 1985.

Seale, William. *Sam Houston's Wife: A Biography of Margaret Lea Houston.* Norman: University of Oklahoma Press, 1970.

———. *Virginia's Executive Mansion: A History of the Governor's House.* Richmond: Virginia State Library and Archives, 1988.

Shonnard, Frederic, and W. W. Spooner. *History of Westchester County, New York.* Reprint ed. 1900; Harrison, N.Y.: Harbor Hill Books, 1974.

Smallwood, Stephanie E. *Saltwater Slavery: A Middle Passage from Africa to American Diaspora.* Cambridge, Mass.: Harvard University Press, 2007.

Smith, Mark M. *Mastered by the Clock: Time, Slavery, and Freedom in the American South.* Chapel Hill: University of North Carolina Press, 1997.

———, ed. *Stono: Documenting and Interpreting a Southern Slave Revolt.* Columbia: University of South Carolina Press, 2005.

Soltow, Lee. "Egalitarian America and Its Inegalitarian Housing in the Federal Period." *Social Science History* 9, no. 2 (Spring 1985): 199–213.

Starobin, Robert S. *Denmark Vesey: The Slave Conspiracy of 1822.* Englewood Cliffs, N.J.: Prentice-Hall, 1970.

———. *Industrial Slavery in the Old South.* New York: Oxford University Press, 1970.

Stein, Linda France, Melanie A. Cabak, and Mark D. Grover. "Blue Beads as African-American Symbols." *Historical Archaeology* 30, no. 3 (1996): 49–75.

Takagi, Midori. *Rearing Wolves to Our Own Destruction: Slavery in Richmond, Virginia, 1782–1865.* Charlottesville: University Press of Virginia, 2000.

Taylor, Alan. *The Internal Enemy: Slavery and War in Virginia, 1772–1832.* New York: Norton, 2014.

Taylor, William R. *Cavalier and Yankee: The Old South and American National Character.* New York: George Braziller, 1961.

Tolbert, Lisa C. *Constructing Townscapes: Space and Society in Antebellum Tennessee.* Chapel Hill: University of North Carolina Press, 1999.

Tyler-McGraw, Mary, and Gregg D. Kimball. *In Bondage and Freedom: Antebellum Black Life in Richmond, Virginia.* Richmond: Valentine Museum, 1988.

Updike, Wilkins. *History of the Episcopal Church in Narragansett.* Boston: Merrymount Press, 1907.

Upton, Dell. "The City as Material Culture." In *The Art and Mystery of Historical Archaeology: Essays in Honor of James Deetz,* edited by Anne Elizabeth Yentsch and Mary C. Beaudry, 51–74. Boca Raton, Fla.: CRC Press, 1992.

———. "Dutch." In *America's Architectural Roots: Ethnic Groups that Built America,* edited by Dell Upton, 48–53. Washington, D.C.: Preservation Press, 1986.

Valentine, Charles A. "Deficit, Difference, and Bicultural Models of Afro-American Behavior." *Harvard Educational Review* 41 (1971): 137–57.

Vlach, John Michael. *Back of the Big House: The Architecture of Plantation Slavery.* Chapel Hill: University of North Carolina Press, 1993.

———. "Graveyards and Afro-American Art." *Southern Exposure* 5 (1977): 162–65.

———. "The Shotgun House: An African Architectural Legacy." In *Common Places: Readings in American Vernacular Architecture,* edited by Dell Upton and John M. Vlach, 58–78. Athens: University of Georgia Press, 1986.

———. "'Without Recourse to Owners': The Architecture of Urban Slavery in the Antebellum South." In *Perspectives in Vernacular Architecture,* vol. 6, *Shaping Communities,* edited by Carter L. Hudgins and Elizabeth Collins Cromley, 150–60. Knoxville: University of Tennessee Press, 1997.

VonToal, Dagmar. "The Shotgun House in Knoxville, Tennessee." M.A. thesis, University of Tennessee, Knoxville, 1998.

Wade, Richard. *Slavery in the Cities: The South, 1820–1860*. New York: Oxford University Press, 1964.

Weld, Ralph Foster. *Slavery in Connecticut*. New Haven, Conn.: Yale University Press, 1935.

Wesley, Charles H. *Negro Labor in the United States*. New York: Vanguard Press, 1927.

William, Michael Ann. *Homeplace: The Social Use and Meaning of the Folk Dwelling in Southwestern North Carolina*. Athens: University of Georgia Press, 1991.

Williams, William H. *Slavery and Freedom in Delaware, 1639–1865*. Wilmington, Del.: Scholarly Resources, 1996.

Williams-Myers, A. J. "The Arduous Journey: The African-American Presence in the Hudson-Mohawk Region." In *The African-American Presence in New York State History: Four Regional History Surveys*, edited by Monroe Fordam, 19–50. Albany: New York African American Institute, 1989.

Wirtz, H. Edmond, and H. Merrill Roenke, Jr. *Rose Hill: A Greek Revival Mansion—History and Restoration*. Geneva, N.Y.: Geneva Historical Society, 1984.

Wood, Julia. *Gendered Lives: Communication, Gender, and Culture*. 12th ed. Belmont, Cal.: Wadsworth, 2016.

Wood, Peter H. "Anatomy of a Revolt." In *Stono: Documenting and Interpreting a Southern Slave Revolt*, edited by Mark M. Smith, 59–72. Columbia: University of South Carolina Press, 2005.

Wright, Giles R. *Afro-Americans in New Jersey: A Short History*. Trenton: New Jersey Historical Commission, 1988.

Wylie, Alison. "Why Standpoint Matters." In *The Feminist Standpoint Theory Reader*, edited by Sandra Harding, 339–52. New York: Routledge, 2004.

Yentsch, Anne Elizabeth. *A Chesapeake Family and Their Slaves: A Study in Historical Archaeology*. Cambridge: Cambridge University Press, 1994.

Young, Amy Lambeck. "Developing Town Life in the South: Archaeological Investigations at Blount Mansion." In *Archaeology of Southern Urban Landscapes*, edited by Amy Lambeck Young, 150–69. Tuscaloosa: University of Alabama Press, 2000.

Young, Amy Lynne. "Slave Subsistence at the Upper South Mabry Site, East Tennessee: Regional Variability in Plantation Diet of the Southeastern United States." M.A. thesis, University of Tennessee, Knoxville, 1997.

Young, Jeffrey. *Domesticating Slavery: The Ideological Formation of the Master Class in the Deep South, from Colonization to 1837*. Ph.D. diss., Emory University, 1996.

Zink, Clifford W. "Dutch Framed Houses in New York and New Jersey." *Winterthur Portfolio* 22 (1987): 278–81.

CONTRIBUTORS

Edward A. Chappell retired in 2016 as the Shirley and Richard Roberts Director of Architectural and Archaeological Research at Colonial Williamsburg, the nation's largest open-air history museum, where he had responsibility for architectural and archaeological scholarship and historic preservation. He recently received the Prentis Award from the College of William and Mary for his efforts to raise the quality of new design and to preserve neighborhoods in Williamsburg. Among his most recent publications are three chapters in *The Chesapeake House,* a study of early domestic buildings in Maryland and Virginia, and "Pride Flared Up" on contemporary Zuni potters in *Ceramics in America.*

Clifton Ellis is Associate Dean for Research and Associate Professor in the College of Architecture at Texas Tech University, where he holds the Elizabeth Sasser Professorship in Architectural History. Ellis earned his M.A. in American history at the University of Tennessee and his M.A. and Ph.D. in architectural history at the University of Virginia. His research interests include plantation landscapes and American vernacular architecture.

Charles H. Faulkner is a retired Emeritus Distinguished Professor of Humanities at the University of Tennessee, Knoxville. He is the author of five books, and over a hundred book chapters, monographs, and journals on diverse subjects such as rock art, cave archaeology, architectural archaeology, and frontier Tennessee history. He is the recipient of the Award of Achievement from the East Tennessee Historical Society, the Career Achievement Award from the Tennessee Council for Professional Archaeology, and the Lifetime Achievement Award from the Southeastern Archaeological Conference.

Rebecca Ginsburg is Associate Professor of Landscape Architecture at the University of Illinois at Urbana-Champaign and the author of *At Home with Apartheid: The Hidden Landscapes of Domestic Service in Johannesburg.* She earned her Ph.D. in architectural history at the University of California at Berkeley. She is currently director of the Education Justice Project at the University of Illinois.

Kenneth Hafertepe is Professor of Museum Studies at Baylor University, and is the author of *Abner Cook: Master Builder on the Texas Frontier* and *The Material Culture of German Texans.* Hafertepe received his Ph.D. in American civilization from the University of Texas at Austin in 1986 and his B.A. from Georgetown University in 1978.

Gina Haney earned her M.A. in architectural history at the University of Virginia. Before founding her own preservation company, Haney worked in preservation for the Aga Khan Trust for Culture. She is founder and principal of Community Consortium and has been the project manager on preservation initiatives throughout the Middle East for the World Monuments Fund. Haney has worked on sites of slavery in Ghana's Cape Coast and in Suriname, formerly Dutch Guiana.

Lisa Tolbert is Associate Professor of History at the University of North Carolina, Greensboro. She earned her Ph.D. at the University of North Carolina, Chapel Hill. Her book, *Constructing Townscapes: Space and Society in Antebellum Tennessee,* was published in 1999. Her most recent work focuses on the social landscape of food shopping in the early twentieth-century South. Part of this research, which constitutes Tolbert's next book project, was published as an essay titled "The Aristocracy of the Market Basket: Self-Service Food Shopping in the New South," in *Food Chains: From Farmyard to Shopping Cart.*

John Michael Vlach began his academic career as an Africanist, spending a year at the University of Ghana before receiving his Ph.D. in folklore from Indiana University, where his dissertation examined the cultural history of the shotgun house, which has roots in Ghana and Nigeria. As the student of a student of Melville Herskovits, the great African historian who was adamant that black culture be seen as a distinctive creation of its own and not as a flawed version of European ideas, Vlach has strived throughout his academic career to give Africans and people of African descent their full recognition. In recent years, his work has focused increasingly on diasporic subjects. He describes himself as "the incredibly shrinking Africanist." His many books include *Back of the Big House: The Architecture of Plantation Slavery, By the Work of Their Hands: Studies in Afro-American Folklife,* and *The Planter's Prospect: Privilege and Slavery in Plantation Paintings.* He has also developed exhibitions for numerous museum shows coast to coast. Vlach retired as Professor of American Studies and Anthropology at George Washington University and as director of the university's Folklife Program in 2013.

INDEX

Italicized page numbers refer to illustrations, and properties named for individuals or families are indexed by surname.

Charleston from, 85; slave insurrections in, 33

Carolinas, 11, 20, 156

carriage houses, 8, 61, 82, 113, 114; domestic space and, 95; housing for slaves in, 6

Carroll, Charles, 71

Carter, Robert "King," House (Williamsburg), 21–22, 48n3, 48n7; attic, 35; kitchen plan, 23; his variable treatment of slaves as form of control, 34

Carter's Grove (James City County, Va.), 27

cellars, 22, 30, 31, 49n14

census, U.S. federal: of 1790, 55, 57, 91; of 1800, 12, 70; of 1830, 62; of 1850, 151nn12–13; of 1860, slave schedule of, 108, 114, 128, 129

Chappell, Edward A., 10, 11, 105n20

Charleston, South Carolina, 5, 12–13, 34, 42, 79, 154; Aiken-Rhett House, 98; backlots of, 82, 87, 90, 97, 106, 155; —, city plats, 96, 96, 104–5n18; —, landscapes of senses in, 97–102; blacks as majority in, 4, 91; Miles Brewton House, 33, 98; as center of East Coast slave trade, 83–84; City Guard, 93–95; domestic space, control of slaves in, 95–96; Heyward-Washington House, 99; Pinckney House, 97, 100; population (1860), 14, 107; Queen Street house, 83; "rival geography" of blacks, 104n12; St. Michael's Church, 3, 92, 93; service wings to main houses, 32; single houses, 82, 83, 107, 110, 116; slave living spaces in, 6; slave population of, 155; urban space, control of slaves in, 90–95

Charleston Courier (newspaper), 3, 87–88, 91

Charlotte Helen Middleton (Mrs. E.P. De-Wolf) and Nurse Lydia (ambrotype by George Smith Cook, 1852), 89

Chase, Samuel, 71

Cherry Walk (Essex County, Va.), 49n21

Chesapeake region, 11, 19, 31; detached plantation wings of great houses, 43; effects of American Revolution in, 29; material culture and social class in, 69; spectrum of housing in, 20; work spaces separated from main houses, 22

Chew, Benjamin, 62, 63, 64

Childress, Jake, 142

churches, 5, 133, 149

cities and towns, antebellum, 2, 5, 16; border cities, 124, 128; as cosmopolitan places, 1; decline in slave population of, 4, 14, 123; density of, 107, 116; "invisible people" in, 136; in northern states, 1–2, 132, 152n16; persistence of slavery in, 123; proximity of black and white residents in, 149, 152n16; scale of slavery in, 7; slave population of (1860), 155; slavery as integral part of urban economy, 154–55; small towns, 15, 140–49; southern cities as crucibles of African American culture, 135. See also slavery, urban, and specific cities and towns by name

Civil War, 4, 9, 14, 117, 123, 124, 145

Cliveden (Germantown, Penn.), 62–63, 63, 64

Coffee, Aaron, 117–18

coffee, 36

Colbert, Burwell, 30

Collins, Patricia Hill, 13, 90, 154

Commack, Long Island, 57

Compromise of 1850, 13

Confederacy, 119, 125

Connecticut, slavery in, 53, 58–59, 67n21

Cook, Abner, 108, 111

cooking, 25, 43; in flankers connected by hyphens, 26–27; integrated position of, 22; living space separated from, 34; outbuilding complex at Mount Vernon, 24. See also kitchens/cookrooms

Cornwall estate (Westmoreland Parish, Jamaica), 45

cotton, 9, 13
counting houses, 35
court records, 15
Cromley, Elizabeth C., 121n7
Cuba, slavery in, 156

Dave (enslaved man in Galveston), 117–18
Decatur, Susan, 32
DeCorse, Christopher R., 157
DeLaland, Francis, 80
diaries, of white slaveholders, 7, 21, 100–101
Dickinson, Perez, 125, 126, 130, 135
Diouf, Sylviane, 156
Door of No Return, The: The History of Cape Coast Castle and the Atlantic Slave Trade (St. Clair, 2007), 156
Douglass, Frederick, 4
Drax Hall (St. Ann Parish, Jamaica), 45
Duff, Hugh, 142
Dunkley, D. A., 47
"Dwelling in the House of Oppression: The Spatial, Racial, and Textual Dynamics of Harriet Wilson's *Our Nig*" (Leveen, 2001), 7–8

economies, regional, 5, 19
Edinburgh Castle (Jamaica), 37
Eelbeck, John G., 140, 146, 147, 150n2
Eliza (enslaved woman in Texas), 112, 121n9
Ellis, Clifton, 11, 154
emancipation, gradual, 52, 67n23
Essex County, Virginia: Blandfield plantation, 27; Cherry Walk, 49n21
Everard, Thomas, House (Williamsburg), kitchen plan, *23*, 24
Ewart, Robert, 40
Exclusion Act (Tennessee, 1831), 126

factories, 4, 10
Falmouth, Jamaica, 10, 19, 36, 44–45; Moulton Barrett House, 42; Duke Street

houses and service buildings, 38, 39, 40, 46, *47;* —, plan, *39;* Lower Harbour Street, house/kitchen, 37–38; —, plan, *37;* Market Street house with "Negro rooms," 39–40; —, plan, *41*
farms, 54, 118, 141, 145; in Knoxville area, 127, 131, 135; as less-documented sites of slavery, 154; in northern states, 53
Faulkner, Charles H., 13
Federal Direct Tax (1798), 11–12, 69, 70
feminist studies, 153, 154
Fields, Barbara Jeanne, 4
fieldwork, as methodology, 153
fireplaces, 24, 30, 31, 36–37, 38, 77
Fithian, Philip, 34
Fitzhugh, Peregrine, 60
"Flatts, The" (north of Albany, N.Y.), 56–57
Folk Housing in Middle Virginia: A Structural Analysis of Artifacts (Glassie, 1976), 153
food delivery, 25, 26, 27, 29–30
Fossett, Edith Hern, 29
Fox-Genovese, Elizabeth, 141, 150n8
Franklin, Tennessee, 15, 140, 145; lax enforcement of laws controlling slaves, 146–47; map of Henry's (enslaved man's) movements through, *143;* slaveholding patterns in, 144, 151nn12–13; slaves as half the population of, 142, 150–51n9
Fredericksburg, Virginia, Kenmore (Lewis house), 28–29, 31
free blacks/people of color, 10, 12, 123, 155; in Annapolis and Maryland, 70, 71, 75, 80, 81, 85; in Charleston, 83, 84, 97; enslavement of, 91; housing of, 20; in Jamaica, 46–47; in Knoxville, 14, 127, *129*, 132–34, *133*, 136; literacy taught to slaves by, 124; in Nashville and surrounding area, 145, 151–52n15; property accumulated by, 149; registration system in Ten-

Knight, Sarah, 54–55
Knoxville, Tennessee, 124–26; Blount Mansion, 130, 131, 132, 135, 136; city directory, 132; composition of economy, 13; demography of slaves and free blacks in, 126–27; free blacks in, *129*, 132–34, *133*, 136; Mabry-Hazen house, 129, 131; map with slave owners' houses, 128–29, *129;* Marble Alley neighborhood, 132, 133, 134; Marble Springs farm, 131, 132; Park house, 129; racial geography of, 14; slave archaeology in, 130–32; slaves in, 127–32; as urban center of the mountain South, 13–14

Lafever, Minard, 111
landscape, natural, 2
landscape, urban, 12, 84, 116–17; of Charleston, 87, 92, 93, 102; of Richmond slave trade, 9; of senses, 97–102; severity of urban slavery and, 13; sound and time in, 88
Latrobe, Benjamin Henry, 26, 32
laundries, 24, 25, 95, 112, 113; combined with kitchens/cookrooms, 31–33, 44, 98, *98, 99, 100,* 110, 111, 115; in Falmouth, Jamaica, 38; in flankers connected by hyphens, 26–27, 32; integrated position of, 22
Law, Robin, 156
Lee, William "Billy," 28
letters, of white slaveholders, 7, 21
Leveen, Lois, 7–8
Lewis, Fielding, 28–29, 31
Lewis, Matthew, 45
Limerick, Ireland, 21
Lions, Joseph F., 40
literature, 2
Livingston, Robert, 55
Löher, Franz von, 7
Lose Your Mother: A Journey along the Atlantic Slave Route (Hartman, 2007), 157

Lott, Hendrick I., 57–58
Lovejoy, Paul E., 156
Lubbock, Thomas S., 108
Lydia (enslaved woman), *89, 90*

Mabee Jan, house of (Rotterdam Junction, N.Y.), 55–56, *56,* 67n25
Mabry-Hazen house (Knoxville), 129, 131
Madison, Dolley, 30
Madison, James, 30–31
Madison, Nelly, 30
Malbone, Godfrey, 58–59, 67n21
Manigault, Margaret Izard, 100
Manning, Patrick, 156
Marble Springs farm (Knoxville), 131, 132
Marx, Karl, 154
Maryland, 22, 34, 47; Catholics and Protestants in, 71; Queen Anne's County, 74, 77; tobacco economy of, 20; Wye Hundred (Queen Anne's County), 74–75; —, comparison of outbuildings with Annapolis, *76. See also* Annapolis; Baltimore
Matthew, Edward George, 42
Maverick, Samuel A. and Mary Adams, houses of (San Antonio), 109–11, *109, 110*
McConnell, Peter, 142, 148
McInnis, Maurie, 9, 155
McLean, Ephraim, 115
McWilliams, Jane, 70
memoirs, personal, 8, 107
Memphis, Tennessee, 14, 127, 132, 135, 136
Mexico, slavery in, 156
Miller, Andrew, 79
Minshall, Jacob, 66n7
Missouri Compromise, 13
Montego Bay, Jamaica, 43
Montpelier (Madison home, Orange County, Va.), 30–31
Monticello (Jefferson home, Albemarle County, Va.), 29–30
Mooney, Barbara Burlison, 7

Mooney, Chase, 125
Morris, Lewis, 55; Morrisania Manor (Westchester County, N.Y.), 55
Morven (Princeton, N.J.), 61–62; icehouse, *62*
Mount Airy plantation (Richmond County, Va.), 27
Mount Vernon (Washington home, Fairfax County, Va.), 24, 28
mutual-aid societies, 5
Myers, Moses, 31

Naragansett Bay, Rhode Island, 53, 54
Nashville, Tennessee, 14, 127, 132, 135, 136; free blacks in, 145, 151–52n15; slaveholding patterns in, 151n12
Negro Seaman's Act, 91, 103n7
Neill-Cochran House (Austin), 113
Nelson (enslaved footman), 100–102
Nelson, Thomas, House (Yorktown), 25–26
New England ell (house form), 111–12, 118, 121n8
New Jersey, 52–53, 59–60, 67n23, 157; abolition of slavery (1846), 156; Peter Berrien house (Somerset County), 60, 64; John A. Haring house (Bergen County), 60, 67n25; Huyler Homestead (Creskill), 59–60, *59*, 67n23; Morven (Princeton), 61–62, *62*
New Orleans, Louisiana, 4, 7, 107, 116, 118; population (1860), 14; slave population of, 155
Newport, Rhode Island, 58–59
New York State, 53, 55; abolition of slavery (1827), 52, 61; "The Flatts" (north of Albany), 56–57; Jan Mabee house (Rotterdam Junction), 55–56, *56*; Morrisania Manor (Westchester County), 55; Philipsburg Manor (Westchester County), 55; Rensselaer Manor, 55; Rose Hill estate, 60–61; Caleb Smith house (Commack),

57, *58*; Springfarm (Tompkins County), 60; Van Cortlandt Manor (Croton-on-Hudson), 55
Nichols, Ebenezer, house of (Galveston), 115
Nicholson, Gov. Francis, 20, 71, 80
Nicholson, Joseph H., 77
Norcum, James, 148
Norfolk, Virginia, 31
North Carolina, 14, 15, 125; Bellamy Mansion (Wilmington), 8–9
Northrop, David, 156
Nugent, George, 36
Nugent, Maria, 36

Olmsted, Frederick Law, 3, 92
Oney (witness in Franklin trial of Henry), 141, 146
Owens, Richard, house of (Annapolis), 78, 79
Owens-Thomas House (Savannah), 32–33

Paca, William, 71
Palmer, E. A., 114
Palmer, John, house of (Williamsburg), 25; kitchen plan, *23*
pantries, 96, *96*, 101, 105n19
Papenfuse, Edward, 70
Park house (Knoxville), 129
Parris, Alexander, 31
Pease, Elisha Marshall and Lucadia, 111–12, 113, 118
Pennsylvania, 54, 62–63, 66n7; Cliveden (Germantown), 62–63, *63*, 64
Petersburg, Virginia, 21, 31; Sterling Castle, 33
Phibbah (enslaved woman in Jamaica), 36
Philadelphia, Pennsylvania, 20, 31, 115
Philipsburg Manor (Westchester County, N.Y.), 55
Pinckney, Thomas, 99
Pinckney House (Charleston), *97, 100*
plantations, 15, 44, 63, 115, 118, 141; absent

in mountainous region of the South, 13–14, 125, 136; coffee, 36; cotton, 9; fieldworkers, 25; harshness in comparison to urban slavery, 13; image in popular culture, 1; "Negro villages" in Jamaica, 45; plantation economy, 5; slavery in popular imagination and, 154; slaves' community building on, 148; sugarcane in Jamaica, 35; town-like landscape of, 145; urban ghettos compared to, 134–35. *See also specific sites/houses by name*
planters (agricultural slaveholders), 4
Porter, Elijah, 144–45
Port Royal, Jamaica, 45
postprocessual theory, 85–86n8
Powell, Benjamin, 25
property deeds, 12
Pruden family, 33

Quakers, antislavery sentiments of, 54

"Racial Boundaries in a Frontier Town: St. Louis on the Eve of the American Civil War" (Mooney, 2002), 7
Randolph, John, house of (Tazewell Hall, Williamsburg), 27; kitchen plan, *23*
Randolph, Peyton, House (Williamsburg), 25, 32, 49n17; kitchen plan, *23*
Rearing Wolves to Our Own Destruction: Slavery in Richmond, Virginia (Takagi, 2000), 4
Rediker, Marcus, 155
"Regulation of Slaves" ordinance (Tennessee, 1817), 126
Rensselaer Manor (New York), 55
Rhode Island, 53, 54
rice, 13
Richmond, Virginia, 4, 5, 7, 21, 79; domestic slave trade of, 9; enslaved workers in Tredegar Iron Works, 155; kitchen-quarters in, 33; population (1860), 14;

107; slave population of, 155; Virginia Executive Mansion (1813), 31
Ridgley, Absalom, house of (Annapolis), 74, *75*
Ridout, John, house of (Annapolis), 22, 26, 71
Ridout, Mary, 77, 78
Ridout, Orlando V., 77
Ridout Row (Annapolis), *73*, 74
River of Dark Dreams: Slavery and Empire in the Cotton Kingdom (Johnson), 9–10
Robertson, David, 103n8
Robertson, William, 44
Robertson Ranch (Saledo, Texas), 106
Robinson, Billy, 79
Robinson, Rowland, 54
Robinson, William, 53
Rochefoucauld-Liancourt, François de la, 73
Rose, Robert, 60–61
Rose Hill estate (New York), 60–61
Rothrock, Mary U., 125
Russell, Elizabeth, 24

Said, Edward, 104n12
St. Ann Parish, Jamaica, 36, 44, 45
St. Clair, William, 156
St. Domingue, 47, 84
St. Louis, small scale of slavery in, 7
San Antonio, Texas, 108, 118; antislavery sentiments in, 107; Samuel A. and Mary Adams Maverick houses (Main and Alamo plazas), 109–11, *109*, *110*; Spanish colonial houses, 108–9
Sanborn Fire Insurance Maps, 106, 115, 121n8
Savannah, Georgia, Owens-Thomas House, 32–33
Schuyler, Col. Philip Pieterse, 57
Schuyler, Philip Pieterse, 56–57
Scott, James C., 65
Scott, Upton, 71

service buildings, 20, 31, 34; in Charleston, 33; in Jamaica, 38, 43; at Peyton Randolph House (Williamsburg), 49n17; in Savannah, 32–33

Sevier, John, 130

Sharpe, Gov. Horatio, 22

Short, John, 144

"Slave and Servant Housing in Charleston, 1770–1820" (Herman), 6, 106

slaveholders/slave owners, urban, 2, 10; housing of, 20; kitchen plans in Charleston and, 97; lives shaped by institution of slavery, 3; in northern states, 52–64; oblivious to presence of slaves, 78–79; Revolutionary War veterans, 29; small number of slaves owned by, 11, 154; in small towns, 144; townhouses of, 6

slave insurrection, slaveholders' anxieties about, 3, 47, 84, 87–88, 92, 102, 103n2; house servants perceived as most dangerous, 98–99; proliferation of slave revolts, 33, 90–91; white women's accounts, 99–102

slave insurrections, 33, 45, 84, 90–91, 100. *See also* Vesey, Denmark

slave narratives, 8, 85

slave resistance, 2, 7, 47, 102, 123; "negro's holiday" and black community, 99, 105n21; proprietary attitudes toward backlot spaces, 97–99, 117; runaway slaves, 81–82, 125; sound of bells ignored, 102

slavery, urban, 10–16, 123–24, 153; apologists and advocates for slavery, 34, 50n22; architecture of, 53, 64; built environment of, 1, 2–10; in decline before Civil War, 4, 123, 155; as fragile institution, 1, 2; harshness in comparison to plantations, 13; in northern states, 52, 156; in smaller towns and hamlets, 15, 140–49, 151n12; studies of, 4, 5, 16n5; work divided by gender, 78

Slavery and Freedom in the Middle Ground: Maryland during the Nineteenth Century (Fields, 1984), 4

Slavery in Tennessee (Mooney), 125

Slavery in the Cities: The South, 1820–1860 (Wade, 1964), 4, 14

slaves (bondsmen, enslaved Africans): African customs of, 77–78, 131; in Annapolis and Maryland, 71, 76–82; in Charleston, 83–84, 87; Christian conversion of, 47; communal ethos of, 148, 149, 152n27; contributions to American history and culture, 16; control of movements of, 88, 90, 103n2, 104n10; curfew for, 3, 88, 90, 91–95; daily routines and living conditions, 11, 131–32; demography of Knoxville and, 126–27; desire for separate space and privacy, 34, 98–99; ethnic diversity among, 91; Federal Direct Tax (1798) and, 70; as gatekeepers and guards, 100–102, 110; housing for, 2; in livery, 27–28, 29, 49n12; manipulation of landscapes by, 3; in northern states, 52, 54, 60–61, 67n21; punishment of, 40, 64, 90, 95, 126; religious services of, 94; ritualized acts of submission, 122n21; skills and talents of, 1, 4, 46, 108; social networks of, 82. *See also specific enslaved individuals by name*

Slaves Waiting for Sale: Abolitionist Art and the American Slave Trade (McInnis, 2013), 9

slave trade: Britain's closing of (1807), 19, 20, 35; Charleston as East Coast center of, 83–84; domestic, 9; slave markets and slave ships, 155

Sloan, Samuel, 115

Smallwood, Stephanie E., 155

Smith, Caleb, house of (Commack, N.Y.), 57; slave house, *58*

Smith, Richard, 54

Smith family (New York), 57
South America, slavery in, 156
South Kingston, Rhode Island, 54
Spanish Town, Jamaica, 36, 45
Speed, Joseph, 60
Spotswood, Gov. Alexander, 81
Springfarm (Tompkins County, N.Y.), 60
Spring Vale (Trelawny Parish, Jamaica), 45
stables, 82, *83*, 95, 112, 115
staircases, hidden, 9
standpoint theory, 13, 90, 154
Sterling Castle (Petersburg), 33
Stewart Castle (Jamaica), 36
Stockton, Richard, 61
Stockton, Robert Field, 61–62
Stone, Margaret, 115
Stono Rebellion (1739), 84, 90
Strickland, William, 53
sugar and rum economy, 20, 35–36

Takagi, Midori, 4
Tennessee, 2, 13–14, 125, 128, 130, 157. *See also*
    Knoxville; Memphis; Nashville
Tenneswood, Samuel, 142
Texas, 15, 111; Anglo-American settlers in,
    102; Governor's Mansion (Austin), 111,
    112, 113, 115, 118, 119–120; Robertson
    Ranch (Saledo), 106; rural slavery in, 107;
    secession from the Union, 119. *See also*
    Austin; Houston; San Antonio
Tharp, John, 39, 43, 45
Thirteenth Amendment, 53
Thistlewood, Thomas, 36, 45, 51n38
tobacco, 13
Tolbert, Lisa, 15, 154
Tredegar Iron Works (Richmond), 155
Trelawny Parish, Jamaica, 36, 40; Arcadia,
    44; Good Hope, 43, 45; Great Hope, 40;
    Spring Vale, 45; Vale Royal, 43, 44; —,
    plan of service and quartering wing, *43*
Tremont House (Galveston), 107

Trollope, Anthony, 7
Tucker, Nathaniel Beverley, 50n22
Tucker, St. George, 29; House (Williams-
    burg), 25, 29

Updike, Wilkins, 54
"Urban Slavery at Work: The Bellamy Man-
    sion Compound, Wilmington, North
    Carolina" (Bishir, 2010), 8–9
Urban Slavery in the American South,
    1820–1860: A Quantitative History (Gol-
    din, 1976), 4

Valentine, Polly, 50n22
Vale Royal (Trelawny Parish, Jamaica), 43,
    43, 44
Van Cortlandt, Pierre, 55; Manor (Croton-
    on-Hudson, N.Y.), 55
Vesey, Denmark, 91, 95, 99, 100
Virginia, 10, 125; Berry Hill (Halifax
    County), 43; Carter's Grove (James
    City County), 27; Governor's Palace,
    24, 25; —, kitchen plan, *23;* Montpelier
    (Madison home, Orange County), 30–31;
    Monticello (Jefferson home, Albemarle
    County), 29–30; Mount Airy plantation
    (Richmond County), 27; Mount Vernon
    (Washington home, Fairfax County),
    24, 28; tobacco economy of, 20; variable
    treatment of slaves as form of control, 34;
    Westover (Charles City County), 27. *See*
    also Alexandria; Essex County; Norfolk;
    Petersburg; Richmond; Williamsburg;
    Yorktown
Vlach, John Michael, 5–6, 11, 106, 156

Wade, Richard, 4–5, 14
walls, 2, 8, 82–83, 87; domestic lots sepa-
    rated from public streets by, 95; slaves'
    assertion of will and, 98–99
War of 1812, 12, 69

www.ingramcontent.com/pod-product-compliance
Lightning Source LLC
Chambersburg PA
CBHW030306100426
42812CB00002B/594